Recovering Native
American Writings
in the Boarding
School Press

"[The texts] go a long way toward showing the degree to which some embraced assimilationist rhetoric and others saw literacy and publishing as means to adapting, surviving, resisting, 'talking back,' and ultimately claiming agency over their own futures in a society that, to differing degrees, saw their existence as a problem to be solved."

— M. F. MCCLURE, *Choice*

"[This volume] brings visibility to the boarding school newspapers, which hopefully will spur efforts at preserving and using these works as an untapped resource that gives voice to Native Americans and expands the history of Native American literature."

— JERRY W. CARLSON, *Nebraska History*

"This collection offers something not only to specialists but also to general readers and especially to classes devoted to Native American studies, Native literature, literacy history, and mass communication. This is an important work."

— HILARY E. WYSS, author of *English Letters and Indian Literacies: Reading, Writing, and New England Missionary Schools, 1750–1830*

"Emery's book is timely and important, as it is critical that both Native Americans and allies push for education about this period in history, especially at such a crucial time in our development as a country. Now, more than ever, with the call for a 'national identity,' we should be looking to our past and what the building of that national identity entails. This means that we should be educating our citizens on how our past governments have attempted to shape the 'American.' Emery's book provides us with a rich resource of stories gathered from the voices of the students who were part of Carlisle founder Richard Henry Pratt's vision."

— LYDIA PRESLEY, *Great Plains Quarterly*

Recovering Native American Writings in the Boarding School Press

Edited by Jacqueline Emery

University of Nebraska Press
Lincoln

Portions of the introduction originally appeared in *American Periodicals,* published by the Ohio State University Press: "Writing against Erasure: Native American Students at Hampton Institute and the Periodical Press," *American Periodicals* 22, no. 2 (2012): 178–98; "Mining Boarding School Newspapers for Native American Women Editors and Writers," *American Periodicals* 27, no. 1 (2017): 11–15.

Library of Congress Cataloging-in-Publication Data
Names: Emery, Jacqueline, editor.
Title: Recovering Native American writings in the boarding school press / edited by Jacqueline Emery.
Description: Lincoln: University of Nebraska Press, 2017. | Includes bibliographical references and index. |
Identifiers: LCCN 2017017419 (print)
LCCN 2017046739 (ebook)
ISBN 9781496204073 (epub)
ISBN 9781496204080 (mobi)
ISBN 9781496204097 (pdf)
ISBN 9780803276758 (hardback: alk. paper)
ISBN 9781496219596 (paperback)
Subjects: LCSH: American literature—Indian authors. | Indians of North America—Literary collections. | Off-reservation boarding schools—United States. | Student newspapers and periodicals—United States. | Indians of North America—Intellectual life—19th century. | Indians of North America—Intellectual life—20th century. | Indians of North America—Education—United States—History—19th century. | Indians of North America—Education—United States—History—20th century. | BISAC: SOCIAL SCIENCE / Ethnic Studies / Native American Studies. | LITERARY COLLECTIONS / Native American.
Classification: LCC PS508.I5 (ebook) | LCC PS508.I5 R37 2017 (print) | DDC 810.8/0897—dc23
LC record available at https://lccn.loc.gov/2017017419

Set in Garamond Premier Pro by A. Shahan.

Contents

Part One
Writings by Boarding School Students

Part Two
Writings by Late Nineteenth- and Early Twentieth-Century Native American Public Intellectuals

Illustrations

Recovering Native
American Writings
in the Boarding
School Press

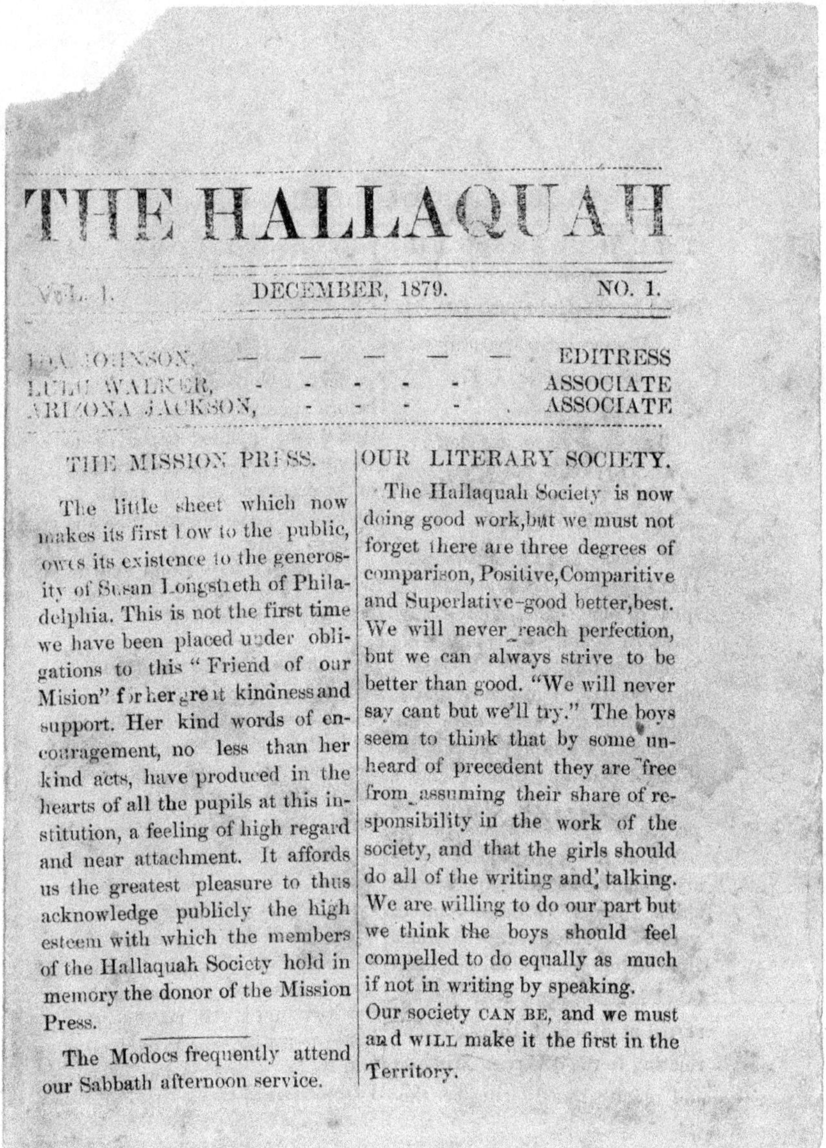

THE HALLAQUAH

VOL. 1.   DECEMBER, 1879.   NO. 1.

IDA JOHNSON, — — — — — EDITRESS
LULU WALKER, - - - - - ASSOCIATE
ARIZONA JACKSON, - - - - ASSOCIATE

THE MISSION PRESS.

The little sheet which now makes its first bow to the public, owes its existence to the generosity of Susan Longstreth of Philadelphia. This is not the first time we have been placed under obligations to this " Friend of our Mision" for her great kindness and support. Her kind words of encouragement, no less than her kind acts, have produced in the hearts of all the pupils at this institution, a feeling of high regard and near attachment. It affords us the greatest pleasure to thus acknowledge publicly the high esteem with which the members of the Hallaquah Society hold in memory the donor of the Mission Press.

The Modocs frequently attend our Sabbath afternoon service.

OUR LITERARY SOCIETY.

The Hallaquah Society is now doing good work, but we must not forget there are three degrees of comparison, Positive, Comparitive and Superlative-good better, best. We will never reach perfection, but we can always strive to be better than good. "We will never say cant but we'll try." The boys seem to think that by some unheard of precedent they are free from assuming their share of responsibility in the work of the society, and that the girls should do all of the writing and talking. We are willing to do our part but we think the boys should feel compelled to do equally as much if not in writing by speaking.
Our society CAN BE, and we must and WILL make it the first in the Territory.

Fig. 1. Front page of the *Hallaquah*, December 1879. Oklahoma Historical Society.

Introduction

In December 1879 three young Native American women at the Seneca Indian School—Ida Johnson, Arizona Jackson, and Lula Walker—launched the first issue of their school newspaper, the *Hallaquah*.[1] This was a rather extraordinary feat, considering these students were printers and editors at a time when such positions were limited for Native Americans and especially limited for young Native women. It is even more remarkable that in the inaugural issue, they proclaimed their intention to make the newspaper serve their own interests and those of the local Native American community and not strictly those of school authorities. Whereas school authorities used boarding school newspapers to promote the civilizing missions of their schools and showcase the transformation of their students, the Indian schoolgirl editors of the *Hallaquah* had something else in mind.[2]

As they announce in their first editorial: "We desire and intend that the *Hallaquah* shall represent the spirit of our school and always speak in behalf of its interest. Supported directly by the Hallaquah Society, it yet is intended to be a true exponent of the Seneca, Shawnee, and Wyandotte Industrial Boarding School, and a news letter to the neighboring people as well as for the pupils" (*Hallaquah* Editorial, December 1879, this volume). Their commitment to using the *Hallaquah* as a vehicle for serving their community and preserving aspects of Native American cultures reflects how students learned to use the tools of the boarding school—their proficiency in English, access to new print technologies, and exposure to the dominant discourses on racial identity—to pose challenges, albeit often subtle ones, to the assimilative policies and practices of the boarding school.[3]

The *Hallaquah* belongs to a vast newspaper archive that remains largely understudied despite the fascinating insight it offers into how Native Americans used boarding school newspapers for their own purposes: to shape representations of Indianness that circulated in U.S. print culture and to foster and maintain indigenous communities of printers, editors, writers, and readers in the late nineteenth and early twentieth centuries. With a few notable exceptions, such as Karen Kilcup's *Native American Women's Writing*, Bernd Peyer's *American Indian Nonfiction*, and Robert Dale Parker's *Changing Is Not Vanishing*, writings by boarding school students and prominent Native American public intellectuals that appeared in boarding school newspapers have lacked critical attention and thus remain virtually unknown and unavailable to most scholars and students of Native American literature. *Recovering Native American Writings in the Boarding School Press* fills this gap in the scholarship by making available a representative sampling of Native-authored letters, editorials, essays, short stories, and retold tales published in boarding school newspapers.

For Native Americans of this generation, the federal boarding school experience in the late nineteenth and early twentieth centuries meant many things, and yet one common thread that binds the thirty-five writers and editors in this collection together was that they employed the periodical as a powerful tool for writing against cultural erasure and for serving the interests of Native communities. Boarding school newspapers, much like the schools themselves, were complex sites of negotiation. Writing for and editing boarding school newspapers, Native Americans developed multiple strategies to negotiate the different and sometimes competing demands and expectations of Native and non-Native audiences in order to gain visibility and the authority to speak. This collection of rich and diverse writings is intended to provide readers with a greater understanding of how boarding school students and Native American public intellectuals demonstrated their agency by fashioning identities for themselves as writers and editors, thus contributing to an expanding history of Native American literature.

Recovering Native American Writings in the Boarding School Press is addressed to readers interested in Native American literature or history, late nineteenth- and early twentieth-century American literature, periodical studies, and U.S. print culture. In this collection readers encounter student-authored texts in a variety of genres from personal letters and autobiographical essays to short stories. The compilation ultimately offers readers insight into the boarding school legacy and its influence on Native American literary production. Besides student writings, selections include writings by prominent Native American literary figures like Gertrude Bonnin or Zitka-la-Ša (Yankton Sioux), Charles Alexander Eastman (Santee Sioux), Arthur Caswell Parker (Seneca), Angel De Cora (Winnebago), and John Milton Oskison (Cherokee), among others, who used boarding school newspapers as a forum for their writings on a range of topics. As the writings collected here reveal, Native Americans used the boarding school press for various purposes—as a vehicle for voicing the interests of their communities, for celebrating tribal identity and preserving oral traditions, and for cultivating networks of Native American editors, writers, and readers at the turn of the twentieth century.

Critical Contexts

Recovering Native American Writings in the Boarding School Press is informed by and contributes to critical conversations in Native American studies that complicate our understanding of the experiences of boarding school students and the influence of boarding schools on Native American literature. The important work of Native scholars Brenda J. Child (Ojibwe), K. Tsianina Lomawaima (Creek), and Robert Warrior (Osage) has allowed us to move beyond seeing boarding school students and prominent Native American writers affiliated with these schools—Bonnin, Eastman, De Cora, Carlos

Montezuma (Yavapai), and others—as simply assimilated victims or simply resistant. Boarding school students had complex and competing responses toward their schooling. These scholars have worked to understand boarding school experiences by reclaiming the voices and writings of students and making them central to discussions of Native American literature.

Despite an interest in recovering student voices, Native and non-Native scholars have been slow to embrace boarding school newspapers in their search for Native-authored texts. One possible explanation for this is the tendency in Native American literary studies to privilege the book over other forms. Warrior's third chapter of *The People and the Word*, titled "The Work of Indian Pupils: Narratives of Learning in Native American Literature," is exemplary in this regard. Central to Warrior's project in the chapter is the notion that Native-authored educational texts, including texts written by boarding school students, are "the backbone of Native American literature" (Warrior, *People*, 100). Warrior searches for student voices in boarding school newspapers like the *Indian Helper*, a white-edited newspaper printed by Native American male students at the Carlisle Indian Industrial School, and although he briefly examines only one student-authored text, an essay by Dennison Wheelock (Oneida), he focuses most of his attention on well-known boarding school narratives that were published in book form: Zitkala-Ša's *American Indian Stories*, Eastman's *From the Deep Woods to Civilization*, and Luther Standing Bear's *My People the Sioux*. These influential books have already garnered significant critical attention, whereas boarding school newspapers remain largely understudied.

By giving only brief consideration to one student-authored text published in a boarding school newspaper, Warrior misses an important opportunity to engage with lesser-known writers and texts that deepen our appreciation of Native educational experiences. Given the privileging of the book in Native American literary studies, it is unsurprising that Warrior's study focuses mostly on retrospective accounts of boarding schools that were published in book form and engages only briefly with boarding school newspapers that contain educational narratives written by students while they were still at school. Scholarship in the main has ignored boarding school newspapers and Native-edited periodicals like the *American Indian Magazine*, the organ of the Society of American Indians (SAI), despite the recognition by a handful of literary scholars and historians that these periodicals served as important outlets for Native American literary production in the late nineteenth and early twentieth centuries.[4]

Another reason why boarding school newspapers remain understudied is that scholars are skeptical of them and the Native-authored texts they contain. Child, whose groundbreaking study of unpublished student letters offers a more complicated understanding of boarding school experiences, acknowledges that boarding school newspapers "present an especially intriguing category for analysis," but she dismisses them as simply promoting an assimilationist agenda (Child, *Boarding*, xvi). Child is right to point out that school authorities often exerted strict editorial control over boarding school newspapers. It is likely that even student-run newspapers like the *Hallaquah* were produced with oversight and possible censorship from school authorities, and thus they should be read with some degree of skepticism. I would argue, however, that all periodicals, including boarding school newspapers, are products of complex negotiations between editors, writers, and readers, and because of that they are objects worthy of study.

New scholarship asserts that boarding school newspapers are an untapped archive for scholars working to recover early indigenous writings and to challenge the restrictive assimilationist-resistance binary that has dominated narratives of the boarding school experience. Scholars who have worked on recovering student-authored texts in boarding school newspapers underscore that this newspaper archive reveals important continuities between student writers and

Native American public intellectuals like Bonnin, Eastman, Montezuma, and Laura Cornelius Kellogg (Oneida), among many others.[5] The present collection contributes to this recent scholarship by emphasizing that boarding school newspapers are important sites for recovering Native American print histories. In it I seek ultimately to demonstrate that Native American boarding school students and public intellectuals capitalized on the periodical's ability to create conversations and debates among a growing network of Native American consumers and producers of print that extended beyond federal boarding schools in the late nineteenth and early twentieth centuries.

The Boarding School Legacy and Early Native American Literature

The writers and editors featured in this collection belong to an emerging canon of early Native American literature that notably includes students who attended missionary-run boarding schools in the eighteenth and early nineteenth centuries. Students of this earlier generation produced a variety of writings using their English-language literacy for their own purposes, as scholars such as Joanna Brooks, Hilary Wyss, and Theresa Strouth Gaul have suggested. The early student writers and the boarding schools they attended serve as precursors to later federal boarding schools and the student writers and public intellectuals connected with them. Briefly tracing some of the similarities between the boarding schools of these two generations and the Native writers affiliated with them allows us to better appreciate the prehistory of the writings reprinted in this collection.

The federal boarding schools of the late nineteenth and early twentieth centuries had their "roots" in the mission boarding schools located in the Northeast in the eighteenth century and in the Southeast in the early nineteenth century (Warrior, *People*, 106). One of the first boarding schools established to convert and educate Native

Americans was Moor's Indian Charity School, founded in Connecticut in 1754 by Eleazar Wheelock. A Congregational minister and mentor to the Mohegan writer Samson Occom, Wheelock established his school to prepare Native American missionaries to convert tribes in New England and beyond. He gave his students a college-preparatory education; however, as Brooks explains, that changed in 1762, when, facing criticism from sponsoring missionary societies, Wheelock "retooled the Moor's curriculum to focus more on preparing his students for the practical aspects of their future duties as missionaries and schoolmasters, small farmers, and domestic servants" (Brooks, *The Collected Writings*, 16). Moor's was eventually relocated to New Hampshire and reconstituted as Dartmouth College.

The next major effort to convert and educate Native Americans in boarding schools was not until 1810, with the establishment of the American Board of Commissioners for Foreign Missions (ABCFM). The ABCFM founded the Brainerd School, which was located in what is now Tennessee and focused on Cherokee education, and the Cornwall Foreign Mission School in Cornwall, Connecticut. Although the Brainerd School and other ABCFM mission schools in the Cherokee Nation served as models for the later federal boarding schools, Gaul points out a crucial difference between them: "Cherokee leaders chose to invite the American Board missionaries into the Nation, encouraged them to open more and more schools, and enrolled their children in the schools" (Gaul, *Cherokee Sister*, 14). Influential Cherokee figures like Catharine Brown and Elias Boudinot attended these schools and later used their English-language literacy and their access to print culture in the service of their communities. Not only did Brown gain an audience for her writings and help shape public opinion, but as Gaul explains, her literary corpus comprises thirty-two recovered letters and a diary, making her, after Occom and John Johnson (Mohegan), "the most prolific Native writer before the late 1820s" (*Cherokee Sister*, 5). Boudinot founded the *Cherokee Phoenix*, the first tribal newspaper, in 1828 and is therefore considered an important figure in the history of the Native American press.

Early missionary-run boarding schools produced texts that represented students as passive recipients of a Native education in English literacy—what Wyss terms "Readerly Indians"—and used student writing for fundraising purposes, as would federal boarding schools in the late nineteenth and early twentieth centuries. In her study of early missionary-run boarding schools, Wyss notes how in the 1760s Wheelock sent student handwriting samples, letters, and other schoolwork to secure continued funding from benefactors in England and Boston. Wheelock also reprinted letters by pupils David Fowler (Montaukett) and Joseph Woolley (Delaware) in his 1766–67 English narratives. Both letters, Wyss points out, "are substantially longer than the version he reprints in his narratives" (Wyss, *English Letters*, 60). Wyss demonstrates how Wheelock exercised control over the narratives by excising details that might reflect poorly on him; for example, Wheelock leaves out Fowler's mention of how much money he will need to live on and Woolley's concern over the shortage of funds. Wyss's examination of how figures like Wheelock used Native writings contextualizes our understanding of how later boarding school authorities like Richard Henry Pratt, founder of the Carlisle Indian Industrial School, used student-authored texts in the school newspapers they edited to create narratives of "progress" and total transformation, as I discuss later.

While Wheelock and other school authorities sought in their missionary literature to represent their students as "Readerly Indians," Wyss argues that Native Americans demonstrated their agency by becoming what she terms "Writerly Indians." As Wyss observes, "Writerly Indians used written discourse to manage their own sovereignty in ways that often challenged, confused, or contradicted missionary desire. At times, however, that sovereignty meshed nicely with missionary goals. Either way, the Writerly Indian figure left evidence of a powerful commitment to the continued existence of Native communities, even in the face of sometimes overwhelming rhetorical and political challenges to that identity" (Wyss, *English Letters*, 7).

Wyss also emphasizes not what Native Americans connected to these early missionary-run boarding schools wrote but that they wrote: "Those Natives who *did* write, no matter what they wrote, fundamentally altered the relationship between missionary culture and Native people through the simple act of self-expression" (7). By suggesting that the act of writing itself should be understood as a demonstration of agency and an effort to control their own repre-sentation, Wyss models a way to move beyond the critical tendency to see early boarding school students and their later counterparts who attended federal boarding schools as passive recipients of an assimilative education.[6]

Wyss's concept of the Writerly Indian provides a useful framework for understanding how the boarding school students and promi-nent Native American public intellectuals featured in this collec-tion used their English-language literacy in ways that at times may have supported the assimilationist goals of the boarding schools and that were at other times unanticipated by school authorities and at odds with the schools' civilizing missions. The *Hallaquah* and other boarding school newspapers thus reflect the complexities of Native writers' positions and contain a range of perspectives—sometimes, within the same issue, writings by Native Americans who assert their tribal identities in an effort to preserve them against the school's programs of cultural erasure appear alongside Native-authored texts that promote the school's assimilationist agendas.

Native American Periodical Networks

Periodicals served as important publication venues for early Na-tive American writers. The Native American press is considered to have begun with the launch of either Henry Rowe Schoolcraft's

Muzzinyegun in 1826 or Elias Boudinot's *Cherokee Phoenix* in 1828. Native American press historians Daniel F. Littlefield Jr. and James W. Parins consider the *Muzzinyegun* the first Native American periodical because Schoolcraft's Ojibwa wife, Jane, and her mother and brother contributed much of the content to the newspaper. Jane wrote poetry as well as articles on Ojibwa folklore and history (Littlefield and Parins, *American Indian*, xii, xx). The same year Schoolcraft's periodical was founded, Boudinot, while on a speaking tour, expressed the need for a tribal newspaper. The American Board of Foreign Missions helped him raise funds to purchase the press and equipment. The *Cherokee Phoenix* was published in English and Cherokee and was established, as Littlefield and Parins explain, "as a direct response to Georgia's efforts to extend her laws over the Cherokee Nation" (*American Indian*, xii). The *Phoenix* published local news, educational essays, poetry, and letters.

Other noteworthy periodicals edited by Native Americans include the *Cherokee Rose Buds* published at the Cherokee Female Seminary in Oklahoma in 1854, Carlos Montezuma's pamphlet *Wassaja*, and the pan-tribal *Quarterly Journal of the Society of American Indians*. Catharine Gunter and Nancy E. Hicks, who edited the *Cherokee Rose Buds*, are two of the earliest known young Native American women to assume the role of editor of their school newspaper. The *Cherokee Rose Buds* was a three-column newspaper of eight pages that contained original poetry, essays, and narratives composed by students. As Littlefield and Parins note, this was not an ordinary school newsletter but a vehicle "for the literary expression of the students, who were exposed to a classical education" (*American Indian*, xx, 407). Montezuma's *Wassaja* was published in Chicago from 1916 to 1922. According to Rochelle Rainieri Zuck, the pamphlet reflected Montezuma's view that "the American Indian press should communicate the material realities of American Indians and focus on the development of strategies and tactics to fight the BIA [Bureau of Indian Affairs]" (Zuck, "'Yours,'" 79). The influential

Quarterly Journal of the Society of American Indians (later renamed the *American Indian Magazine*) was launched in 1913. Arthur C. Parker served as editor-general until Gertrude Bonnin assumed the editorship in 1918.[7]

As publishing opportunities for Native Americans began to expand in the late nineteenth and early twentieth centuries, prominent figures like Bonnin, De Cora, and Eastman found outlets for their short stories and autobiographical essays in magazines with a predominantly non-Native readership like the *Atlantic Monthly*, *Harper's Monthly*, and *St. Nicholas: An Illustrated Magazine for Young Folks*. These early Native American writers were boarding school graduates with connections to Carlisle. Indeed, it was partially through their affiliation with Carlisle and its periodical networks that they learned how periodicals could serve as a powerful tool for shaping public perceptions of Native Americans. They used their periodical writings, in the words of A. Lavonne Brown Ruoff, to educate "white audiences about the intellectual and creative abilities of Indian people, the value of their tribal cultures, and white injustice to Native peoples" (Ruoff, Foreword, x).

At the same time, they sought to reach a broader audience that included Native American readers in their efforts to cultivate and sustain pan-tribal networks of communication. In this way they resembled their eighteenth- and early nineteenth-century precursors who established northeastern networks by adapting print and English-language literacy practices to serve as tools for resistance and change, as the work of Lisa Brooks (Abenaki), Matt Cohen, and Phillip H. Round demonstrates.[8] Bonnin, De Cora, Eastman, boarding school students, and other writers of their generation recognized early on that boarding school newspapers and Native-edited periodicals provided the best venues for reaching a mixed audience of Native and non-Native readers. That is why, according to Bernd Peyer, boarding school newspapers and Native-edited periodicals like the *Quarterly Journal of the Society of American Indians* constitute a major archive for nonfiction prose as well as fiction and poetry in the late nineteenth and early twentieth centuries (Peyer, *American Indian Nonfiction*, 26). Native Americans used these periodicals as outlets not only for self-expression but also for community building. Student editors of the Seneca Indian School's *Hallaquah*, Hampton Institute's *Talks and Thoughts of the Hampton Indian Students*, and the Carlisle Indian Industrial School's *School News* as well as editors of the *Quarterly Journal* employed reprinting, a common journalistic practice at the turn of the twentieth century, in their efforts to strengthen communication between disparate networks of Native American editors, writers, and readers. They also announced and supported other periodicals edited by or written for Native Americans. The editors of the *Quarterly Journal* even published several pieces on boarding school newspapers.

For example, in the "Editorial Comment" in the January–March 1915 issue Arthur C. Parker notes that in every boarding school newspaper he has examined "there is an expressed spirit of cheer and of helpfulness." Parker goes on to emphasize the value of boarding school newspapers and their mission. That mission, as he explains, is not only to give students who want to learn instruction in printing but also to keep students, parents, and the public informed of the educational work of the school. Parker further asserts, "All of these purposes are worthy ones, and the school paper deserves the support of the field it reaches and the appreciation of the public" ("Editorial Comment," 5–6). Parker's editorial ultimately reveals his belief that boarding school newspapers and the *Quarterly Journal* served as tools for fostering and sustaining pan-tribal networks of periodical producers and consumers.[9]

Native American editors and writers also used boarding school newspapers to debate pressing issues that were important to the survival of Native American communities in the face of the assimilationist imperative of the boarding school and the dominant culture more broadly. This newspaper archive thus troubles the assumption that Native Americans voiced static or homogenous perspectives on issues like assimilation, citizenship, and education; indeed, these issues were widely debated in Native writings that appeared in boarding school newspapers. It is because boarding school newspapers offer disparate and often competing perspectives that they provide a richer sense of the conversations and debates that transpired between and among boarding school students and prominent Native American public intellectuals at the turn of the twentieth century.

Given the complicated institutional contexts of the production of boarding school newspapers, it should come as no surprise that the writers and editors featured in this collection engaged in the assimilationist and progressivist rhetoric of their day in complex and sometimes contradictory ways. Although many of them voiced critical perspectives that posed challenges to the assimilative thrust of federal boarding schools and the dominant culture more broadly, most of the time their resistance was subtle. As Gale P. Coskan-Johnson explains in her insightful literary recovery of Charles Eastman, "Revolution is only occasionally 'blood in the streets'; what we are more likely to find here, given the overwhelming hegemony of American cultural and military forces in the United States at the time, is something trickier, more sophisticated, and heavily veiled—something that would protect the speaker from retribution and so allow her or him to continue speaking" (Coskan-Johnson, "What Writer," 111).

Boarding school students, who lacked the relative cultural authority of prominent Native American public intellectuals like Eastman, had to develop even trickier and subtler strategies in their writings in order to express their critical perspectives and their commitment to Native communities and to change. In a more telling example, even a writer like Bonnin, whom Dexter Fisher described as "the darling" of the northeastern literary establishment, found herself engaging in pen wars with school authorities who sought to silence and discredit her in print (Fisher, "Zitkala-Ša," 229). The editorial comments accompanying Bonnin's essays reprinted in this collection serve as a reminder of the obstacles she and other Native Americans were up against in the contest over representations of Indian identity in the boarding school press and the complex rhetorical strategies they used in their writings in order for their voices to be heard. Like Eastman, who, as Coskan-Johnson writes, "engaged in a rich Native American public discourse that circulated in and out of national discussions of identity and politics," so too did Bonnin, boarding school students, and other writers of this generation (Coskan-Johnson, "What Writer," 130).

The Boarding School in Context

With a few notable exceptions, like the *Hallaquah*, which was published at a reservation boarding school, most of the writings in this collection were first printed in newspapers published at off-reservation boarding schools. Missionaries assumed the primary responsibility for educating Indian children until the 1870s when the federal government took direct control over Indian education, and policy makers began to shift away from day and reservation schools in favor of off-reservation boarding schools. This shift can be explained in part by a change in public attitudes toward Native Americans, especially among eastern reformers, who saw education as the solution to what had long been deemed the "Indian problem." Samuel Chapman Armstrong and Richard Henry Pratt were among a cohort of reformers known as the "friends of the Indians" who believed strongly in Indians' ability to be educated in preparation for citizenship.[10] Both Armstrong and Pratt set out to prove that Indians were educable by establishing the first federal off-reservation educational programs designed to eradicate "from students every available trace of Native identity and replac[e] it with a facsimile of whiteness" (Warrior, *People*, 112).

The genesis of the federal government's system of off-reservation boarding schools for Native Americans was Pratt's educational venture at Fort Marion in St. Augustine, Florida.[11] Pratt's program for Indian prisoners at Fort Marion sought to prove that Native Americans could be educated and civilized. He taught the prisoners English and aimed to instill in them habits of discipline, work, and cleanliness. The containment and seclusion of the fort provided what Pratt believed were ideal conditions for civilizing Native Americans; he would later recreate this model at the Carlisle Indian Industrial School in Pennsylvania (Fear-Segal, *White Man's Club*, 15–18).

Pratt's experiment with the prisoners at Fort Marion set a precedent for the creation of the first formal federal off-reservation educational program for Indians. In 1878 Samuel Chapman Armstrong opened the doors of Hampton Institute in Virginia, founded in 1868 to provide freed slaves with a vocational education, to some of the recently released Fort Marion prisoners.[12] One year later Pratt founded the Carlisle Indian Industrial School, which became the prototype for federal off-reservation boarding schools across the United States.

The aim of federal boarding schools like Hampton and Carlisle was the same: to provide Native American students with the teachings of civilization in the form of a practical, vocational education. In keeping with the civilizing mission of these schools, students were first taught how to speak, read, and write in English.[13] The government established an English-only policy in boarding schools that reflected a belief in the superiority of English over Indian languages. The imposition of an English-only education was highly politicized: the policy, which was strictly enforced from the 1880s until the 1930s, solidified the notion that the acquisition of English was the primary purpose of education for Native Americans.

As soon as students understood English they were to begin studying other academic subjects like math, geography, and U.S. history. Students received a "half and half" education, meaning that their academic education was accompanied by vocational training designed to enable them to become self-sufficient workers. Students spent part of the day learning trades or performing manual labor and a few hours each day in the classroom. Girls received a domestic education to prepare them to become wives and maids. Boys learned how to use tools and acquired skills associated with farming, blacksmithing, and carpentry. Some male students received training in printing and worked in the printing offices.

From the beginning of their educational experiments, Armstrong and Pratt set out to sway skeptics about the educability of Indians. As Pratt once explained, his was a twofold educational program: "We have two objects in view in starting the Carlisle School—one is to educate the Indians—the other is to educate the people of the country . . . to understand that the Indians can be educated" ("Indian School Commencement," *Sentinel*, 2). Both Hampton and Carlisle established printing offices to aid in their attempts to demonstrate that Indians were educable. Male students were responsible for printing all the publications produced at the printing offices at Hampton and Carlisle. Carlisle's weekly *Indian Helper* advertised this fact, announcing on the front page of every issue that it was "printed by Indian boys." The newspapers themselves attempted to prove to a skeptical public that by providing training in printing to Indian students, the boarding schools were offering them a means of attaining economic self-sufficiency.[14]

In addition to showcasing the printing skills of their students in the various school publications, Armstrong, Pratt, and other school authorities frequently published student writings in the pages of the school newspapers to demonstrate to white readers that students were successfully learning the language of civilization. Alongside the student writings and writings about fully assimilated Indians, they printed before-and-after photographs capturing the cultural transformation students underwent at the schools. Together, the photographs and writings told a narrative of assimilation designed to convince white readers that Hampton's and Carlisle's educational programs could not only transform "savages" into students but could do so quickly. In this way the white-edited newspapers played a crucial role in gaining the financial and political support of white readers. Armstrong and Pratt sent copies of their newspapers to "every member of Congress, all the Indian agencies and military posts, and the most prominent American newspapers" (Enoch, "Resisting," 122). For Armstrong, Pratt, and other school authorities, the boarding school press was an important medium for gaining the support of whites in order to ensure the success of their educational experiments.

Armstrong and Pratt relied heavily on the periodical press to gain public approval of and financial support for their educational programs, especially among those who might influence the government's policies on Indian education. The white-edited school newspapers served as an important link between school authorities and Washington and helped shape government Indian policy from the late nineteenth century through the early decades of the twentieth (Littlefield and Parins, *American Indian*, xxviii). They also provided a means for Armstrong, Pratt, and other school authorities to respond to critics of Indian education.

As early as the 1880s critics began to voice concerns over the system of education practiced at off-reservation boarding schools. According to historian Robert A. Trennert, after 1900 "critics became more vocal and persistent, arguing that the Indian community did not approve of this type of education, that most students gained little, and that employment opportunities were limited at best" (Trennert, "Educating," 288). Commissioner of Indian Affairs Francis E. Leupp (1905–1909) argued that the educational system not only failed to produce self-reliant Indians and to provide students with a useful education but also protected them in an artificial environment in boarding schools, where they received the comforts of civilization at no cost and without developing a work ethic.

In order to demonstrate that their educational programs could Americanize Indian students, school authorities printed representations of students in the pages of their newspapers that showcased their "progress." Coverage of Indian Citizenship Day pageants, sporting events, and graduations was meant to signal to white readers that students were capable of being transformed.

Besides playing a role in promoting the educational work of the schools, the white-edited newspapers at Hampton, Carlisle, and other boarding schools performed specific roles for their Native American readers. These newspapers functioned first and foremost as a pedagogical tool for boarding school students and graduates. As Jessica Enoch points out, Carlisle's white-edited *Indian Helper* "taught current and former Carlisle students the rules of etiquette, English, and white behavior, reinforcing the pedagogical objectives learned in the classroom" (Enoch, "Resisting," 122). Hampton's white-edited *Southern Workman* also performed a pedagogical role for students: not only was the *Workman* the main text in all the reading courses offered at Hampton, but like the *Indian Helper*, it printed success stories of model students and graduates for other students to emulate (Anderson, *Education of Blacks*, 50). Furthermore, the white-edited newspapers printed at Hampton and Carlisle served as a disciplinary and surveillance device designed to keep student readers in their place.

Boarding school newspapers, much like the schools themselves, were complex sites of negotiation. Whereas school authorities used the white-edited school newspapers to publicize their efforts to erase their students' Indianness by imprinting them with the markers of a white middle-class cultural identity, students often used the school newspapers to defend and preserve Native American identity and culture against the assimilationist imperatives of the boarding schools and the dominant culture. Writing for, editing, and printing school newspapers, students learned how to negotiate the demands placed on them by school authorities who oversaw these publications.

Writers and Themes

Of the thirty-five writers and editors whom I have selected to include in this collection, some may be unfamiliar to readers. The students I have selected are notable because they contributed regularly to their school newspaper and some of them even served as editors. Although many of the students who contributed to boarding school newspapers did not continue to publish after they graduated, there are a few exceptions. Hampton Institute graduate Harry Hand (Crow Creek Sioux) founded his own tribal newspapers, the *Crow Creek Herald* and the *Crow Creek Chief*. Hand died only one year after he founded the *Chief*; however, his ambition to serve his community by starting his own newspapers speaks volumes about his belief in the power of the periodical press. Elizabeth Bender (White Earth Chippewa), also a Hampton graduate, continued to publish nonfiction prose in the boarding school press. Through her active membership in the SAI, Bender met and married Henry Roe Cloud (Winnebago), a founding member of the organization. Roe Cloud founded the American Indian Institute, where Bender taught as well as contributed to the institute's newspaper, the *Indian Outlook*. Other more prominent writers like Charles Eastman (Santee Sioux) and Angel De Cora (Winnebago), who were boarding school graduates and active members of the SAI, may be familiar to readers, yet many of the writings they published in boarding school newspapers have never before been published in a collection. *Recovering Native American Writings in the Boarding School Press* provides readers with a greater understanding of how these writers engaged each other about a range of topics from education and citizenship to tribal art.

A crucial topic for many writers collected here is education, and a number of them set out to reflect on the boarding school experience. Boarding school students and graduates responded in multiple ways to their schooling; some took a rather positive view of it, as we see in writings by Henry C. Roman Nose (Southern Cheyenne), Mary North (Arapaho), Luther Standing Bear (Pine Ridge Sioux), and Samuel Townsend (Pawnee), all of whom contributed to the *School News*. Although the *School News* was edited by Townsend and another Carlisle student, Charles Kihega (Iowa), it is likely that the newspaper's content was closely monitored by Pratt and Marianna Burgess, who supervised the printing office. This may explain why, in their writings, students seem to reflect the views of school authorities and are less critical of their boarding school experience, which was, in the words of historian David Wallace Adams, an "education for extinction."

Roman Nose's autobiographical essays appeared in the *School News* from June 1880 through March 1881. He was one of the Fort Marion prisoners who accompanied Pratt to Hampton and then to Carlisle, where he stayed two years to learn the tinning trade. In his autobiographical essays Roman Nose chronicles his journey from Fort Marion in St. Augustine, Florida, to Carlisle. He also charts his progress from his Indian boyhood marked by hunting and battles to his success as a Carlisle student, which he attributes to his learning English: "They stayed in prison there three years and we had no school, but Capt. Pratt showed us ABC and now we understand these letters. We did not know how to spell anything . . . but [we] have certainly been much benefited" (Roman Nose, "Experiences 1880," this volume).

Like Roman Nose, North and Standing Bear emphasize the benefits of their schooling. North contrasts her life as a Carlisle student with her life on the reservation: "When we were at home in Indian Territory we had nothing to do but play and go to the river and go in swimming and now we are way off from home at school and learning something" (North, "A Little Story," this volume). She tells us that what she is learning is how to write a story, which will give her practice expressing herself in English. In contrast to North, Standing Bear reveals in a letter to his father some of his struggles

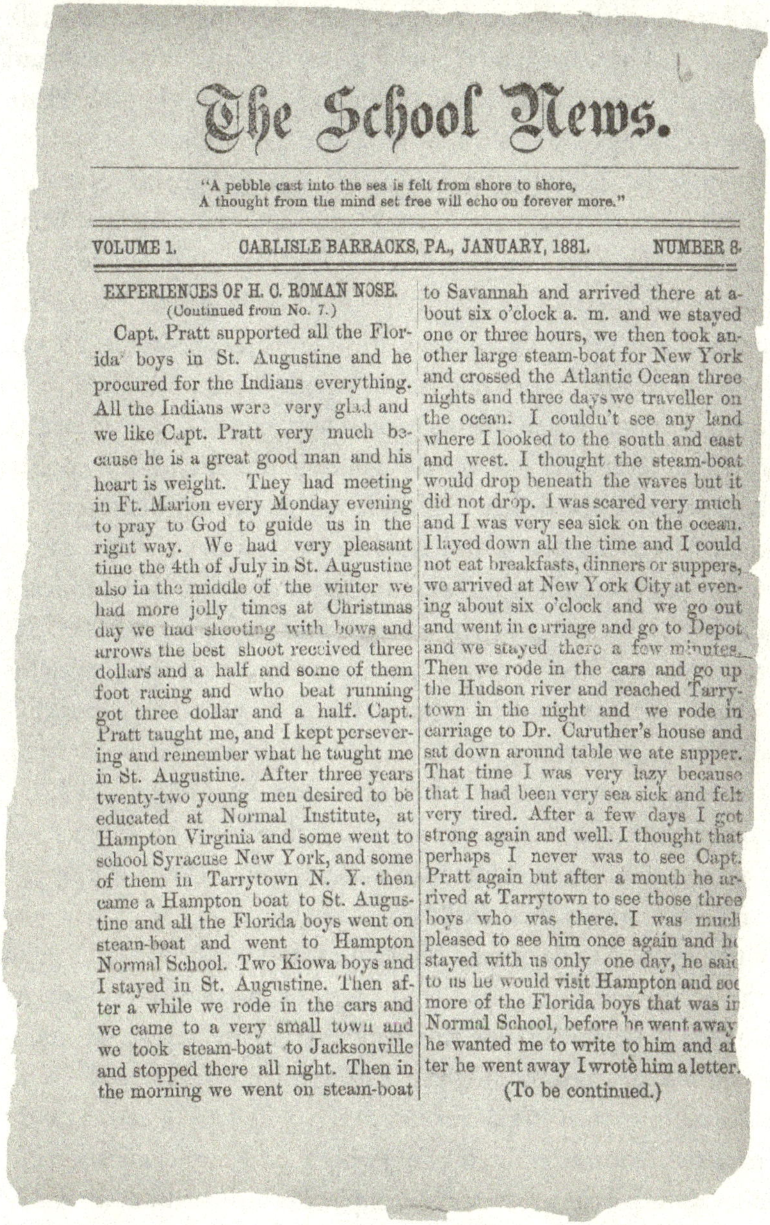

The School News.

"A pebble cast into the sea is felt from shore to shore,
A thought from the mind set free will echo on forever more."

VOLUME 1.   CARLISLE BARRACKS, PA., JANUARY, 1881.   NUMBER 8.

EXPERIENCES OF H. C. ROMAN NOSE.
(Continued from No. 7.)

Capt. Pratt supported all the Florida boys in St. Augustine and he procured for the Indians everything. All the Indians were very glad and we like Capt. Pratt very much because he is a great good man and his heart is weight. They had meeting in Ft. Marion every Monday evening to pray to God to guide us in the right way. We had very pleasant time the 4th of July in St. Augustine also in the middle of the winter we had more jolly times at Christmas day we had shooting with bows and arrows the best shoot received three dollars and a half and some of them foot racing and who beat running got three dollar and a half. Capt. Pratt taught me, and I kept persevering and remember what he taught me in St. Augustine. After three years twenty-two young men desired to be educated at Normal Institute, at Hampton Virginia and some went to school Syracuse New York, and some of them in Tarrytown N. Y. then came a Hampton boat to St. Augustine and all the Florida boys went on steam-boat and went to Hampton Normal School. Two Kiowa boys and I stayed in St. Augustine. Then after a while we rode in the cars and we came to a very small town and we took steam-boat to Jacksonville and stopped there all night. Then in the morning we went on steam-boat to Savannah and arrived there at about six o'clock a. m. and we stayed one or three hours, we then took another large steam-boat for New York and crossed the Atlantic Ocean three nights and three days we traveller on the ocean. I couldn't see any land where I looked to the south and east and west. I thought the steam-boat would drop beneath the waves but it did not drop. I was scared very much and I was very sea sick on the ocean. I layed down all the time and I could not eat breakfasts, dinners or suppers, we arrived at New York City at evening about six o'clock and we go out and went in carriage and go to Depot and we stayed there a few minutes. Then we rode in the cars and go up the Hudson river and reached Tarrytown in the night and we rode in carriage to Dr. Caruther's house and sat down around table we ate supper. That time I was very lazy because that I had been very sea sick and felt very tired. After a few days I got strong again and well. I thought that perhaps I never was to see Capt. Pratt again but after a month he arrived at Tarrytown to see those three boys who was there. I was much pleased to see him once again and he stayed with us only one day, he said to us he would visit Hampton and see more of the Florida boys that was in Normal School, before he went away he wanted me to write to him and after he went away I wrote him a letter.

(To be continued.)

Fig. 2. Front page of the *School News*, January 1881. General Research Division, New York Public Library, Astor, Lenox and Tilden Foundations.

to learn English: "We are trying to speak only English nothing talk Sioux. . . . I have tried. But I could not do it at first. But I tried hard every day. So now I have found out how to speak only English. I have been speaking only English about 14 weeks now I have not said any Indian words at all" (Standing Bear, Letter to Father, this volume).[15]

The writings of Roman Nose, North, and Standing Bear bring into focus how students negotiated an English-only policy designed to result in their loss of their respective first languages. These students, like so many educated at Carlisle and other boarding schools, were subject to a strict English-only policy that prohibited them from speaking Indian languages on school grounds. Their writings reveal that they did not overtly challenge the English-only policy but rather believed that English-language literacy offered them, their fellow classmates, and even their elders an opportunity for social and economic gain (Standing Bear urges his father to learn English). This was the same message Pratt espoused in his efforts to convince Native American parents to send their children to his school: "Cannot you see it is far, far better for you to have your children educated and trained as our children are so that they can speak the English language, write letters, and do the things which bring to the white man such prosperity, and each of them be able to stand for their rights as the white man stands for his?" (Pratt, *Battlefield*, 223). Pratt underscored the link between literacy, advancement, and citizenship. He and other school authorities wedded their belief in the promise of literacy to the ideology of social evolutionism. As Amelia Katanski explains, they believed that literacy would "transform students as they 'progressed' from tribal 'savagery' to Western 'civilization'" (Katanski, *Learning to Write "Indian,"* 4). At the same time they considered literacy not only a marker of civilization but also an indicator of students' complete transformation or loss of Indianness (Katanski, *Learning to Write "Indian,"* 131).

What Pratt and other school authorities failed to understand, however, was that most students were not simply going to give up their first languages and Native identities and sever their ties to their tribal communities once they acquired English-language literacy. For many students learning English did not result in a total transformation. Rather, those who learned English and became proficient in it gained the power to use it to serve their communities. In this way they resembled prominent boarding school graduates like Bonnin and Eastman, who as Warrior explains, "wanted what the schools they attended offered. Yet they also wanted to have a stake in their own destiny" (Warrior, *People*, 116). By fashioning identities for themselves as writers in the pages of boarding school newspapers, students gained control over their self-representations and revised what it meant to be educated Indians, just as Samuel Townsend did in his editorials in the *School News*.

In his July 1880 editorial Townsend challenges white stereotypes about Native Americans as uneducable and uncivilized:

Some white folks say that the Indians do not know anything and can't learn anything, but the Indians are learning something. Great many of the white folks never read about the Indians and they do not know anything about us, but sometimes they talk bad about us and they say that the Indians have no brains to think with and they can't learn anything. Sometimes they say Indians can not be civilized. Maybe those white folks don't know anything. (Townsend, Editorial, July 1880, this volume)

Here Townsend argues that Native American students were learning and gaining much from their education. He also reverses what white critics say about the ignorance of Native Americans: he argues that those critics are ignorant about Indians' ability to earn an education and integrate into the dominant culture on an equal basis. In the same editorial Townsend uses cross-cultural comparisons to stress that like whites, Native Americans "can do most anything" so long as they are given an education.

Furthermore, he argues, Native Americans are not to blame for the slow spread of civilization. He insists instead that the blame rests with the lack of federal funding for boarding schools: "If every Indian boy and girl were in school it would not take long to civilize all the Indians. The reason it takes so long is because Washington does not give enough money to put all the Indian children in school." Admittedly, Townsend's rhetoric echoes some of Pratt's thinking about the fundamental role of education in civilizing Native Americans. However, more significantly, Townsend's editorial demonstrates that he is not a passive recipient of his boarding school education; indeed, he uses the *School News* as a venue for "talking back," to borrow a phrase from historian Frederick E. Hoxie. By talking back to members of the dominant culture, Hoxie writes, "Natives made it clear that they refused to accept the definitions others had of them—savage, backward, doomed" (Hoxie, *Talking Back*, viii). For Townsend, "talking back" meant challenging, albeit in subtle ways, white stereotypes of Indians and the assumption that white culture was superior.

Writing more than thirty years later, long after Pratt was forced to resign from Carlisle in the wake of increasing criticism of his approach to Indian education, John Milton Oskison (Cherokee) praised Carlisle and other boarding schools for what they were doing for Indians.[16] In "The Indian in the Professions" Oskison challenges the notion that Carlisle graduates return to the blanket by offering examples of how educated Indians have entered a number of professions, including "teaching, nursing, the law, the diplomatic service, the ministry, medicine, politics, dentistry, veterinary surgery, writing, painting, acting." Furthermore, he writes, "The professions are wide open to us. We have the strength and the steadiness of will to make good in them" (Oskison, "The Indian in the Professions," this volume). For Oskison and others, an education at Carlisle, and better yet, a degree from a college or university, "could be a means to do what he and the SAI urged the Indians to do: take their future into their hands and speak for themselves as Indian individuals and Indian peoples" (Larré, "John Milton Oskison," 11).

Several writers in this collection argued for higher education for Native Americans. For example, in an address Charles Eastman delivered at a Carlisle commencement and which appeared in the February–March 1899 issue of the *Red Man*, he narrates the story of how he became an educated Indian.[17] Eastman, who graduated from Dartmouth and earned his medical degree at Boston University, writes, "[S]ome twenty-five years ago, I took my blanket and my bag and started from Sioux Falls, in South Dakota, to the Santee Agency up above Yankton on the Missouri River, some one hundred and thirty miles, on foot in search of education" (Eastman, "Address at Carlisle Commencement," this volume). Although it begins with his account of schooling, Eastman's address is not merely an account of his success as a model boarding school graduate. Rather, Eastman uses his audience's interest in him as an educated Indian for his own purposes. Unlike Pratt and other school authorities who opposed higher education for Native Americans and imagined a future in which they were absorbed into white culture as landholders and farmers, Eastman articulates an alternative vision. He envisions a future in which educated Indian leaders with "purer and higher ideals" would "press steadily onward and upward, that we [Indians] may some day take a distinctive part in the great civilization of this western nation." Echoing the rhetoric of uplift commonly associated with African American public intellectuals like W.E.B. Du Bois, Eastman reveals that he believed strongly that a higher education would prepare Native Americans for their future roles as leaders of the race.

Also believing in the advantages of higher education, Arthur C. Parker (Seneca) argues for an Indian college or university. In his essay "Progress for the Indian" Parker writes, "The great need of teaching the Indian to appreciate and measure his own culture in the full knowledge of others is apparent. To this end the writer strongly believes in the necessity of an Indian college or university. In such an institution graduates of the higher schools might be trained in the art, literature, history, ethnology, and philosophy of their people" (Parker, "Progress for the Indian," this volume). In their periodical writings, Oskison, Eastman, and Parker, among others emphasized the importance of higher education to an indigenous future.

For most of the writers in this collection, being an educated Indian meant challenging the notion of the vanishing Indian with their own counter-representations of Indians as capable of change. Elizabeth Bender represents her people in a moment of transition in "The Land of Hiawatha," an essay that appeared in the June 1907 issue of the student-edited *Talks and Thoughts of the Hampton Indian Students*.[18] She subtly disrupts the discourse of the vanishing Indian celebrated in Henry Wadsworth Longfellow's poem "The Song of Hiawatha" by representing the Chippewas not as disappearing culturally but rather as capable of change. Her negotiation between a desire to preserve Ojibwa traditions and an embrace of cultural change becomes more complex toward the end of the essay as she mentions the inevitable passing of "old ways," meaning hunting and gathering, and praises "civilization, with cozy homes and well kept farms" (Bender, "Land of Hiawatha," 4). Bender embraces the transformation of a hunter-gather culture to an agricultural one and speaks positively of her tribe's transition to farming: "Most of the Chippewas are engaged in farming, and are quite industrious. The reservation life has somewhat retarded their progress, but in spite of obstacles and hardships they are making a brave struggle" (Bender, "Land of Hiawatha," 4). By emphasizing that Indians could change and were changing, Bender challenges the myth of the vanishing Indian, while at the same time she insists that Chippewas are retaining their cultural ties.[19]

Other writers featured here also challenge representations of Indian cultures as vanishing by showcasing how indigenous traditions like storytelling, dancing, and art remain important to Native communities. Students like Harry Hand, Joseph Du Bray (Yankton Sioux), and Anna Bender (White Earth Chippewa) transcribed oral traditions into English and then preserved them in print in *Talks and Thoughts*. Hand's illustrations also accompanied some of his writings. The students' retold tales often depict how stories are passed down from a revered storyteller to the younger generation. By retelling oral traditions in boarding school newspapers, these writers contribute to the efforts of more well-known writers like Francis La Flesche (Omaha) and Gertrude Bonnin (Yankton Sioux), who sought to preserve oral traditions for future generations of Native Americans while educating white readers about the value of their tribal cultures.[20]

Bonnin often portrayed Native traditions positively in her periodical writings. For example, in her 1902 article "A Protest Against the Abolition of the Indian Dance" she likens Native American culture to a frozen river waiting to "rush forth from its icy bondage" (Bonnin, "Protest," this volume). Meanwhile, white assimilationists hack away at the ice, hissing "immodest" and "this dance of the Indian is a relic of barbarism." Bonnin rails against the notion that the Indian dance is "barbaric." Turning a critical gaze upon the dominant culture, she challenges white readers to see their assumptions and values reflected through the eyes of an educated Native American woman writer. She suggests that "the yellow-haired and blue-eyed races" who wear corsets in their evening gowns as they dance to orchestral music may in fact be "barbaric." She then writes, "In truth, I would not like to say any graceful movement of the human figure in rhythm to music was ever barbaric." In this way, Bonnin seeks to humanize Indian dancers in the minds of her white readers. At the same time, she argues against efforts among assimilationists to destroy Native cultural traditions by abolishing the Indian dance. She suggests that the Indian dance still has value in tribal culture, especially among the older generation.

TALKS AND THOUGHTS

OF THE HAMPTON INDIAN STUDENTS.

"Genius, like humanity, rusts for want of use."—Shakespeare.

VOL. VII. No. 10.　　　HAMPTON, VA., MARCH, 1893.　　　25 cts. Per Year.

Wo-kda-ke-sa, or The Story Teller.

The Story Teller.

The picture here presented, is from a sketch by one of our students, Harry Hand. The picture shows something that is very often seen among Indian homes. In the evening, after supper, the men would get together, bring their pipes with their long stems and kinnikinick bags, sit in a circle and smoke; while one of the group would tell a story of war or hunting. When they have this, if there are any children present, the old Indian would say, now children, you listen, so that you will see what I ought to have done and what I ought not to have done, so that if you ever meet with the same thing you can remember what I said so that you can improve on them." It is very interesting to listen to them. We have read of many adventures of white people among Indians, but we never read of adventures told by Indians among white people. Why? Because the Indians have no newspaper through which to let the reading public know their side of many stories.

They usually put the pipes and kinnikinick and some matches in the center of the circle so that whoever wishes can fill a pipe up and have a smoke. The true stories they tell are free for all but when they tell fairy stories the story teller has to be given something by some of the listeners. Only those who give something have the right to tell the stories; but they must not tell them unless something is given to them. We think if the Indian fairy stories were gathered and translated by a good translator and published in book form they would compare favorably with "Arabian Nights."

On the right of the picture will be seen something hanging very much like washed clothes hung on clothes-line. In olden times when there were plenty of buffaloes the Indians did not salt the meat they wanted to keep, like white people do at Chicago and other places, but they sliced the meat into thin pieces and then hung out in the sun or above the fire to dry. This way was very good as it kept long time.

HBA

Fig. 3. Harry Hand's illustration on the front page of *Talks and Thoughts*, March 1893. General Research Division, New York Public Library, Astor, Lenox and Tilden Foundations.

Like Bonnin, Eastman and Angel De Cora argue for the importance of Native cultural traditions in their respective writings published in the *Red Man*.[21] For example, in his essay "'My People': The Indians' Contribution to the Art of America," Eastman comments on the study of Native arts and crafts in boarding schools. He explains that without this instruction, most students would "grow up in ignorance of their natural heritage, in legend, music, and art forms as well as practical handicrafts" (Eastman, "'My People,'" this volume). He goes on to praise the work of De Cora and her husband, William Deitz (Sioux), at Carlisle for attempting "to discover latent artistic gifts among the Indian students, in order that they may be fully trained and utilized in the direction of pure or applied art." Reminding readers that "as recently as twenty years ago, all native art was severely discountenanced and discouraged, if not actually forbidden in Government schools and often by missionaries as well," Eastman writes, "the present awakening is matter for mutual congratulations." Eastman's assertion that Native artists have a distinctive tradition challenges the very notion of the Indian as "primitive" and thus doomed to extinction. Likewise, De Cora writes about her art students at Carlisle: "There is no doubt that the young Indian has a talent for the pictorial art, and the Indian's artistic conception is well worth recognition, and the school-trained Indians of Carlisle are developing it into possible use that it may become his contribution to American Art" (De Cora, "An Autobiography," this volume). By publishing in a boarding school newspaper devoted to the continuation of Native artistic traditions, Eastman and De Cora joined other Native writers who celebrated the intellectual and artistic achievements and contributions of Native Americans to American culture.

Note on Structure and Procedures

This collection is divided into two parts: the first features writings by boarding school students; the second consists of writings by prominent Native American public intellectuals, many of whom were boarding school graduates and members of the SAI. Part 1 is subdivided into letters, editorials, essays, and short stories and re-told tales to highlight the variety of genres students used to offer their unique perspectives and express their commitment to their Native communities.

The writers in this collection are arranged in chronological order, according to when their writings appeared in the boarding school press. I include their tribal affiliation and a brief profile indicating where they went to school and what they did after they graduated. Some of this information I gleaned from accounts of students and prominent figures in boarding school and other newspapers. I also relied on excellent resources like *A Biobibliography of Native American Writers, 1772–1924*, by Daniel F. Littlefield Jr. and James W. Parins, and Bernd Peyer's *American Indian Nonfiction*. Entries that contain little information suggest that little is known about the writers.

I mined roughly fifteen boarding school newspapers for this collection, but I did not use all of them. Accessing some of these newspaper archives proved difficult if not impossible. The *Peace Pipe*, a biweekly newspaper published at the Pipestone Indian School in Minnesota from 1912 to 1916 is a case in point. The only existing copy of the newspaper I know of, which has been indexed and is held at the Minnesota Historical Society, is the April 1916 issue. Although the newspaper regularly published student writings, the ones that appear in the April 1916 issue are short, one- to two-paragraph compositions students wrote for their classes. I also ruled out other school papers because, like the April 1916 issue of the *Peace Pipe*, they do not contain substantive writings by students. In selecting student writings for this collection, I typically included ones that were of substantial length.

I chose to focus on the following boarding school newspapers because they contain writings by students and prominent Native Americans that offer insight into their perspectives:

Carlisle Indian Industrial School Publications

Carlisle Arrow. Published weekly. 1908–1917.
Eadle Keahtah Toh. Published monthly. 1880–1882.
Indian Helper. Published weekly. 1885–1900.
Indian Craftsman. Published monthly. 1909–1910.
Morning Star. Published monthly. 1882–1887.
Red Man. Published monthly. 1888–1900, 1910–1917.
Red Man and Helper. Published weekly. 1900–1904.
School News. Published monthly. 1880–1883.

Chilocco Indian Industrial and Agricultural School Publication

Indian School Journal. Published monthly. 1900–1980.

Hampton Normal and Agricultural Institute Publications

Southern Workman. Published monthly. 1872–1939.
Talks and Thoughts of the Hampton Indian Students.
　　Published monthly. 1886–1907.

Santee Normal Training School Publications

Word Carrier. Published monthly. 1884–1903.
Word Carrier of Santee Normal Training School.
　　Published monthly. 1903–1936.

Seneca Indian School Publication

Hallaquah. Published intermittently. 1879–1881.

In terms of editing the texts reprinted here, I have maintained the original spelling and punctuation except for obvious typographical errors. I have also made minor edits to the student-authored texts for readability, using brackets to indicate alterations to the original text.

I see this book as a contribution to recent efforts among scholars to preserve and analyze indigenous archives. Many of the boarding school newspapers remain inaccessible to scholars and students. Some of these periodicals have disappeared entirely and are no longer available. Those that do still remain in hard copy are often in poor condition and in desperate need of being preserved. By publishing them in this collection, I have sought to preserve them. It is my hope that bringing visibility to these archives will spur increased efforts at preservation, especially through digitization, as well as encourage further scholarly investigation into early Native American literary production in the boarding school press and other newspaper archives.

I also see this book as an opportunity to transform the way Native American literature is taught in the college classroom. I hope this collection will encourage students to engage in more meaningful discussions about the boarding school experience and its impact on the history of Native American literature. When used in the classroom alongside boarding school narratives by prominent turn-of-the-twentieth-century writers like Bonnin, Eastman, and Standing Bear, as well as twenty-first century works like Sherman Alexie's *The Absolutely True Diary of a Part-Time Indian* (2007), this collection will reveal interesting parallels and points of contrast that will help students gain a deeper appreciation of how the boarding school legacy has shaped and continues to shape Native American literature.

Part One

Writings by Boarding School Students

LETTERS

Arizona Jackson (Wyandot)

Arizona Jackson, along with Ida Johnson and Lula Walker, founded, printed, and edited the *Hallaquah* at the Seneca Indian School. The inaugural issue of the monthly was published in December 1879. Johnson was the first editor; Jackson and Walker were associate editors. Jackson later became editor and remained on the staff while she attended Earlham College in Indiana in 1880. She then taught at the Modoc Day School in Oklahoma; she resigned her post after eight years in June 1891. (*Annual Report of the Commissioner*, 235; *Earlham College Bulletin*, 1916; Littlefield and Parins, *American Indian*, 144–45)

Letter to Laura, 1880

S., S. and W. Mission, I.T.

JANUARY 1880

Dear Laura,

It has been so long since you were here, that I must write to inform you how much our school has improved.

During the week, we have school, Literary Society, Prayer meeting, Sabbath School, Mission Church and Gospel Temperance meeting.

Our school begins at half past eight in the morning and closes at four in the evening.

We have but two schoolrooms at the present time. The advanced students from the fourth reader and upward attend the higher department. While those below the fourth reader grade are in the Primary. There are three teachers including the music teacher.

I believe it is so arranged that while one of the teachers is absent or otherwise engaged a pupil from the most advanced class is required to take the primary room.

The evenings of Monday, Tuesday and Wednesday are occupied in writing. Thursday night is our Hallaquah Literary Society, which is participated in with interest by most of the students and a number of outsiders.

On Friday night all the employees and students, together with the missionaries and outsiders collect together and hold a prayer meeting. We have a very nice Sabbath School on Sabbath morning, and in the afternoon is the meeting of the Mission Church, which now numbers nearly forty members. In the evening we hold a Gospel Temperance meeting which I think has proved a great blessing to our people, and from which greater things are expected in the future.

Rev. Jeremiah Hubbard of Timbered Hills held meetings here on the 17th, 18th, 19th and 20th inst. We had a real pleasant time.

They are making new additions to our Mission, a kitchen, sitting room for the girls, and a new school house. For these reasons I think it desirable for me to attend school here as long as I possibly can. I will now close hoping that you will be interested in my detailed account.

Your Friend,
A. J.[1]

Letter to the Editors, 1881

Earlham College, Ind. Jan. 1881.

Dear Editors of the *Hallaquah*:
I have for sometime past been wanting to write you, for the purpose of expressing my thanks for the honor conferred on me by allowing me to still hold my place on the Paper. I certainly shall do my best in contributing to the little "Star," which I see is

going to shine brighter than ever, and I hope prove beneficial to all interested therein.

Respectfully,
    Your Friend
    Arizona Jackson[2]

Letter to Susan Longstreth, 1881

Earlham E.C. February 25, 1881

My Dear Friend S. Longstreth[3]—I have about 15 minutes in which to write this now, and will see how far I can go. For the last two weeks we have been very busy in examinations, which is I am glad to say over with. The result of mine was, in U.S. History, 90; English, History, & Algebra, 85; Physical Geography, 94; English Composition, 98; and Deportment, 98.[4] It is only five weeks until our vacation. I am contemplating going home with an Earlham friend who lives not far from Indianapolis if I can. I did think of staying here, but since I was told how terribly lonesome it is here during vacation, I would rather not stay.

I suppose you have read something of Gough's lecture in our *Hallaquah Times*.[5] It was not as much of a temperance lecture as I expected. Yes, it has done some awful wrongs (whiskey has) to the Indian. About 15 or 20 years ago, most all of the Wyandots (my tribe) who lived in Kansas were very wealthy, then they began to drink, and quite a number almost ruined themselves thereby. But now there are but very few men of our tribe who drink and they are those of the lowest class. I have never known the women to drink, and I guess but few ever did.

I've found out that after I'd been here a day, the first of last term, whenever a student came, the first thing they sought was the Indian girl. Some of the girls came and asked me where she was, and seemed to be surprised when I told them that I was the

Indian girl. That shows that they saw me different from what they expected. So many that know nothing of Indians can't think of them in any other way, than being savages, uncivilized, and anything but the right thing.

I received a letter from home which stated that they were having glorious meetings, and many have joined including myself. I did so by sending my name; and I ask your prayers that I may be ever faithful. Ethel is well and will send her love with mine to you. Do you know Huldah Bonwill's address?[6] I would very much like to know that I may write to her. I will close hoping when this reaches you it will find you well, as it leaves me at present. As ever your little friend,

Arizona Jackson[7]

Samuel Townsend (Pawnee)

Samuel Townsend, who attended Carlisle from 1879 through the late 1880s, was often represented in print as an educated Indian for his participation in performances designed to raise funds for the school. For example, an 1887 *New York Times* article titled "Educated Indians. The Carlisle School's Way of Solving the Indian Problem," mentions the original speech on "Work a Civilizer" that Townsend delivered before an audience at the Academy of Music in New York City. Besides delivering speeches at such events, Townsend was considered an exemplar of the vocational work being done at the school.

While at Carlisle, Townsend was trained in the school's printing office. He printed the school's publications and was the first editor of the *School News*, the only student-edited newspaper printed at Carlisle. A four-page, two-column monthly, the *School News* was printed and edited by students and was intended to showcase the progress they were making in the vocation of printing and in learning English. Townsend's apprenticeship in Carlisle's print shop afforded him the opportunity to learn the fundamentals of publishing. His experience printing and editing the *School News* prepared him for his career as a printer for the *Chippeway Herald* at the White Earth Boarding School in Minnesota and later as the night foreman for the *Daily Oklahoma State Capital*. ("Educated Indians" 5; Littlefield and Parins, *American Indian* 101, 317, 320, 335–37)

Letter by an Apprentice, 1880

This is a very pleasant morning; the sun is shining very bright.

In this school there are many different tribes going to school. Some of these boys are learning to read and write very fast. And another thing they are learning they can make a speech in the chapel.

I am learning how to print papers. Every morning and evening I go there to the printing office and work a little and when the school bell rings I go to school. I am both trying to read and write well. I can set one stick full in a day. I like the trade I am learning.

[A] few days ago Sioux chiefs were here to see their children at Carlisle School. They were very glad to see them, and were glad to see so many different tribes.[8]

Luther Standing Bear (Oglala Sioux)

Luther Standing Bear (1868–1939), who originally bore the name Ota K'te, meaning "Plenty Kill," was born in South Dakota. He was one of the first pupils to enter Carlisle in 1879. While there he learned the tinner's trade. He left Carlisle in 1885 and lived at or near the Rosebud and Pine Ridge reservations, working as clerk, teacher, rancher, and lay minister. He joined Buffalo Bill's Wild West show in 1902. In 1905 he was chosen chief of the Oglala Sioux. He became an Indian actor with the Thomas Ince Studio in Hollywood in 1912 and appeared in several silent films and grade-B Westerns.

He launched his literary career in the late 1920s, publishing four books in six years: *My People the Sioux* (1928), *My Indian Boyhood* (1931), *Land of the Spotted Eagle* (1933), and *Stories of the Sioux* (1934). His earlier writings, including the two letters he published in the *School News* reprinted here, reflect his embrace of the assimilationist teachings of Carlisle. His later works, especially his 1931 essay "The Tragedy of the Sioux," take a far more critical view of government boarding schools such as Carlisle, which he considered to be "a curse and a blight" for Indians. (Hale, "Acceptance," 25–41; Littlefield and Parins, *Biobibliography: Supplement*, 288; Peyer, *American Indian Nonfiction*, 399–400; blight quote from Standing Bear, *Land of the Spotted Eagle*, 268)

Letter on Baltimore, 1881

Luther Standing Bear gives us something about his visit to Baltimore.[9]

I have something to say about Baltimore. I went there February 3rd. Great many people in Baltimore, because it is a big city. Now

43

I will tell you what I did and saw. It is very beautiful in Baltimore, so I like to speak and play in the church.

I think those people like Indians because when our speaking was all done, I shake hands with white men and women and boys and girls. Some men said, "O, you can play. How long in Carlisle? How old are you? What is your name? Can you work?" And some boys and girls said, "I want to be your friend. Can you speak English?" I said no. "O, you can I guess." But I speak to them nothing. Now I am sorry for just the same as my home.

I like what we had to eat and sleep and play in piano. When I am very glad I saw the Mayor of Baltimore. He is the head man in Baltimore. Then I think he likes Indians that is the reason I was very happy to shake hand with him and I was very glad I saw him. He is very kind and nice and big house and very beautiful stone house. I like to saw it always I remember the beautiful large house he let us all see. And when I am going in the cars it was about 100 miles. Now then I will try talk to you about Indian boys and girls. You must let us try hard everything. You must not play in the school. You must not talk bad at the teachers. Always you can be good boys and girls. Now always let us try to speak English and work and write and be good and be right and let us do right everything that is best way and Capt. Pratt what he says. We must hear and do it and me too. Now I will try to do all he says.[10]

Letter to Father, 1882

Indian Training School, Carlisle,

MARCH 31ST, 1882.

Dear Father Standing Bear[11]:—
Day before yesterday one of the Sioux boys died.[12] His name is Alvan. He was a good boy always. So we were very glad for him. Because he is better now than he was on Earth. I think you may be don't know what I mean. I mean he has gone in

heaven. Because he was a good boy everywhere. I hope you will understand exactly what I mean, and you should think that way. I want you must give up Indian way. I know you have give it up a little. But I want you to do more than that and I told you so before this. But I will say it again you must believe God, obey him and pray to Him. He will help you in the right path and He will give you what you want if you ask Him. Dear father I know it is very hard for you to do that out there. But you can try to think that way. You must try day after day until you can do it. Then you will be always happy. Now I shall say a few words about what we have done here. We are trying to speak only English nothing talk Sioux.[13] But English. I have tried. But I could not do it at first. But I tried hard every day. So now I have found out how to speak only English. I have been speaking only English about 14 weeks now I have not said any Indian words at all. So I wish you will try to do like that after while you will go forward in which is no sorrow and no trouble. You could not do nothing if you don't believe me what I told you in this letter. So I wish dear father you must turn round and try to walk in the right way. Now dear father I would like to know if you have that store. Do you keep it yet or not? I will help you when I go back home. That is all I have to say.

Good-bye from your son.[14]

EDITORIALS

Ida Johnson (Wyandot?), Arizona Jackson (Wyandot), and Lula Walker (Wyandot)

Ida Johnson edited the *Halaquah Times*, the publication of the literary society at the Seneca Indian School in the early 1870s. She was assisted by her associate Julia Robitaille (Wyandot). Only two undated handwritten issues are known to exist. Johnson was also the first "editress" of the *Hallaquah*. She attended Earlham College in 1883 and later became a teacher in the Indian Service.

Arizona Jackson and Lula Walker founded the *Hallaquah* with Ida Johnson and were associate editors for the first three issues; all three young women assumed the editorship in the March–April 1880 issue. A brief profile of Arizona Jackson is in the Letters section of this book. Although there is little biographical information known about Lula Walker, I do know that she was born in Kansas and was an older sister of Bertrand N. O. Walker. (Carlisle Indian School Digital Resource Center; *Earlham College Bulletin*, August 1916, 93; Littlefield and Parins, *American Indian*, 143–45)

Hallaquah Editorial, December 1879

We desire and intend that the *Hallaquah* shall represent the spirit of our school, and always speak in behalf of its interest. Supported directly by the Hallaquah Society, it yet is intended to be a true exponent of the Seneca, Shawnee and Wyandotte Industrial Boarding School, and a news letter to the neighboring people as well as for the pupils.

We do not aspire after "literary honors," but we expect—"to shine in our corner,—you, in yours." Interesting extracts from letters relating to our, and other Mission work will be inserted at different times. News relating to the different Missions and neighborhood will be the prime feature of this paper, and any "locals" relating to the same will be gratefully received and acknowledged.

Everything in "getting out" a paper is new to us. We never before attempted to write an editorial for printed paper or to set up a line of type, and we never before expected to make so much "pi" in so short a time and do it so easily.

We pray you—"Don't view us with a critic's eye but pass our imperfections by."

Hallaquah Editorial, January 1880

We are very much encouraged by the interest manifested in our little paper, by our friends far and near. Our exchange list is headed by the *Olathe Gazette*; and we have read in other papers the kind words with which it has been received. So much encouraged are we that we are induced to publish another number, hoping it will meet with as much favor if not more, than the first issue.

We publish a written number every Thursday evening. A portion of which is read at intervals, during the exercises of the literary society, and is found to be one of the best means of securing and maintaining an interest among the pupils and those who attend from the outside.

Hallaquah Editorial, February 1880

With the Matrons' help we have set up all the type for this issue and we now hope to be able before long to do all the work ourselves. News-paper making isn't play, and then it is not at all pleasant after we have done the best we can and the type are all distributed to find someone who tells us, "Why didn't you do this way, or that way it would have been so much better."

But then we have some very good friends who have told us that the last paper was better than the first one and that shall help us to try to do our best on this one.

Send us a few subscriptions; we want to buy some new type, rules, ink, and paper.

Hallaquah Editorial, March–April 1880

Our little "STAR" is still shining in its corner as bright as ever though it was a little late making its appearance before the public this month. The reason it is so late is that two of the Editors were absent; also we were late getting moved into our new Office; and now we are moved a little further from the Matron we will have more of the work to do ourselves, which of course will do us more good than harm: we are getting along so well without very much help this month that we expect to try to do all of the work alone for the next issue.

Hallaquah Editorial, May 1880

After this issue of the *Hallaquah*, there will be but one more number of this volume. We had thought that every number we had published, that the next one would be easier, but each time we find new difficulties to overcome and as two of the Editors are away this time, there is more work for one to do than usual, and that is somewhat mixed up with tonic powders, quinine, and about fifty girls to look after.

Lucy Grey (Seneca), Arizona Jackson (Wyandot), and Bertrand N. O. Walker (Wyandot)

The January 1881 issue of the *Hallaquah* announced two new members of the staff: Lucy Grey and Bertie Walker. Lucy Grey (ca. 1864–1881) was born in Kansas, lived with her uncle's family in Oklahoma, and was adopted by the Senecas. She entered the Seneca Indian School in March 1880.

Bertrand N. O. Walker (ca. 1870–1927), or Bertie as he was known in school, was born in Kansas, the youngest of eight children. When he was a child he moved with his family from Kansas to Indian Territory. He attended the Seneca Indian School and a public school in Missouri. He later taught for ten years in federal boarding schools in California and Arizona and at the Seneca Indian School.

Walker's literary ambition stirred in him at an early age. When he was just eleven years old he became an editor of the *Hallaquah*. He later aspired to be a poet and published the majority of his poetry under his Wyandot name Hen-toh in the Chilocco Indian School's *Indian School Journal*. Several of his poems have been reprinted in Robert Dale Parker's collection of American Indian poetry, *Changing Is Not Vanishing* (2011). Besides poetry, Walker published animal stories in *Tales of the Bark Lodges* in 1919. He also published a collection of poetry, *Yon-Doo-Shah-We-Ah (Nubbins)*, in 1924. (*Hallaquah*, August–November 1881; Littlefield and Parins, *Bio-bibliography: Supplement*, 298–99; Littlefield and Parins, "Introduction," vii–xvi; Walker, "A Personal Sketch," 89–93)

Hallaquah Editorial, January 1881

In this issue we do not propose to offer any apologies, nor make any promises; and we do not want any statement of facts which we may make, regarded in the light of either. We are late again this month: everybody is, under similar circumstances. It's the *way to be*, when you can't help it. Any fears that may have been entertained by our patrons that the amount of their subscription was likely to prove, at least an unprofitable investment, if not an entire loss, have cast their shadows in our minds nearly a month ago, but we are giving you a fair dividend in the Jan. number, and dare to expect not only a renewal but at least one "new name" with each. A vacancy on the "Staff" caused by the absence and resignation of one of our number, is filled, you will notice by "One of the Boys."[1] In this connection we are free to announce, that we are indulging in "Great Expectations" and venture to hope *you* will not be disappointed.

Hallaquah Editorial, February 1881

Much of the time that would have been employed in printing this No. of the paper, has been occupied in attending the meetings which have been held at the Mission during the past two weeks. We are glad to be able to offer our subscribers as good an excuse as this is, for the delay this month.

Hallaquah Editorial, March 1881

We commenced setting up the type for this month's paper, much sooner than we ever did before, and we expect to get it out in better time, and with less hurry, and trouble, than usual. We have had a much larger number of contributions to select from than heretofore. We are encouraged by the 15 new names on our subscription list, handed in by our friends in this Agency. And we are yet hopeful of the 400 we have asked for in our letters to friends in the States, but one of which has been heard from yet.

Hallaquah Editorial, April 1881

While we were at home on a visit the last of March, some one very kindly cleaned up our office and rearranged all of the furniture:

adding one entirely new large case of type and eight small ones, in a serviceable if not beautiful cabinet; veneer and varnish is all that is needed to make it elegant. And therefore for all of this we return our thanks to them for their kindness. We confess to some curiosity as to how we are going to appear in our new dress; of course we don't expect that we shall use our new type to the best advantage the first time, but we shall profit by experience.

Hallaquah Editorial, May 1881

Every attempt to write the few lines for this particular part of the paper seems more difficult than the last one, and we don't know why; wonder if it is this way with every one who tries to write Editorials. We are thankful to the several friends who have sent us lists of new subscribers this month. We shall print nearly 400 copies of this number. One more paper will close our labor for this session, after which the little Star will have to be kept shining by other hands and brains than ours.

Hallaquah Editorial, August, September, October, and November 1881

During the temporary suspension of our paper we have had considerable malarial sickness in the school, and November will long be remembered for its epidemic of pneumonia which prostrated 13 of our number and took from us our beloved colleague, schoolmate, and sister, Lucy Grey.[2] She was sprightly, lovable. She was dignified, earnest. She was an Indian school-girl, editor, [and] a lover of the Lord Jesus. We miss dear Lucy, and our loss in her death is immeasurable. Silence is more fitting than our words. See a just tribute to her worth by our matron in another part of the paper.[3]

Samuel Townsend (Pawnee)

Samuel Townsend was the first editor of Carlisle's *School News*, a monthly, which ran from June 1880 until May 1883. Charles Kihega (Iowa) took over as editor in 1881. Kihega was assisted by Ellis Buffington Childers, a member of the Creek Nation.

The *School News* was the only student-edited newspaper printed at Carlisle. In his first editorial Townsend introduces the student-run *School News* to readers by distinguishing it from the white-edited newspapers at Carlisle: "We put everything in this paper that the Indian boys write for us. Not any white man's writing, but all the Indian boys' writing." Townsend's first editorial suggests that from the beginning, students were aware that the *School News* was fulfilling a unique role for its readers. Although it was written primarily for current and prospective students, Townsend envisioned a broader audience for the newspaper: "We print this paper for the boys and girls at this school, and for any body else who would like to read about what we are doing." (*School News* Editorial, June 1880; Littlefield and Parins, *American Indian*, 335–37)

School News Editorial, June 1880

We know that this is a small paper. It is the smallest that we ever saw. We are going to try to make it good. We put every thing in this paper that the Indian boys write for us. Not any white man's writing but all the Indian boys' writing.

Some speeches and some letters.

They gave us the paper they write and then we take it to the printing office and print it. We want to show the people how they can do. Some have been going to school but a few months and some have been going to school for several years and they can do most everything now. This little paper we print everybody thinks is so funny and sometimes they laugh at it. We do sometimes laugh at it because it is so small.

We will try to make it good, so everybody will want to read it and will give us twenty-five cents a year for it. We will print it every month.

School News Editorial, July 1880

Some white folks say that the Indians do not know anything and can't learn anything, but the Indians are learning something. Great many of the white folks never read about the Indians and they do not know anything about us, but sometimes they talk bad about us and they say that the Indians have no brains to think with and they can't learn anything. Sometimes they say Indians can not be civilized. Maybe those white folks don't know anything. Great many white people are willing to help the Indians and to make them civilized so that they can make their own living. If those other people would only come here to Carlisle school they would find something here that the Indians have done and see all the fields that they have cultivated, and if they would go out to Indian Territory and visit some of the Indians there who are like the white people— Cherokees, Chickasaws and Choctaws, who have their own houses and their own farms, who can do most anything, they would soon change their minds and never say anymore that the Indians are not worth anything. If every Indian boy and girl were in school it would not take long to civilize all the Indians. The reason it takes so long is because Washington does not give enough money to put all the Indian children in school. White people put their children to school when they are young. We know the white children learn very fast because they go to school every day and that is the reason they know much, and when they grow up to be men they know all about everything. If Washington would only give enough to put all the Indian children in school, Indians would soon be civilized. That is so what John Downing says on our first page: "Indians have more friends among the white people who are willing to help the Indians now than ever before." Now if Washington would tell all the Indian boys and girls to go to school and if they would stay in school until they know something, until they know how to work and read and write, in thirty years the Indians would not be much like they are now they would know about the white man's road and they would make their own houses. When all the Indians are civilized why they can make cars and do most anything.

School News **Editorial, August 1880**

It is better for the Indians to send all their children to school for if they don't send their children to school they will not know anything. Now the Indians don't know how to make wagons, plows, hoes, and harness; they don't know how to make anything. They have to buy these things from the white people. That is the reason the white people like to make wagons and plows and everything because they think they can get lots of money. If the Indians knew how to make wagons and plows and all these things they would get lots of money from the whites and would keep all their own money saved. The Indians don't know how to make anything, that is the way they spend all their money. Long time ago the Indians used to go to hunt buffalo. When they found some buffalo they killed them and take the skins off and take it to some town and sell it and get money for it but now almost all the buffalo are gone. What will the Indians do? Why they have to work hard; plow the ground and do something, for if they don't they will starve to death and their children too. It is better they should send their children to school and learn to read and write, and not only read and write but learn how to work at a trade. That is the way the white boys do; they learn a trade and when they grow up to be a man, they can go on working and make some money of it. If the Indians do the same way they would not be poor. The men who make the wagons and plows and clothes and everything get much money from the Indians, because the Indians must buy these things from the men who make them. If the people of the United States will help the Indians they will soon find the way. From all over the parts of the country Washington sends teachers to Carlisle and Hampton and to the agencies to educate the Indians, but there are not enough schools like this one, where the boys and girls learn to work at everything. We learn from books and we learn about God too.

School News **Editorial, October 1880**

Some Indians don't want to be ignorant they want to know something. They want to know about the things that the white men do. Indians can't learn anything without some wise people teaching them so the people of the United States must give the Indians more help and give them more education. They can't do the things like the white people because the white people have more knowledge but the Indians have not this kind of knowledge. The Indians are ignorant. Some of them are trying to know something. They put themselves among the white people. Some of them have thrown away the things they used to wear and wear now the white people's things. Only a few tribes are using paints and wearing blankets and other things but some other tribes have thrown away the Indian things and have caught hold of the things like the people of the United States and are glad to have them. Some white people like to have the things that the Indians wear because they think Indian things are a curiosity to look at. Uncivilized Indians ought to go to school and learn something. They don't know how to travel. If they were traveling in the cars they would not know which way to go they would be lost, if no white man was with them.

Some bad people teach the Indians how to drink whiskey. Indians never drank whiskey but they have learned it from the bad people.

School News **Editorial, December 1880**

The children want to hurry to learn how to read and write, so they can read all the hard words in the books and they can read every book, and so they can write letters home to their parents. They try hard to learn all they can how to spell long words. That is the reason they try hard because they want to show their parents how they can read and write and speak the English language. They won't have to try so hard to learn English when they are with their tribe because they talk the Indian language all the time but now these boys and girls if they want to talk to their parents they must write English letters. So you see that is good for them. They feel that they must try hard to write but then they go to school in their tribe they have nobody to write to. Only a few white friends sometimes, but now these children write to their homes very often. Some boys and girls who have been to this school about one year can write very good English letters. We hope our parents will not forget to write to us, and we hope some of the boys and girls at the agency school will write to the boys and girls at this school. When these children write a letter to their home they can tell them a great many things about the east that these children never saw. It is a good thing for the Indian boys and girls to go to school but we think it is the best thing to come east to school because we can not see out at our tribe and we learn much faster.

School News **Editorial, January 1881**

Sometime the Indians will become entirely civilized people just as good white people. If the boys and girls want to be the rulers among their people they must get the best education and learn how to work too. We don't think these children at this school or at any other school either will ever rule their parents and the old Indians only if they do their best, when these children go back to their homes far west if they act right and show the Indians about the way they

Editorials   59

learned at school the old Indians will see that is the best way to do. If there were many big schools like this and Hampton school we think the Indians would get along very nicely. When all the Indians become educated there would be no more wild Indians but all civilized and educated people. Great many white people think that it is best for the Indian boys to learn to be minister. It is good to be a minister but the best thing for most of the Indian boys to learn is to work. Some of the boys get tired of too much work. White men never get tired of working. Some of them are just like the Indians lazy like to do nothing but the greatest white men that ever lived became great through hard work. We learn to be good while we are learning to work and if we can spend some time in school that is very good, but work and hard work is what makes men of the Indian boys. There will be no use for a lazy Indian in a few years, so learn to work and to be good, and honest and true. Let the boys who expect to be ministers learn to work, too.

School News Editorial, February 1881

The new President Mr. Garfield will take his place in Washington on the 4th of March and Mr. Hayes will go out because he has been President of the United States for four years. Mr. Hayes did the best he could to make the Indians civilized and he did the best he could to help the Indians, now we hope Mr. Garfield will put all the Indian children in school right away and not wait. Just a few children in school can't do much good but EVERY Indian child who is old enough would be glad to go to school, and the ONLY way to civilize the Indians is to educate the children.[4]

Annie Lovejoy (Sioux), Addie Stevens (Winnebago), James Enouf (Potawatomi), and Frank Hubbard (Penobscot)

Annie Lovejoy was from the Flandreau Agency in South Dakota. She edited *Talks and Thoughts* from 1891 to 1892. After graduating in 1892, she enrolled in nursing school. Addie Stevens (born ca. 1873) entered Hampton in 1883. She left the school for a brief period and returned in 1888. She edited *Talks and Thoughts* for two years. James Enouf (born ca. 1865) attended Hampton from 1889 to 1892. He edited *Talks and Thoughts* for one year. He later became postmaster at Curry, Oklahoma.

Frank Hubbard, a Penobscot from Oldtown, Maine, attended Hampton for three years beginning in 1890 and served as editor for two years in 1891 and 1892. The August 1893 issue of the *Southern Workman* reported that Hubbard was one of only two Indians to graduate that year. The *Workman* described Hubbard and the other graduate, Frank Bazhaw, a Potawatomi, as "earnest students, faithful in all their duties, and worthy examples and helps to other scholars." On commencement day, according to the *Workman*, "Hubbard gave a very interesting account of his tribe, its early customs, and present needs." After graduating, he worked in various printing offices in Oldtown and in Bangor, Maine. He accepted a position as teacher at the Rosebud Boarding School in South Dakota and was later transferred to the Oglala Boarding School in Pine Ridge, where he founded and managed the *Oglala Light* until 1906. As manager, he wrote and edited copy and oversaw the print shop. (Brudvig, *Hampton*; Littlefield and Parins, *American Indian*, 280, 356–58; Littlefield and Parins, *Bio-bibliography: Supplement*, 209, 289–90; *Southern Workman*, August 1893, 131; *What Hampton Graduates Are Doing*, 78)

Our Motto Changed, *Talks and Thoughts*
Editorial, January 1892

Dear Readers:—We wish to call your attention to the change of our motto, "Come over and help us," in our little message courier, which heretofore has appeared in both English and Indian print.[5]

We decided to take this motto off, not that we are tired of it, but because we wish to print a new motto at each publication of our little paper which change, we think, will improve the heading of its little page. So in this number, we print our first new motto which we have selected ourselves, hoping that our readers will find it a suitable one.[6]

We omit the Indian print, that our readers may get our thoughts in the English language, which the Indian finds so difficult to master. We do not mean that we can lay aside our Indian language all at once, for well you know, how we love the language in which we have grown up, but we wish you to know that we realize the need of the English language, and that we are trying very hard to master it, in order that we may soon be traveling the white man's road, and likewise, may help to build up the kingdom of One who has so graciously placed us here.[7]

ESSAYS

Henry Caruthers Roman Nose (Southern Cheyenne)

Henry Caruthers Roman Nose (ca. 1850–1917) was one of the Fort Marion prisoners Richard Henry Pratt brought with him to Hampton in 1878 and then to Carlisle when it opened in 1879. Roman Nose, who renamed himself Henry after Pratt, stayed at Carlisle for two years to learn the tinning trade. Roman Nose's writings appeared in the *School News* from June 1880 through March 1881. His autobiographical essays are representative of student writing that was used by school authorities to recruit students and to demonstrate that students who returned to the reservations could continue to practice the teachings of Carlisle. In his autobiographical essays, Roman Nose chronicles his journey from Fort Marion in St. Augustine, Florida, to Carlisle. He also charts his progress from his Indian boyhood marked by hunting and battles to his success as a Carlisle student, which makes his writings an early example of what literary scholar H. David Brumble III calls the "Carlisle success story." (Brumble, *American Indian Autobiography*, 143; Littlefield and Parins, *Biobibliography: Supplement*, 277–78; Smith, *Indians of the United States*, 181)

An Indian Boy's Camp Life, 1880

When I was ten years old in Indian Territory, I commenced to kill buffalo calves, shooting them with bow and arrows, and then when I grew up about fourteen years old, I had killed big buffalo good many.

One day that time I killed about seven buffaloes.

At my old home in Indian Territory I would go out and search for birds, and when I had found them I shot them with bows and arrows. I had to kill many of them. When I was a little boy I would like swimming very much and I had to catch a great many turtles in the water, that time I was very glad to catch it and we got to eat the turtles. When I was 13 years old my father he took me to war against the Pawnees. I was sick and I could not [get] good sleep every night but every day I [was] anxious to go back home in Indian camp.[1]

Roman Nose Goes to New York, 1880

I had a pleasant visit to New York. I was very much delighted to see my friends in New York and Tarrytown. The people, they were very glad to see me also. I stayed there about ten days. I had a very jolly time. In three days I traveled very much in New York and I saw a great many beautiful things, the houses and everything. New York is a very good city, very handsome. I like it very much. Oh I forgot to tell what I saw there. I went to the top of the Equitable Life Insurance building on Broadway. I went upon an elevator. I saw three cities, New York, Jersey City, and Brooklyn. The top of building was nearly two hundred feet above the ground. Then I went to the aquarium. I saw a great many strange kind of fish, we call them spotted codling, Lake Dog, gar pine long nose, spot and lake cat fish very long, Gold and silverfish, winkle, Spotted sole, crabs, toadfish looks like frog, Spider crab, crab lively, Rock fish, Turtles, alligators and monkeys.

I cannot tell all that I saw in New York City, because I do not understand how to spell and call them.

When I returned here I was glad to see my Indian friends of different tribes in this Indian Training School at Carlisle Barracks. I went to camp at the Warm Springs and stayed a week. We had a very nice time at the camp in the woods. The Indian boys are making bows and arrows every day, and shooting with bows [and] arrows very much. Capt. Pratt told me that he would allow me to go to Indian Territory and see my old relations. I will stay there two or three weeks with my family and friends. Then I will come back again to Carlisle Barracks and stay here a few more years. I go to school here and acquainted some things each day. I am very anxious to learn my Bible. I will always try to work and learn something every day. When I get through school and work then I will return to my old home in Indian Territory. When I get there I think maybe I will help all my Indian people and teach them about the good way of the white man road and to love God. They will pray for him to make good Indian men and women. I will teach the Indians what I have learned at school and I will teach them how to work in the white man's ways. I like tinsmith shop very much and I want to learn well how to make tin cups, buckets, pails, etc.[2]

Roman Nose Goes to Indian Territory, 1880

August 2nd I went out west to the Indian Territory. First I arrived at Harrisburg and I found cars for Pittsburgh and I got there in the night about twelve o'clock. I changed cars again and went to Indianapolis. I arrived at Indianapolis in the morning about twelve o'clock and stopped there a few minutes. Then they went to St. Louis. The cars go very fast. I arrived at St. Louis in the night about nine o'clock and changed cars again. I got out there and I looked for the cars from Kansas City. I found them and I went in, and went to Kansas City. I arrived there at nine o'clock in the morning, changed cars again. I went out and I found cars going to Wichita and Wellington. I arrived at Wellington half past three o'clock in the morning and stayed in the depot all night. Then in the morning I went to Wellington and I told a man that I wished a stage to go to Cheyenne agency, Indian Territory. The man said they had no stage this time to go to Cheyenne agency. Then I went back again in depot and stayed there five hours. [When the] train came I went in the cars to Caldwell. I got there about one and half PM. I saw a good many of the Cheyenne young men and women in Caldwell and I was very much delighted to see them. I did not know any of them because I have not seen them for five years. I stopped in Caldwell a few minutes with the Cheyenne young men and they spoke to me where I was going. I told them that I was going to Cheyenne and

Arapahoe agency. Then after I was through, I took mail wagon to Cheyenne agency, Darlington.

I had arrived at Cheyenne and Arapahoe agency at ten o'clock AM. I was very much pleased to see my father, brothers, and sisters and uncles, cousins, and all my relatives. Also they were happy to see me. I stayed in Darlington three weeks. I rode horse every day and I traveled all around the Indian camps when I stayed there I was very tired. All the Cheyenne chiefs and young men, I spoke to them about the good ways of the whites. I told them all about the Indian children at Carlisle Barracks, PA. I told them what they had learned here at school and at work. All the Cheyenne chiefs were very glad to hear that Capt. Pratt has taken good care of the Indian children here. All the Cheyenne chiefs and Arapahoe chiefs they thought Capt. Pratt a great and good man. I told them Capt. Pratt is a great man and I know his heart is true and faithful. I asked all the chiefs for the children to come here to Carlisle school. The North Cheyenne do not want to send the children to school here. But some Cheyenne and Arapahoe [were] kind to me and gave me twenty-one Cheyenne children and ten Arapahoe children to bring to this school. If I did not go down to Cheyenne agency, John D. Miles could not get the children to bring to Carlisle Barracks. Some Cheyenne do not want their children to come here to school. September sixth I came back here. I was very glad to see Carlisle Barracks and all my friends, the white people and different tribes of the Indian children. Under the instruction of Mr. Curtin who will try very hard to teach me to make tinware as soon as possible, I will then go home and open a business for myself at Indian Territory and prove to the Indians or to those opposed to Indian advancement that Capt. Pratt and his Training School has accomplished something and will accomplish more with proper encouragement and interest from those what are or ought to be most deeply interested.[3]

Experiences of H. C. Roman Nose, 1880

I will now endeavor to tell you of my experiences and travels from the time I was taken to Florida up to the present day.

It is very warm weather at the South, in wintertime it is not very cold and they have no snowing there. I often judge by Florida and St. Augustine, because I had commenced to find good friends there, all the white people in St. Augustine. When we stayed there, some time they told us they were very sorry and felt our hearts sadness. But Capt. R. H. Pratt helped us to support our sad hearts and took us away from all sadness and bad thoughts and sinners. He can show to us our hearts properly and he is anxious to make Indian men do right and guide them in the right way and he taught them all about the good ways of the whites. We promise to listen to Capt. R. H. Pratt to what is said. [We] stayed in prison there three years and we had no school, but Capt. Pratt showed us ABC and now we understand these letters. We did not know how to spell anything. It is not bad we stayed in prison three years there. But [we] have certainly been much benefited. We stayed altogether in Fort Marion. The white people call Indians Florida boys.[4] Capt. Pratt had two small boats for Indians to go out on the ocean hunting birds and fishing. They caught very large sea fishes. Sometimes we rode in sail boat beyond St. Augustine about eighteen or twenty miles to camp, hunt and fish and swim in the ocean. We lived in tents like soldiers. We made bows and arrows and we were seeking for sea beans near ocean beach and we obtained lots of them and brought them to Fort Marion and we polished them and after necessary polishing, we sold them and bows and arrows also. And we drew Indian pictures for the white people who visited Fort Marion and they bought sea beans, bows and arrows, and pictures.[5] Indians sold sea beans each at twenty five cents and bows and arrows one dollar and a half. Some two dollars and a half and best bows and arrows for five dollars. I commenced to learn how to row a boat there and some Florida boys learned very well. All the Florida boys commenced to learn to say Capt. Pratt when we anxious something to buy went in Capt. Pratt's office and asked him if we could go down town to St. Augustine and he would say all right and he would give them the pass to St. Augustine.[6]

Experiences of H. C. Roman Nose, on Captain Pratt, 1881

Capt. Pratt supported all the Florida boys in St. Augustine and he procured for the Indians everything. All the Indians were very glad and we like Capt. Pratt very much because he is a great good man and his heart is weight. They had a meeting in Ft. Marion every Monday evening to pray to God to guide us in the right way. We had very pleasant time the 4th of July in St. Augustine also in the middle of the winter we had more jolly times at Christmas day. We had shooting with bows and arrows the best shoot received three dollars and a half and some of them foot racing and who beat running got three dollar and a half. Capt. Pratt taught me, and I kept persevering and remember what he taught me in St. Augustine. After three years twenty-two young men desired to be educated at Normal Institute, at Hampton Virginia and some went to school in Syracuse New York, and some of them in Tarrytown NY. Then came a Hampton boat to St. Augustine and all the Florida boys went on steamboat and went to Hampton Normal School. Two Kiowa boys and I stayed in St. Augustine. Then after a while we rode in the cars and we came to a very small town and we took steamboat to Jacksonville and stopped there all night. Then in the morning we went on a steamboat to Savannah and arrived there at about six o'clock a.m. and we stayed one or three hours. We then took another large steamboat for New York and crossed the Atlantic Ocean three nights and three days we travelled on the ocean. I couldn't see any land where I looked to the south and east and west. I thought the steamboat would drop beneath the waves but it did not drop. I was scared very much and I was very seasick on the ocean. I laid down all the time and I could not eat breakfasts, dinners or suppers. We arrived at New York City at evening about six o'clock and we go out and went in carriage and go to Depot and we stayed there a few minutes. Then we rode in the cars and go up the Hudson River and reached Tarry-town in the night and we rode in carriage to Dr. Caruthers' house and sat down around table. We ate supper. That time I was very lazy because that I had been very seasick and felt very tired. After a few days I got strong again and well. I thought that perhaps I never was to see Capt. Pratt again but after a month he arrived at Tarrytown to see those three boys who was there. I was much pleased to see him once again and he stayed with us only one day. He said to us he would visit Hampton and see more of the Florida boys that [were] in Normal School before he went away. He wanted me to write to him and after he went away I wrote him a letter.[7]

Experiences of H. C. Roman Nose, on Going to Hampton, 1881

He didn't reply to my letter and I did not hear from him but he went out west and when [he] came back to Washington then he obtained my letter and he replied immediately and said in his letter, he wanted me and the other boys to go to Hampton School but I didn't like to go to Hampton I wanted to stayed at Tarrytown, New York. I started to Hampton and we arrived at New York City a.m. and saw a great many of the white people in New York. We had a very pleas-ant time just the same as the 4th of July 1878, at Dr. Deems house we had dinner who is my friend, then after dinner I had to shake hands with him and also his family and I bid them good-bye. Then we went in a steamer and stayed a little while. Then the steamer left at half past three o'clock p.m. one night and one day we went on the ocean. We arrived at Norfolk near five o'clock p.m.

We took another steamer and went to Hampton. We arrived at the Fort in the night. We went in carriage to Hampton about a mile and a half from the Port. By permission we went through the cornfield and Capt. Pratt told us that this field and the other fields were all worked in by the Florida boys plowing and hoeing every day. We arrived at General Armstrong's house and got out of the carriage and went to where the Florida boys stayed in two houses. I was very much delighted to see my Florida friends again and we shook hands with them all. Then we went into the room and stayed all together and they told me all about what they had been doing at Hampton Institute. We said that it is very hard toiling every day. We had hard work all the summer, learning how to work on the farm. The Normal School opened at Hampton on the first of October. Then we went to school every morning and afternoon and learned something every day and we worked very hard two days, in a week Friday and Saturday. One of the Kiowa boys learned very fast. His name is "Ki-e-sh-co-ly." His English name is Hunting Boy. The rest of the Florida boys didn't learn very fast. The reason that didn't learn more rapidly was because some of them was too old to learn. We studied hard there one year and learned some thing every day in the spring. Capt. Pratt took several boys and went to Washington and saw President Hayes. He said he was very glad to see those boys. We stayed several days at the Smithsonian Institute and then returned to Hampton, Virginia and at the desire of Capt. Pratt and General Armstrong twelve of the Florida boys went to a small town called Lee in the state of Massachusetts. We left Hampton after dinner and walked to the Fort to where the boat stopped and waited there about one hour and then took the steamboat to Norfolk. We arrived there about half past 4 o'clock p.m.[8]

Experiences of H. C. Roman Nose, on Getting an Education, 1881

We then took another steamer for New York where we arrived safely. Capt. Romayn went with the boys to Norfolk and when we got out there he said to the boys, Capt. Pratt will meet you in New York.

After we shook hands and bid him goodbye, he said, boys I hope all of you will have a good time where you are journeying. Then he returned to Hampton Normal Institute. In the night at about nine o'clock, we took the steamer for New York and after one day and one night on the ocean traveling, we reached New York. Some of the boys were very seasick and I [was] too. Capt. Pratt met us in steamboat and he said, boys you sleep in the boat until morning and called the boys to get up and get ready to start a restaurant to get some breakfast, then we took a walk to Grand Central Depot and took the train to Lee. We arrived at Lee at half past two p.m. We got out and went in the carriage to different places. We stayed there all summer and learned mowing with scythe and milking and churning butter and worked every day for months and in October 1879, we left Lee and arrived here at Carlisle Barracks. We saw the Sioux boys and girls had to wear Indian clothes. The Florida boys did not like that kind of clothes. It looked like wild Indian people who had learned nothing but just play every day and night and punishing each other and fighting with sticks and hurting their bodies. But Capt. Pratt threw away old Indian clothes and he gave them new white man's clothes and assisted them very patiently to make the boys and girls of different tribes go one way that is the right way the white man's way.[9] Now we are following the white man's way and endeavoring to get [an] education and do something useful and teach the red man [to] avoid temptation. First I did not know anything about the white man's ways. I am very happy now that I can be useful, polite, and love God. I do not say I am always polite and good because I don't know sometimes when bad thoughts come or sin. But God will keep us from sin and he will aid us in the right way and I pray that he will bless all our benighted race and show them their error and at last lead us with the white man's good way is the prayer of Henry C. Roman Nose.[10]

Mary North (Arapaho)

Mary North, a member of the Arapaho Nation, attended Carlisle from 1879 to 1884. After leaving Carlisle she worked briefly in the Indian Service in Genoa, Nebraska. In 1910 she was a housekeeper in Kingfisher, Oklahoma, and in 1913 she was an assistant matron at the Cheyenne and Arapahoe School in Darlington, Oklahoma. (Carlisle Indian School Digital Resource Center; Littlefield and Parins, *Biobibliography: Supplement,* 260)

A Little Story, 1880

We all have good times and we went out to the Camp meeting and heard the people talk about God, and we sang two or three hymns and the people it was very much glad to hear us sing. When we were at home in Indian Territory we had nothing to do but play and go to the river and go in swimming and now we are way off from home at school and learning something. I think that is better than swimming and picking berries. I know picking berries is very good, but you will get your hands scratched and then you will be tired to go another time. Now I am very glad to go to Carlisle school and learn something that is all right, and we have good time here too, and I am trying to write a story and I will do the best I can and write it till I get done.

When I get letters from home I always look at them and they would say push hard and learn all you can.[11]

Joseph Du Bray (Yankton Sioux)

Joseph Du Bray (born ca. 1872) entered Hampton in 1890 when he was approximately eighteen years old. The editorial note opening his essay suggests his classmates and school authorities considered him to be a model student. During his five years at Hampton, Du Bray was a frequent contributor to *Talks and Thoughts*. He also served a brief stint as an editor in 1892. After graduating from Hampton in 1895 he became a student at the Theological Seminary in Alexandria, Virginia. He was ordained as a reverend and worked on the Pine Ridge and Sisseton reservations. (Littlefield and Parins, *American Indian*, 358; Littlefield and Parins, *Biobibliography: Supplement*, 203; *Southern Workman*, November 1919, 623)

Indians' Accustoms, 1891

> Editorial Note: The following story was written by one of our Indian boys in a contest for a prize. He attended a mission school three years before coming here, this being his first year with us. We print it in his own words.

Before the Indians become civilized they used to have foolish accustoms. I will tell you a few of them. When a man some place in a family he has no right to call his father-in law's name. If he does call his father-in-law's name or his mother-in-law's name, he will get his ears pulled. A man or a woman has no right to call his son-in-law's name. For instance if Gen. Armstrong is your father-in-law, you have no right to say, "Where is Gen. Armstrong?" If you said this way you will get your ears pulled.

Here is another foolish accustom. If you go to an Indian woman and ask her, What is her name, she will not tell you, but she will point at her husband and tell you to ask him.

A lady has no right to get mad at her oldest brother. If a young lady get mad at her brother, the young man will go out where no-body see and kill himself.

Some Wanitipi (winter) in a valley. That is the Indians have so many (papa) dried meat that they do not need to move place to place, as they do when they have no papa. As the Indians wanitipi in a valley. A young lady get mad at her oldest brother. The young man didn't kill himself, but he determined to go to the Padani tipi and get killed by the enemy. He started off by himself. After he took three days journey he came to a river. The banks are high and rocky. As he walked along the shore of the river he saw some rain-cloud coming from the west, so he looked for a refuge. It was almost sunset too. He went a little way up the river. He found a hole at the bank and he examined it. He made up his mind to stay there all night. After he went into the hole it began to rain hard as it could. Somebody come in and sit by him. The man was so afraid he fainted. After he sat there a little while he filled his pipe and smoked it. This man was a Padani.

The Sioux thought he would smoke too. He filled his pipe and smoked it. When morning came they came out of the hole and talked [to] each other with their hands, for Padani and Sioux are different languages. The Padani said: "Scalp me," as he gave his knife to the Sioux. The Sioux said: "Yes I will," as he sang the war-whoop—"Hi hi hi hi bi hi hi han." He scalped the Padani.

Now [it was] the Padani's turn to scalp the Sioux. As he got his knife back he sang the same war whoop and scalped him.

After they scalped each other they killed a deer and got the skin off. They cut the skin big enough to cover the wounded place to keep the blood from running. The Padani went home with the Sioux and he gave him 100 ponies. They made good friends by scalping each other.[12]

How to Walk Straight, 1892

I heard an interesting story the other day. It was about crabs. There was once a council of crabs met together in a certain place and talked about this subject: How shall we make our children walk straight? They said that they are too old to learn how. So all the old crabs went home ready to tell their children how to walk straight.

One day one of the crabs tried to teach his child. He told the young crab how he must put one foot just in front of the other and walk straight. The young crab tried several times but didn't succeed, because nobody show[ed] him how.

The young crab can learn how if he goes some where and stay with some one who know how and is able to show him day by day. After the young crab once learn he will always walk straight and be able to teach, or show, his brother how to walk straight. I am going to compare this story with the "Indian question." The walking straight business is a very difficult lesson to learn. We all see that the young crab tried to walk straight but did not succeed because no one could show him how. We also see that the old crab had dreadful time to show his son, but yet he didn't make his son walk straight because he does not know how himself.

The young crabs are the Indian youths and the old crabs are the old Indians. The old Indians want to make their children walk straight ahead through the path of civilization and Christianity. They tell their children and they try to show them how, but often times walk sideways instead of walk[ing] straight themselves.

The old Indians are too old to learn how to walk straight in the way of civilization, but the youths are not too old, therefore they need to go somewhere, where some one will not only teach, but *show* them.

If the Indian youths once learn how to walk straight, they will always do it and show their brothers or their race.

So, good walkers, come and show us how to walk the way of civilization.[13]

The Sun Dance, 1893

I am going to explain or tell you what [the] Sun Dance is. I was asked good many times by my northern friends while I was up there. Sun Dance is a kind of religious festival among the Indians of old times.

They meet together in a special place which is appointed by the greatest men of that time. This festival is held once a year. It comes on summer time when all the plants and flowers spread out their beautiful green leaves to the nice warm air and the sun light. The Indian name for Sun dance is *Wiwanyag wacipi*. *Wi* means sun, and *wanyag* means to see or looking, and *Wacipi* to dance. So it is really means, to look at the sun and dance. Their dance is kept for seven days only. The place in which this dance is held is made of branches of trees and bush. They also have a long pole right in the middle of the camp. This pole has good many ropes tied to it way on top.

These ropes hang down to the ground. When the dance is begun, some of the men cut a hole or two in their flesh just below the collar bone, and then take one or two of the ropes and tie it to the flesh where [it] is cut, and dance all day long. They keep their eyes on the sun from morning until night and at the same time they bless the Great Spirit. Some of the men cut holes in their backs and draw a head of a cow or a horse all day long. They do this to show their people that they can endure hardness and also to please the Great Spirit or their God who they thought have made the sun, moon and stars.[14]

Robert Placidus Higheagle (Standing Rock Sioux)

Robert Placidus Higheagle (born ca. 1873), whose Indian name was Kahektakiya, entered Hampton in the early 1890s and was editor of *Talks and Thoughts* from 1893 to 1894. After graduating from Hampton, he became a teacher at Lower Brule and then returned to Standing Rock Reservation, where he taught school. During this time, Higheagle also assisted Frances Densmore, an expert in tribal music, in her efforts to record and transcribe traditional songs of the Teton Sioux for the Bureau of American Ethnology. (Barrett et al., *American Indian Biographies*, 216–17; Littlefield and Parins, *American Indian*, 358; Littlefield and Parins, *Biobibliography: Supplement*, 229)

Tipi-iyokihe, 1895

In the olden times, when the Indians used to live together in their villages of white tents, which sometimes extended for five or six miles, there prevailed certain customs that were very much like those of civilized nations. Among these there existed one among the Sioux tribe called Tipi-iyokihe.

The village was built up in a circular form. In the center of the circle no animals were allowed, only people. Sometimes some rich Indian would present a large tent, large enough to accommodate two or three hundred people. In one of these enormous tents the old men would gather. Another would be given up to old women, and another to children.

Each tent had its special amusements. The tent for the young people was generally used for dancing, while those used by the older people were given up to councils and other public exercises. These tents were not obtained by taxing the Indians, but were given by individuals who were interested in certain classes of people. In some cases the donor gave it for fame; while others gave for their kind spirit towards others, that were not able to enjoy the advantages of the giver. Some of these benevolent men are yet in the minds of our people. In some places these very tents have been kept and are now used for better purposes. I remember before coming here some of those tents were used for outdoor prayer-meetings, where many souls were converted.

This old custom resembles that of many benevolent people in the North. They have shown their interest in certain classes of people and their welfare.

Here in this school I think that these friends are doing this same good work in helping us to get an education. When I go around and see the different buildings and the grand work that is carried on in them, I thank God that there are people who are interested in us and are trying to elevate us.[15]

Samuel Baskin (Santee Sioux)

Samuel Baskin (born 1870) was from Santee, Nebraska, and entered Hampton in 1890 at the age of twenty. After graduating in 1895, he attended Kimball Academy at Meriden, New Hampshire. He later worked as a mechanic at the Santee Normal Training School in Nebraska. (Littlefield and Parins, *Biobibliography: Supplement*, 171; *Southern Workman*, April 1918, 208)

What the White Man Has Gained from the Indian, 1896

(Delivered on Indian Day)

We all know that what has brought us to be what we are and where we are, is the spirit of American civilization, and it is constantly blotting out our Indian manner of living and in place of it, has given us American rights, homes, citizenship. So we come together this afternoon to show our appreciation to our friends and to our God. But we must also look back to our old time Indians and thank them too for what little they have given toward building up this great nation of ours.

Let us go back to our first acquaintance with the white people and see what lessons they have learned from our fathers. The red man, as you all know, was found in this country a wild man but there is one thing about him, he was very active in his own country. I mean he knew the waters, the hills, the woods, and the forces of nature, such as the rain, and the snow, the sun, and the stars of the heaven and he respected them for they were his schoolmasters.

He made his canoe from a log, or birch bark, in which he navigated the waters. He made his snowshoes on which he could travel and hunt in time of winter and not be shut in to starve. He made his sugar from the maple by boiling the sap. He cleared the woods not with such tools as we have today but by burning down the trees, for his tools were made of chipped or finely polished stones; yet with these he was able to plant his corn, tomatoes, squashes, beans, and tobacco. I suppose tobacco is something I ought not to count, but in the time of Capt. John Smith, it was one of the chief products of cultivation and since then has been a profitable trade to the world.

The Indian's method of planting, hunting, cooking, and fishing was imitated by the early settlers and so saved them from starvation and enabled them to gain a foothold in this country. These are some of the lessons the white made learned when he first came to this country. We might say we were the first instructors of this country and afterwards we received the white man's method of living. The knowledge of nature and knowledge of books, these two elements have combined and have made America what it is today.[16]

Alonzo Lee (Eastern Band Cherokee)

Alonzo Lee entered Hampton in 1894 and left without graduating in 1900. He published several essays on the Cherokees in *Talks and Thoughts* and was editor from 1896 to 1897. (Littlefield and Parins, *American Indian*, 358; Littlefield and Parins, *Biobibliography: Supplement*, 243)

The Trail of the Serpent, 1896

When I came to Hampton in September 1893, the Government still near our reservation was just being built.[17] This still is the greatest downfall on the Cherokees that ever occurred in our part of the country. As we all know, the red man has a great appetite for strong drink and when he is tempted will generally take it unless trained to withstand the temptation.

The men who are running this still are old moonshiners. They are getting all the Indians' money, yes, more than that they are taking the red man's life.

It seems to me the government is helping the Indians up with one hand and down with the other. We get our education by the help of the government and our whiskey from a government licensed still. Which is the stronger influence, we can know only when we go back home and try to change the discouraging state of things described in a letter from a former Hampton student.

"I am glad that the Cherokees there are doing well. I wish they could all get good places there or up north and never come back to this dreadful place. The Indians drink nearly all the time. Last week two white men and a Negro jumped onto a drunken Indian and cut him terribly so that he died before morning. They have the Negro in jail but the two white men are not caught yet. There is a reward for six hundred dollars out for them. The Indians hunt them day and night. Whiskey is killing Indians and making this place unfit to live in."

I think all the educated Cherokees ought to go back home and try to help their friends up and out of darkness into light. We may find it discouraging at first but if we will stick to it we can do a great deal of good.[18]

Indian Folk-Lore, 1896

In Georgia there is a swamp that has a large quicksand in it. The red men who remained in Georgia in the beginning of this century declared that the swamp was holy ground, that in the vast morass were islands inhabited by a peculiar race of Indians who did no evil and who were ruled by beautiful winged women. This was the land of peace and pleasure.

No hunter could ever visit these islands. When his boat entered the river that penetrated the swamp the shores vanished from before him until, starving and homesick, he died. Then his body was carried to this happy land.

On the Blue Ridge there is a peak that the Indians also held as a holy place. Upon this peak is a rock in which were to be found deeply indented tracks of animals and human feet. There were nearly five hundred of these footprints, of every size, from that of a baby up to a large mark ten inches in length.

The Indians thought the Great Spirit had destroyed all the living creatures but one family, who escaped in a large canoe to this high peak. Whenever a hunter succeeded in climbing the mountain and reaching the top, heavy rain fell. The Great Spirit wept remembering the destruction of so many living creatures with water.

Modern civilization, churches, and ministers are rapidly destroying such superstitions as these which our forefathers believed. It is worth our while to preserve them, for they have value. They furnished a clue to the past history and religion of the Indians.

In these few lines are remembrances of the flood and a promised heaven. Nothing is useless which shows that red, or white, or black, we are children of one father and therefore we are brethren.[19]

An Indian Naturalist, 1897

A good many Cherokees live in the northeastern part of Tennessee and once I visited a friend there for two weeks.

One bright sunny day my friend said,

"Come, I am going to take you to a show."

"Is it far?" I asked as we started out.

"The first house up the road about five miles," replied my friend. "That is near for this part of the country."

"Is this neighbor the show?" I inquired as we walked along the path.

"Yes, he's an odd stick and the people about here think he is not quite bright, but I think he is a first-rate fellow. He and his mother have lived here many years. She is a root and herb doctor and he is a naturalist. Hark! He is at home, you can hear his shingle-saw going. He has a little sawmill on the brook and makes his living by putting up fine shingles. He keeps cows and raises an acre of corn and potatoes every season."

When we entered the door the old man was singing and seemed very happy. He was glad to see us and had my friend and me take a seat.

"Is old snoozer waked up yet?"

"Yes, he crawled out last Monday."

"What did he think of the weather?"

"Wal, he didn't know what to make of it. I laid down and laughed to see him snuff and smell the air and was so hot he almost melted. He was as poor as a shadow too."

"Who is old Snoozer?" I ventured to inquire.

"It is my old groundhog," said the Indian. "Come with me and you shall see him."

We crossed the fence and went into a lot to the woodchuck's hole. Then the Indian puckering up his lips gave a sharp whistle, prolonged in low quavers, almost exactly the sound which every country boy has heard a woodchuck make. Immediately we heard a slight rumble down in the hole, and the next moment a black head appeared in sight. Seeing his master, the chuck came out from the ground and rising on his hind feet, sat up and dropped his forepaws like a cat. Woodchucks are usually so shy that it seemed odd indeed to see this one sit docile at the threshold of its burrow and allow his master to scratch its head and pat its back. It seemed to enjoy these caresses and once or twice gave vent to a droll little chuck in its throat.

"We will go and see Drog next," remarked the naturalist.

He led the way along the bank of the brook past the house and the little low barn. We went on for fifty or sixty yards up the brook, till we came to an old pine log lying among the rocks. Our show-man then stopped and uttered a note which I cannot well describe, unless by the letters Oo-ee-ooo; droned out in a musical way. There suddenly dashed out of the hollow log a short legged and slim little creature, more trimly built than the woodchuck but not so large. It was reddish brown in color over the back, but light orange along the under part of its body. The tail was slightly bushy, the ears erect; the eyes like black beads in all of its movements. The naturalist called it a Sweet Marten.

From here we went down the brook to the mink's hole.

"Do you feed your minks?" I inquired.

"No, they go off nights and get their own food. They killed the last old hen I had a few nights ago, but they always come back and stay under the banks during the day."

He walked up near the bank of the brook, chirped a few times, then whistled between his teeth in a way that would be difficult to imitate. In response to this invitation first one little head appeared beside a rock then the second from beneath an old root. Again he whistled.

"There is one more but perhaps he is off on a hunt," he said.

These two would allow the naturalist to approach them, but were more shy of us. Nearly every one has seen a mink, so I need not describe them. Next we went to see a bear, which was tied down near the mill.

As we were walking along down the brook, the Indian said, "There was [a] party of sportsmen up here last summer, and they brought a stock of nice supplies including two or three kegs of beer. They played a great deal with my bear; he was only a yearling then. They gave him beer and got him so that he would stand up, take a bottle in his paw, and drink it. They spoilt him for good, for after they had gone he would not eat anything, only sat and whined for that nasty beer."

By this time we had reached the spot where the bear was. His last season's coat of hair was still clinging to his sides in rusty patches and, as the Indian said, he would not play any now.

By this time it was getting late and we had five miles to walk home. I had learned many things from the old man, for he not only loved and cared for his pets, but he knew all their habits and, it seemed to me, even their thoughts.[20]

Transition Scenes, 1899

From the earliest history of this country the Cherokee Indian has inhabited the South Atlantic States. In 1836 the white people decided that they must have this land, and the Government sent General Scott to convey the whole Cherokee nation west of the Mississippi River. About two thousand of these Indians refused to leave their homes but they were forced to go. Before many days they succeeded in escaping from the soldiers at night and fled back into the mountains. There they stayed in hiding until several years later they were permitted by the Government to remain.

These people are always spoken of as the disloyal part of the Cherokee Nation because they would not share the fate of their brothers, but who can dishonor them for love of home? Men of every race and of every age since the birth of Adam have been ready to fight, or even die, to defend their homes. It is human nature to love the place where you are born and brought up.

They had left their tribe and were no more a part of that great nation. Thus they became known as the Eastern band of Cherokees, and in 1838 they were admitted to the state as citizens of North Carolina.

The land these Indians now own was bought by them from the state of North Carolina. The reservation contains 8000 acres, lying in the beautiful valley of the Ocona Lufta River. The soil is fertile and is cultivated in some places to the summit of the hills.

The chief occupation of the Indians is agriculture, including stock-raising and gardening. Some of them make good baskets while others manufacture fine pottery. They raise and sell to the surrounding towns, corn, wheat, rye, oats, potatoes, and most all kinds of vegetables.

They are peaceful, law abiding citizens, and are anxious to improve their condition in every good and prosperous way. They work for their white neighbors and are considered honest men in all their transactions. I once heard a tax collector say that if white men would pay their taxes as promptly as the Indian, he would have no trouble to raise tax money. When they know that it is their duty to do a thing they go ahead and do it.

I came to this school in 1894 and did not get an opportunity to go back until last Christmas. Four years, I am glad to say, have brought several changes for the better. The Indians are making progress in spite of the many difficulties they come in contact with.

Better homes are being built. The little log cabins are being replaced by comfortable frame houses with glass windows. The farms are better cared for, cultivated to larger and finer crops, barns are made to shelter grain as well as livestock; church is better attended, and those who claim to be Christians seem anxious to hear the Word of God. I noticed, too, that Christmas was kept as a holy day by the Christian people.

If it wasn't for one thing, bright days would be dawning on the hilltops of North Carolina. That cloud is the curse of whiskey, which stops progress in every race. The Indians are noted for their thirst of strong drink, and down there it is a great temptation. A government still on one side and a half dozen moonshiners on the other, makes it as easy to get a drink of whiskey as a glass of water. If the liquor business is not stopped it will surely bring disaster to the red man of North Carolina.

These Indians are getting their education from the government schools; they are getting their whiskey from the Government stills. The Government is holding them up with one hand and pulling them down with the other. But in spite of this temptation there are a few men with purposes as true as steel. But they need an army of such men and women to stand for better work and higher living.[21]

Anna Bender (White Earth Chippewa)

Anna Bender (1885–1911), a Chippewa Indian from the White Earth Reservation in Minnesota, attended Lincoln Institute in Philadelphia and Pipestone Indian School in Minnesota before entering Hampton Institute's Indian Program in 1902, when she was seventeen years old. As a student Anna, or Annie as she was known at Hampton, showed a lot of promise, according to a report from the school to the White Earth Agency. She served as editor of *Talks and Thoughts* from 1903 to 1905 and published nonfiction essays and retold tales based on tribal legends, including "The First Squirrel" and "The Big Dipper" (see Short Stories and Retold Tales, this volume). After graduating from Hampton in 1906 she enrolled at Haskell Institute in Kansas and graduated in 1908. She then became a clerk at the Chemawa Indian School in Salem, Oregon, where she died at age twenty-six. (Littlefield and Parins, *Biobibliography: Supplement*, 174; Molin, "'Training the Hand'")

A Glimpse of the Old Indian Religion, 1904

The religious idea has always been strong in the Indian, and he believed that there was a God, sometimes called the Great Spirit, who ruled all nature and himself.

In the early part of the seventeenth century Jesuit priests and Puritans both testified that the tribes which they met believed in a god and many uncivilized tribes of the present day believe in a Supreme Being who is ruler of the universe. They have different ideas as to where God stays, some think in the skies, others in the earth, and still others at the four cardinal points.

In many tribes during a religious ceremony, or when gathered around a council fire, where the sacred pipe is smoked, the first puff is blown to the sky, the next to the earth, and then to the points of the compass, usually beginning with the east.

The tobacco which was smoked was a sacred weed and was wholly used for religious purposes, and not as a drug as it is now used. Often times they burned sweet grass, so that their prayers might ascend with fragrant smoke.

Many people think the Indian worshipped idols such as the sun, the trees, animals and stones, because he sacrificed before them, but he believed that the Great Spirit commanded all these powers, the greatest of which is the sun, as it gives off heat and light, and they believed that God had helpers who caused the sun to rise in the east and set in the west.

Some Indians said grace before meals, not as we do, but they broke off a piece of food and offered it to the sun with a short prayer.

The Indian child was taught to say little prayers by his parents and when he became older he made up his own.

When a youth, it was a part of his religious duty to go off on the plain or in the woods all by himself where he would not be interrupted, and there fast and pray four days. In this absence he must receive some vision, for they believed the Great Spirit communicated with them in dreams. This dream must be in the nature of a contest which must be carried out before he won the name of a brave.

The first buffalo killed by a young brave was always offered for a sacrifice.

When a man he always committed himself to the Great Spirit's protection before entering upon any perilous undertaking. He prayed all night that he might have good luck and while he was gone with other braves the priest went about the camp shouting the names of the different warriors, so that the people would remember to pray for them.

During the time they were gone they never forgot their prayers at night. If it was a hunting expedition the first game killed was burned for sacrifice, and it was considered a great sin among many of the tribes if this ceremony was left out.

The Indian believed in evil spirits who bring disease and trouble and which can be frightened away by rattles and by the burning of sweet grass.

Medicine men were not doctors, although they knew something of medicine, but were the religious leaders of their people. All the dancing and singing in former times were religious duties, so that is why some of the old Indians will not dance just for others' curiosity, because it means so much to them and they reverence it. The younger generation, however, do these dances and think nothing of it.

Each Indian composes his own death song, and on his death bed he sings it if he is able.

He believes in a heaven where the soul goes after death, which is called the "Happy Hunting Grounds," as nearly as can be interpreted, where there will be no more sorrow and trouble.

The Christian thinks of the "Golden City," but the Indian never saw a city so that could not suggest anything of that kind to him.

He thought that his horses and dogs who had been faithful to him in life would come with him in this happy land.

This is the reason why they sometimes shoot his animals when he dies and his wife will sometimes kill herself so that she can accompany him on his journey and enter with him into his heaven.[22]

An Indian Girl in Boston, 1904

This fall I visited friends who live in Boston. They were very proud of their city and wished my sister and me to see all the places of interest. We went into the new State House which has a gilded dome and saw the flags that had been through the different wars. There were also paintings around the walls near the ceiling. One of them especially took my fancy. It was that of John Eliot preaching to the Indians. A guide allowed us to enter the room where the governor stays, which was very grand, also the council chamber.

From here we went on our way and passed the old State House with the lion on one side and the unicorn on the other. We did not go in but proceeded to Faneuil Hall with its market below, the assembly room above, just as it was years ago. This room was very interesting. On the platform, occupying almost the entire wall, was a large painting of a company of men listening to the eloquent and patriotic speech of Daniel Webster. Many such speeches have been delivered in this room. Upstairs are numberless paintings of various battles. At this place we found a guide who knew General Armstrong, so when he discovered that we were from Hampton he pointed out everything of historic interest. Although he was quite an old man he did not hesitate to trudge down with us to the north end of the city where stands the old North Church in whose tower flashed the lantern that warned the Americans of the approach of the English. We three mounted its winding, rickety stairs, and sometimes had to bend beneath the rafters across our way. From this height we viewed the city while our guide pointed out the course that Paul Revere took and the movements of both armies. When we came down we were shown a tithing rod which was used to keep people awake during the three-hour sermons in church.

The place we next visited was the Public Library. This is a large, beautiful building surrounding a grassy court. In the center stands a sparkling fountain with benches all around where people may enjoy the pleasure of reading with this scene before them.

As we mounted the broad stairs we were confronted by two huge stone lions. The room we entered had the story of the Holy Grail pictured on its walls. Another had the painting of the Prophets. Both were beautiful.

We left this interesting place for Harvard College and the museum which contains the world-famous glass flowers. Fancy could not picture a more pleasing sight. I could hardly believe they were really glass when I saw the tendrils of some of the vines. The coloring was exactly like the real flowers.

However interesting the flowers, we were obliged to continue our sight-seeing to the department of preserved bones, of stuffed birds and of animals. Different kinds of monkeys were placed in a row leading up to man. It was surprising to see the gradual change of the monkey to man. I could see the reason why some people get the idea that we were once monkeys. I was glad to see that as the skeletons increased in size from monkeys through different races of man, the Indian stood last and the tallest.

The last place we visited in Boston was the Art Museum. Many of the things here I had seen pictures of, and it reminded me of a lecture on sculpture we had last winter.

The next day we spent visiting Lexington and Concord, the two cities which figured so illustriously in the early history of the country.

On our way home we passed the home of the poet Longfellow, once the residence of George Washington.[23]

Elizabeth Bender (White Earth Chippewa)

Elizabeth Bender (1888–1965), a Chippewa Indian from the White Earth Reservation in Minnesota, entered Hampton Institute's Indian Program in 1903. Like her sister Anna, Elizabeth published nonfiction essays in *Talks and Thoughts*. In the essay that follows, Elizabeth describes a trip she took with Anna "From Hampton to New York." As Elizabeth explains in her essay, she and Anna were not simply on a sightseeing trip. They were "chosen" to go north to sing Ojibwe songs and speak at "parlor meetings . . . for the benefit of Hampton." Even though school authorities wanted to emphasize that students were being successfully civilized, they often referenced the tribal past of students and displayed them as "examples" or "objects" whenever it proved beneficial for drumming up financial support for the schools. There are several possible reasons why Elizabeth and Anna were chosen to represent Hampton's Indian Program. They both excelled academically; were active in a number of organizations, including the Josephines, a female literary society; and published their writings in the school's student-run *Talks and Thoughts*. From the perspective of school authorities, exemplary students like Elizabeth and Anna were a walking testament to Hampton's Indian Program.

Elizabeth Bender would continue to publish nonfiction essays in the boarding school press after she graduated from Hampton in 1907. After completing postgraduate work in teaching at Hampton, she taught among the Blackfeet on the Fort Belknap Reservation in Montana, which she recounts in her 1916 essay "A Hampton Graduate's Experience" (see part 2, this volume), and at Carlisle. Later in life she was active in the women's club movement and in programs aimed at developing Indian education. Through her membership in the Society of American Indians she met and married Henry Roe Cloud, a founding member of the society and founder of the American Indian Institute, where Bender taught as well as contributed to the institute's newspaper, the *Indian Outlook*. In the 1940s she was named chair of the Indian Welfare Committee of the State Federation of Women's Clubs, and in 1950 she was named American Mother of the Year, the first Native American woman to win that honor. (Littlefield and Parins, *Biobibliography: Supplement*, 174; Molin, "'Training the Hand'"; Tetzloff, "Elizabeth Bender Cloud")

From Hampton to New York, 1905

Early in January my sister and I had an opportunity to go north to speak and sing at some of the parlor meetings that were held in Philadelphia and New York for the benefit of Hampton.

We left Old Point Comfort one evening and reached Baltimore the next morning. As we were being transferred from one depot to another we had a good view of the burned district and the many large new buildings that are being put up. One who had not seen or read of the terrible fire would hardly know the difference the new buildings are going up so rapidly.

From Baltimore we went on to Philadelphia and as soon as we reached there we started to go about the city. First of all we visited the Lincoln Institute. There are about forty Indian scholars, mostly little tots. We got there just as they were having dinner and they seemed to be very happy indeed, to judge by the broad smiles on their faces. We also visited Independence and Carpenter Halls and they are about the most interesting places I have ever been to. In the evening we attended the meeting which was held in a private house for the benefit of the school. Bishop McVickar presided and it was very interesting.

The next morning we left for New York and remained there about ten days. Between the meetings we had a good deal of time to go about the city and we visited the Metropolitan Museum of Art,

Museum of Natural History, the Aquarium, Zoological Garden, Academy of Design, the Settlements, and also went to a lecture on Holland and to a concert where a young Hungarian violinist played with great skill. In the Aquarium were every kind of fish imaginable. They were swimming around in large glass cases and seemed to be as much at home as in their native haunts.

The Museum of Natural History interested me the most for it contained so many Indian ornaments, weapons, domestic utensils, medicines, and I believe every imaginable thing that the different tribes of America have used. It seems so strange that nearly all the tribes should differ so very greatly in the way of dress and of living.

We spent one whole day at the Zoological Park. It was great fun watching the many kinds of monkeys, some seemed almost human. In one of the houses were all sorts of reptiles. One of them was twenty-two feet long, and the keeper said that they had one that was twenty-eight. We did not remain there very long for it gave us the creeps. There were ever so many kinds of animals and birds which one could not stop to mention, some of them I had never heard of before.

In spite of all these good times we were not sorry when the time came for us to come back to Hampton, and we think we were very fortunate to have been the ones chosen to go, for we had a chance to see so much and meet so many interesting people.[24]

J. William Ettawageshik (Ottawa)

J. William Ettawageshik (ca. 1889–1942) was one of several male printers at Carlisle. After graduating from Carlisle in 1911 he became assistant editor of the *Outlook* in Onaway, Michigan, as reported in the February 1913 issue of the *Red Man*. In 1914 he worked as a printer for the *Enterprise* in St. Ignace, also in Michigan. (*Red Man*, February 1913, 265; Littlefield and Parins, *American Indian*, 320; Littlefield and Parins, *Biobibliography: Supplement*, 209)

My Home Locality, 1909

Harbor Springs, in the northern part of the lower peninsula of Michigan, in a county called Emmet, is my hometown. It has a population of about nineteen hundred people. It is a delightful place, both in summer and in winter. It is well up-to-date. The name comes from the "harbor" which is nearby and "springs" from the many beautiful springs which are near the place. Putting harbor and springs together brings the name, Harbor Springs.

The surface around this locality is hilly. The hills average from 100 to 300 feet high. The highest of these hills are 950 feet and are called Emmet Heights. There are a few small rivers and their names read as follows: Maple river, Bear river, Indian river, and Five Mile river. They are mostly used for water-power and fishing. Three of these rivers flow into Lake Michigan and one into Lake Huron.

The climate is very mild in summer. There is plenty of rain in summer and much snow in winter.

Lumbering, fishing, farming, and manufacturing are the chief industries. The agricultural products are: oats, rye, barley, potatoes, sugar-beet, and wheat. Forest products, sugar, bark, maple, beech, hemlock, elm, oak, cedar, and tamarack. Sugar comes from the maple tree, bark from the hemlock and oak. This bark is used in tanning leather; maple, oak, beech, hemlock, and elm are made into lumber. Cedar into railroad ties and shingles; tamarack into telegraph poles. Pulp wood is also found in large quantities and it is made into paper in a town nearby. From the lake large quantities of fish are caught. Lake trout, white fish, and perch are chiefly caught for food. There are twenty other different kinds of fish in the lake and in the streams.

The scenery is grand, both in summer and in winter. The harbor is very beautiful and safe. Steamers stop at this place on their way to Buffalo, or to Chicago, both freight and passenger.

The scenery and climate are very suitable for a summer resort. Bay View, Petoskey, Wequetonsing, and Harbor Point and Harbor Springs are known as Petoskey resorts. In the lake there is excellent fishing, yachting, and swimming. There are also other amusements besides these. Golf, driving, and observation. Harbor Point has the most beautiful and best golf course in the northern part of Michigan. Many people come here to spend their vacation.

The most interesting part of this locality is in a park known as Hiawatha Park. It is situated on a little lake called Wayagaimug, or Round Lake. At this place Hiawatha is dramatized by the Ojibwa Indians. It is given daily, except Sundays, through the months of July and August.

Education is compulsory in this locality. All children over seven years of age, both Indian and white, must go to school or else be kept at home. This rule is enforced by the town officers. District schools are located in convenient places throughout the township. Sixty per cent of the people have education. Harbor Springs has both primary and secondary schools. After finishing secondary schools or high schools, they are admitted into a college in a town nearby.

Reservation is an almost unknown word to many of the Indians and the whites. The people are mostly of French descent. There are about 100 Indians living in this town. They are scattered among the white people. They work together and make the laws for the town in the same way. Indian boys and girls attend the same schools as the white children. Indians have equal rights with, and make laws and vote the same as their white brothers.[25]

Caleb Carter (Nez Percé)

Caleb Carter (born 1888), whose Indian name was Ip-nau-sau-lau-kaskt, attended Haskell Institute for three years before entering Carlisle in 1909. His student file indicates that he did not attend Carlisle continuously. After graduating in 1912 he moved to Kansas to become a farmer. (Carlisle Indian School Digital Resource Center; Littlefield and Parins, *Biobibliography: Supplement,* 187)

Christmas among the Nez Percés, 1911

Come with me to spend Christmas with that famous Indian tribe which led Generals Miles and Howard a merry chase through the Rockies not so many years ago, covering a distance of over thirteen hundred miles, regardless of the numbers pitted against them.

We will find that the Nez Percé Reservation is in the northern part of Idaho on the Clearwater River, a tributary of the Columbia River, almost directly across the boundary line between Oregon and Washington, on the Idaho side.

Our invitation came several weeks beforehand, stating the place at which the Indians were to gather for the festivities, and fixing the date, several days before Christmas. No one is barred from the celebration, for the poor and the rich are alike welcome.

On the day appointed, we find all the invited guests assembled in camp which is not to break until the middle of January. The first event on the program is the delivering of an address of welcome by the chief in a big tent where all the guests are gathered.

When Christmas Day actually comes, there is a very great bustle throughout the encampment and all seem to be as busy as ants; some are helping to barbecue the beef, others are preparing the program for the afternoon's entertainment, and still others are fixing their war bonnets, leggings, and other articles of apparel worn on such occasions.

At last dinner is announced and the "heap big eat" commences. It is no dog feast, you may be sure; but it is exactly what you would expect to find at some elaborate banquet among white people, with a few natural differences. For instance, here there are dried venison, dried salmon, and other dainties which only an old-time Indian has the secret of preparing.

After dinner is over and the tables cleared away from the big tent, the chief commands each person present to prepare for the annual dance—the "Tukyawa"—a dance which has been handed down among the Nez Percés from generation to generation. It may be said that this dance answers to our Memorial Day observance on May thirtieth. All the old costumes are brought out to be worn by the relatives of absent ones, for the dance is to be in commemoration of those whose places in the tribe have been filled by others. The dance starts with a special song—of very ancient origin—a song so sad that it brings tears to the eyes of all who are within hearing, for the Indians are a very sympathetic race and their dead are very dear to them. When this one song is ended, and the dancers have gone several times in a big circle around the tent, like soldiers marching in file, then all the sad part of the celebration is over.

Now the guests may do anything they choose to do, and they usually choose to dance. The dances are, for the most part, round dances, or the war dance, each of which is announced by the chief.

During a war dance, the attention of a stranger would naturally be fixed on the decorations of the dancers, and they would notice how curiously this one or that one has painted his body or his shield. These decorations all tell a story, and, should you ask an old-timer who has to his credit about sixteen or seventeen scalps, the meaning of the emblems painted on a certain shield, he would, perhaps, tell you that during the war with General Howard, or the

Crows, or any other tribe, this particular buck scalped his enemy alive; or, that he came off victorious after being surrounded by his enemies. It is like reading shorthand at "Old Carlisle" to interpret these symbols.

During the war dance, if some dancer should lose some part of his ornament, a feather usually, the following performance would ensue:

First, the tune changes, the drum sounds like the roar of a cannon, war whoops arise, and the whole tumult gives the hearer the impression that a real Indian scrimmage is taking place. Now, everything but the singing ceases and the dancers dance in time with the music around the feather lying upon the ground. As soon as the drum starts up again, the dancers suddenly stop and seat themselves in a circle, until the discord ceases. This is kept up for some time.

Suddenly one brave steps to the center of the circle, where the feather is lying; and, as he approaches it, he performs certain maneuvers resembling those which actually took place at some critical moment in his career. Nearer and nearer he draws to the feather, while all, who are closing the circle in on him, watch him closely. At last, the brave strikes the feather with his tomahawk. Then the music stops, all reseat themselves, and the warrior tells of the brave deed which his movements have been suggesting, the record of which is painted on his person. Perhaps it is a tale of a miraculous escape from death; perhaps he tells how he saved some one from losing his scalp to the enemy; probably he shows a scar or two as a result of the encounter. When he has finished his story he returns the feather to the owner. Meanwhile, his relatives are piling money, blankets, shawls, and numerous other articles for him to distribute to his listeners, to show how grateful he is that on this Christmas Day he is still alive, when he might have fallen a victim to his dreaded foes.

During these war dances many things are given away. Visitors, if they happen to be of a different tribe, usually get the most of these.

If a lady has asked you to dance with her during the round dance, she pays you, either with a blanket or a sum of money, and you must take the gift or she will feel herself insulted, for it is a time-honored custom of this tribe to make gifts in this manner—from a few cents in value to a span of horses or a wagon.

We have spent the day witnessing many curious customs, handed down from our ancestors; our visit is over and we return to our homes.[26]

How the Nez Percés Trained for Long Distance Running, 1911

Strange and improbable as this description seems, it is every word of it true, as the writer is of the tribe mentioned in the title of his paper and has always been familiar with the customs about to be described.

The men of the tribe who were set apart by their physical qualifications to train for runners, used to commence their training in the latter part of October, at which time they began to take early morning baths in cold mountain streams. These baths were kept up through the whole winter season until the spring weather made the water cooler.[27]

Next on the schedule to be followed by those in training are the warm baths, taken in a hole in the ground where the water is heated by hot rocks, mixed with cold baths described above. If the warm bath is not taken, the sweat bath is substituted, and is prepared as follows: first, a skeleton of a small hut is made from willow boughs; this is covered with twigs and dirt, a small opening being left in front for a door, over which blankets are hung. Near this door, a small round hole is dug and filled with red-hot stones. After all the trainers have had a plunge in the cold water they enter this little sweat house and close the door. Then one of the number pours warm water on the red-hot stones, causing the steam to rise and surround the occupants of the tightly-closed room.

After awhile the victims emerge and take another plunge into the cold water. This process they keep up until the stones are cold and useless for the manufacture of steam.

After a light dinner, consisting of merely a little soup, the same program is repeated; and this is done daily for at least three months of the year, sweat baths being indulged in in the early morning and late evening—usually after sunset.

The way in which a young buck's endurance was tested was like this: An old warrior selects a tree with a limb affording a tempting opportunity to swing on it by one's hands. When the night comes for the testing, the old buck calls the young brave to jump out from his hot bath-hole, to leap and catch the limb with both hands, and to cling to it until he is ordered to "let go." If he drops unconscious before the signal is given, it is a sign that the training has not been sufficient, and he is ordered to return to his daily routine until such time as he can cling to the limb for the desired number of minutes. After this testing, the program for those in training is extended by the addition of short runs, every morning and evening, for a distance of five or six miles. As the youths begin to show endurance, this distance is gradually lengthened.

Then comes another testing: A small hill, so many paces high, is chosen, up which they are required to run, on jumping out of the hot bath. If the person tested does not reach the top and back again, he is considered not yet in proper condition. Sometimes the candidate runs halfway up the hill, then falls and rolls down the slope unconscious.

Such training gives to the Indian incredible strength, agility, and power of endurance. As an example, one needs only to cite Lawyer, who was killed near Cul de sac, Idaho. Compared with his white brothers, he appeared to be about forty at the time of his death, but in reality he was past seventy years of age. It is said that at one time, before the Nez Percé war, he chased a black bear for over sixty miles, over mountains and across canyons. He might have succeeded in catching "Bruin," but it grew too dark for the chase, so he calmly trotted back home again.

I wonder how the young Indian of today would like this sort of training?

Now, an Indian cannot even break through the ice, while skating, without endangering his life.[28]

SHORT STORIES AND RETOLD TALES

Joseph Du Bray (Yankton Sioux)

See the Essays section for a profile of Joseph Du Bray (born ca. 1872).

A Fox and a Wolf: A Fable, 1892

There was once upon a time a wolf and a fox were travelling through a civilized country. The wolf was very proud and talked as though he was the only one that knew everything on this universe. He even told the fox that he could speak all kinds of languages.

The fox was very polite and gentle to him, but not in his heart; then the wolf put his confidence in him without delay. Thus they journeyed together very happily for three months, although the fox [was] thinking about how he could get the proud wolf into trouble all the way.

One day as they went through a beautiful forest country, they saw a mare and a colt by the highway. When the fox saw the beautiful colt he wished to have it for dinner. The fox said to the wolf, "Go and ask the mare how much she wants for her colt." The wolf answered and said, "You better go yourself, because you are small, light, and you can run swiftly; you can escape from the owner if he should come."

The fox went to the mare and said, "Hallo! Mare, you have a nice colt, how much do you want for him?" The mare answered and said, "Certainly I have a nice colt; if you wish to know the price, you must lift my hind leg and look into my foot." The fox refused to do it and went back to the road where the wolf was waiting. The fox told the wolf all the words the mare said and also told him that he had seen the price mark in her hind foot, but could not make out on account of having no education and said, "You know how to talk and read different kinds of languages, so please go and see

how much she wants for her colt. I am very hungry, aren't you?"
The wolf went and asked the same question which the fox asked.

The mare answered the question by saying, "You lift up my hind leg and you shall see how much I take for him." So the wolf went to her and was about to raise her leg [when] the mare kicked him with both her feet and mash[ed] his nose. The fox laughed and mocked him and went on his way as happy as ever.

The poor wolf was left behind by his own friend, one who he put his confidence in.

Moral—Never think yourself better than others, and never put your confidence in a person because he is polite to you and smiles before your face. They are happy when trouble comes to you.[1]

Harry Hand (Crow Creek Sioux)

Harry Hand entered Hampton in 1889 at eighteen, after spending six years at the Crow Creek Agency School, and was a regular contributor to *Talks and Thoughts*. He wrote stories about war and hunting that were passed down from elders, including "The Brave War-Chief and the Ghost" and "A Buffalo Hunt," both reprinted here. He also wrote about trickster figures like the spider in "The Spider, the Panther, and the Snake." Besides highlighting the importance of the art of storytelling to Native education, Hand's writings and illustrations bring into focus how some boarding school students used the periodical press to preserve in print the oral and pictorial traditions of Native American culture. Hand not only celebrates and affirms his indigenous oral and pictorial heritage but also illustrates the humanity of Native Americans to readers of *Talks and Thoughts*.

After leaving Hampton in 1894 Hand returned to the Crow Creek reservation, where he founded his own newspaper, the *Crow Creek Herald*. Hand and another Hampton alumnus edited the newspaper. In April 1898 Hand founded the *Crow Creek Chief*, which published news about Crow Creek returnees and commented on broader issues that influenced Indian affairs in South Dakota. He died just over a year later, in the summer of 1899. (Fear-Segal, *White Man's Club*, 130–34; Littlefield and Parins, *Biobibliography: Supplement*, 223)

The Brave War-Chief and the Ghost, 1892

I don't know whether this story is true or not, but some Indians say it is a true story.

Well, many years ago, when there were no white people in the west, the tribes of Indians used to make war against each other. At one time, a chief picked out nearly all the young men of an Indian village and said he wanted to go to war with the Crow Indians. These Indians that wanted to go to war were Sioux Indians. Well, there were about 40 young men under that brave chief. They were all under the age of 30.

They started from their village on foot, for they expected to take the ponies away from the Crows. At the end of the four days' journey they came to a place, where, they said, a ghost lived. They said that was a very horrible place, for even more than 100 brave warriors were scared and driven away from that place by that ghost. That was a very beautiful place with many trees and plenty of water, for there was a large creek too. Every time the Indians go to war they stopped at that place, but the ghost always bothered them at night and scared them so they always had to flee.

Well, they put up a very large wigwam made of small trees and leaves. As soon as it was dark they built a fire and sat around it, ready to enjoy their pipes. But as they began to talk about what they were going to do when they reached the Crows' camp, they heard someone crying in the woods. Then they began to feel frightened, for they were not much acquainted with ghosts or ever go to war before, so they were coward fellows. They heard strange stories about that ghost before they started on their journey. The ghost kept coming closer and closer to the wigwam. He screamed and did all sorts of things to scare them. Nearly all the young men lay senseless on top of each other, because the ghost frightened them. The brave chief, as he was called, sat calmly by the fire enjoying his big pipe.

When the ghost came to the door the chief told him not to make such noise but to come in quietly. The ghost came in. He was nothing but a skeleton of a man and had a blanket wrapped around him. The chief handed his pipe to him, but while he was smoking the chief laughed hard for the smoke came out of every hole in the skull of the ghost. One of the young men recovered his sense and the chief told him to get a piece of meat for his friend. He took a kind of membrane of fat which was nearly as large as a blanket. He said he was going to cook it for his friend, the ghost. He held it over the fire and when it was burning he took the ghost's blanket away and wrapped the burning fat around him. The poor ghost cried out and fled, but the chief took his war-club and chased him. The moon began to shine just at the time so the chief kept on chasing him and broke all the bones to pieces. The next morning all the young men determined to go home. The chief had to go on by himself. He reached the Crows' village. Two men were guarding the horses at night but while they were sleeping he killed and scalped both of them and drove all the horses home. When he came home they had a war-dance and he gave some of the horses away. The people gave another war-bonnet to the chief, for they said, he was a brave man. It was a very dangerous thing to wear a war-bonnet during a battle. The enemies would shoot first at the man that wore a war-bonnet. They always wanted to kill the most brave men and they had to wear war-bonnets.[2]

A Buffalo Hunt, 1892

Once upon a time two Indian families went out to hunt. At the end of two days' journey from their village, they camped at a place where [there] was plenty of grass for their ponies and plenty of water. These two men were brothers. Their grandfather, the old war chief, was a medicine man too, and when they camped he put up his medicine flag and hung his drum and things on the staff so that his sons would have good luck in their hunting. They had only a little meat left hanging on the *iwotkeyapi*, or pole laid across two forked sticks to dry the meat on, and were very anxious to see a big fat buffalo come that way. By and by one came very near and the young men chased it on their horses. One of them used a spear and the other used a bow and arrow. Their grandfather stood outside the tipi watching them, and the women were ready to help at any time. After they had killed the buffalo they took the skin off, which was used for a blanket afterwards. In those days buffaloes were very useful. The Indian used to make spoons out of the buffalo's horns and some of the horns were used as a cup to drink out of. Some skins, with the hairs on, were used as blankets. Others were tanned and made into moccasins and something like a satchel called in Indian *unksuna*.

Well, while the two were killing that buffalo they saw a large rattlesnake. They killed it and one of the men took the rattle off and carried it into his tipi. The next morning they woke up and were very much frightened by rattlesnakes that were lying around the tipi. It is said that whenever the rattle of a rattlesnake is taken into a tipi all the other rattlesnakes come at night and lie around.

After that the man who killed the buffalo took most of the meat and returned home to his village; the other went out to hunt some more and camped with his wife in another place. One day as he was making arrows in his tent he asked for some soup, so his wife put some in a cup and set it down by him. While the man was whittling an arrow he happened to look into the soup and there he saw the reflection of a man's face in the grease that stood on top of the soup. The man was a medicine man and in some way he had got up on top of the tipi without making any noise and was looking down at him. He was a Crow man and a great enemy to the Sioux. The man told his wife not to look, but to hand his bow to him. When she handed it to him he made believe try[ing] the arrow into the bow, then looked up suddenly and shot the man in the head and killed him. They then scalped him and carried his scalp home, and had a great rejoicing in the village.[3]

The Story Teller, 1893

The picture here presented is from a sketch by one of our students, Harry Hand. The picture shows something that is very often seen among Indian homes.

In the evening, after supper, the men would get together, bring their pipes with their long stems and kinnikinick bags, sit in a circle and smoke; while one of the group would tell a story of war or hunting. When they have this, if there are any children present, the old Indian would say, "Now children, you listen, so that you will see what I ought to have done and what I ought not to have done, so that if you ever meet with the same thing you can remember what I said so that you can improve on them." It is very interesting to listen to them. We have read of many adventures of white people among Indians, but we never read of adventures told by Indians among white people. Why? Because the Indians have no newspaper through which to let the reading public know their side of many stories.

They usually put the pipes and kinnikinick and some matches in the center of the circle so that whoever wishes can fill a pipe up and have a smoke. The true stories they tell are free for all but when they tell fairy stories the story teller has to be given something by some of the listeners. Only those who give something have the right to tell the stories; but they must not tell them unless something is given to them. We think if the Indian fairy stories were gathered and translated by a good translator and published in book form they would compare favorably with "Arabian Nights."

On the right of the picture will be seen something hanging very much like washed clothes hung on clothesline. In olden times when there were plenty of buffaloes the Indians did not salt the meat they wanted to keep, like white people do at Chicago and other places, but they sliced the meat into thin pieces and then hung out in the sun or above the fire to dry. This way was very good as it kept [a] long time.[4]

The Adventures of a Strange Family, 1893

Once upon a time there was a man living with his five sons in a place by themselves. One of the sons was a rock, one a buffalo, one a bear, one an owl, and the fifth one, an eagle.

One day they wanted to select places to live in. They determined to scatter themselves so each one could select the place that he wanted. Well, they started out on their journey with their father. When they came to a high rocky hill, the eagle told his father that he wanted to live there. So the eagle stayed there while the others went on.

When they came to another hill that had trees on its side, the owl wanted that place, so he stayed there. One of the trees had a hole in it.

The others came to another hill that was not rough or rocky. The rock made up his mind to stay there on the hill. So the others kept on their journey. They came to a beautiful valley where there was plenty of grass and water. The buffalo determined to stay there, so he did.

The man and the bear went on their way. The bear selected his place on the side of a hill, where there was plenty of trees and a cave. His home was thus near a watering place of the animals that would come to drink there.

Last of all the father went alone on his journey. When he had gone quite a long distance, he saw a deer and he killed it with his bow and arrows. While he was dressing the meat an old woman came to him. The man asked her if she wanted the forelegs of the deer. She said she did not want them. Then the man asked her if she would like to have the hind legs. But she said she didn't want them, the hind legs. Then the man told the woman to select the kind of meat that she did want. While the man was cutting up the meat the old woman all at once took the quiver and the bow, saying that she wanted those, and went off with them. It was so unexpectedly done that though the man ran after the old woman, she, being a swift runner, escaped and disappeared in the woods.

The man kept on looking for the old woman. After a while he came to a smoky lodge in the woods. The old woman was in that lodge. The man stood outside and asked her to give him his bow and quiver back, but she told him to get away or else she would cut off his head. Then the man turned himself into a mouse by magic and went inside the lodge and took his bow and the quiver. He then made himself a man again and ran off. The old woman took out her sword and said, "Where are you going? You have to die today." She ran after the man.

When the man came back to the place where the bear was, he called to the bear to come out and help him. The bear came out and cut the sides of the woman with his claws. The old woman said, "You old rascal, you hurt me. What did you do that for?" Then she cut the bear's head off. Meanwhile the man had gained quite a long distance. When the old woman was within a few yards of him, the man called to the buffalo for help as he had then reached the place where the buffalo lived. The buffalo came and hurled the woman in the air with its horns.

The old woman called the buffalo names and cut its head off. The man called for help again when he came back to the rock. The rock rolled itself down the hill and knocked the old woman down. The old woman got up and called the rock names and cut it into two parts with her sword.

He called for help again when he reached where the owl was. The owl flew up in the air and then swooped down. The old woman had a blue mark on her forehead. She would die even if the smallest insect touched it. The owl tried to hit that spot with its beak but missed it. The owl tried it again, but this time its head was cut off.

Last of all the eagle came out to help his father. If the eagle should fail to hit the mark on her forehead, he and his father would surely die. The eagle flew way up in the air and swooped down and hit right in the center of the blue round mark and cracked the old woman's head. So she died; and the man and his son, the eagle, came back to their old home and lived there.[5]

Chapman Schanandoah (Oneida)

Chapman Schanandoah (born 1870) attended Hampton in 1888 and left a year later. He reentered the school in 1892 and stayed for two years. He enlisted in the U.S. Navy in 1897, and in 1904 he served aboard the USS *Raleigh*. After leaving the navy in 1912 he moved to Buffalo. (Littlefield and Parins, *Biobibliography: Supplement*, 282).

How the Bear Lost His Tail: An Old Indian Story, 1893

It may seem rather strange, come to inquire about this story among the different tribes of Indians. We seem to know it so alike, even if we do speak different languages. This story must have happened when we spoke the same language.

As we know such as prairie dogs, rattlesnakes, and owls live together and don't quarrel; so some of the animals first lived together and spoke the same language, until they got quarreling and cheating each other, when they parted for good.

The Bear and the Fox once lived together in the same place. Mr. Fox always depended on Mr. Bear very much. Especially when he got in trouble with someone else, he would call on Mr. Bear sure. So one winter Mr. Bear thought that he was so wise and strong, and everybody was afraid of him that he would get Mr. Fox to support him all that winter.

Mr. Fox thought that he had to work very hard to get his own living and so he was not going to do all the work. Mr. Bear had brought home a nice fat deer one day; so he told Fox that he would not share with him anymore, as he used to. "Very well," said Fox. All the more Mr. Fox would get such good things to eat that Bear could not get. One day he brought home a nice mess of fish. He had picked them up along the river. Mr. Bear wished very much to have a taste of those nice fishes. Mr. Fox told him that he might get all the fish he wanted if he would do what he did. Bear asked him very kindly just how he got them. He would be friends with him again. So Fox said, "You go with me some cold night and do what I did, you shall get all you want." The night came and it was very cold. Mr. Bear was very anxious to go. They started at last and they came to the place where some fisherman had been through the day and there were nice holes to fish in. So Mr. Fox told Bear that he would have to wait some time before he could get a fish. Fox said, "You put your tail in that ice hole until it gets hard and you will see that you can get all the fish you want." Bear did just as he was told, not to lift up his tail till Fox came back. Mr. Bear patiently waited nearly all night. At last Fox came back with a party of dogs to scare the bear. Bear had no more than heard the cries of the dogs, before he jumped with all his might, leaving his nice long tail in the frozen ice.

Mr. Fox never forgot this and he never went back home to see how his old friend Bear got along.[6]

Robert Placidus Higheagle (Standing Rock Sioux)

See the Essays section for a profile of Robert Placidus Higheagle (born ca. 1873).

The Brave Deaf and Dumb Boy, 1893

An Indian named Step made a feast and invited good many Indians, as he wished to tell them about this dangerous escape in a war long time ago. His first statement was that he would have been dead long ago if he had lived in a savage state as he did many years ago. He then began to tell them the following story. He stated that a long time ago some men and himself went to war with a deaf and dumb boy. They went on foot, as they expected to capture some horses from their enemies.

Thus they continued marching until they arrived at a very high hill which they named Dog's Ears Hill. From this hill they could see a long distance off. Looking down they saw herds of buffaloes and wild horses in a forest. They were not only pleased, but were very much surprised when they saw these objects before their eyes. So they concluded that they would divide their party in such a way, so that they would surround them. Down in the forest they went and were having a pretty tough chase. But all at once they were yelling and began to climb the tallest trees. What was the matter? (Here I wish to say that he mentions a kind of animal which I don't think is found in this continent. He described it and it seems as though it must be an animal that is found in Africa called gnu—an animal something like a horse with two horns. So I will call it a gnu). They saw a gnu right among the herd—been engaged in chasing the herd before the men did. The animal stopped chasing the herd and began to attack these poor fellows. About six of them climbed on a single tree. But the gnu came around and began shaking the tree with its horns and the men were in great fear. Every time they attempted to shoot the animal, it acted more furiously. By and by the animal shook the tree with all its might and one of the men fell off.

This was the deaf and dumb boy the youngest but bravest in the crowd. Before the animal had the chance to attack him he climbed up another tree that was near by. From the tree he made signs to the other fellows, which meant that as he does not expect to see a hundred years he would give up his life for the others, and he descended to the ground and began to shoot at the animal. He shot him in the brain, which made the animal senseless for a time. While this was taking place the men came down from the tree and ran away in full speed. The boy himself ran away with the others. They all ran in the same direction. But before they were gone some distance another gnu attacked him. The young fellow knew that he was going to die this time so as soon as the gnu attacked him he fell down to the ground. The animal caught him in his horns and threw him up in the air. When he fell to the ground he was not hurt, but he lay there pretending to be dead. The animal came around, pawing him. By and by [the animal] began to feel if [the boy's heart was beating]. The boy, even if he was deaf and dumb, was very ticklish. It is said that he could laugh at any time he gets [tickled]. So when the animal came around to feel his heart beating, he got so tickled that he had to burst into a loud laugh. He tried very hard to resist but he could not. So when the animal found out that he pretended to be dead he caught him in his horns and did the same thing to him as before, only a little harder than before.

But the young fellow got the best of him and was saved. While he was having this tough time with the animal his companions had gone away from him. He found their tracks and followed them. He soon overtook them and was very glad to see them again. It is said that they made him a chief on account of his bravery.

The next day they had war with their enemies and it is said that they were victorious. After they had overcome their enemies they captured all of their horses. Thus they went home in a good style.

The reason why he told this true story was, he wished to impress upon their minds that a person, even if he is deaf and dumb, can accomplish much, just by patient endurance of suffering that may befall him.

The Indians drew good many morals from this story. One was that a person, even if he could not hear, could attempt to defend himself in the time of danger.[7]

The Legend of Owl River, 1895

"In the land of the Dakotas," there is a certain river known as the Owl River, from the fact that a famous event had happened there concerning the above named bird.

It was customary among the Indians of old to do anything in their power to bring up their children as brave as themselves. One of the common punishments inflicted to remedy cowardice was that, when a male child cried over anything instead of acting like a man, he was sent out of the community until he could overcome his stubbornness.

One night, when the Indians camped out near the above mentioned river (which did not have a name at that time) a boy was crying over something. Owls were plentiful in the neighboring woods and were wide awake as usual. They were the means by which the mothers could pacify their children by telling them strange anecdotes about them. But this child did not care to hear anything concerning the owls but kept on crying. His mother told him that if he did not stop crying she would send him out where the owls would come and carry him away. It was a general belief at that time that owls had enormously large ears—so large as to enable them to carry away in them a young child with perfect ease. Of course the mother was just saying this in fun, as mothers would often do, in order to quiet the child, but her words were of no avail. Finally she sent him outdoors into the darkness of the night and told the owls to come and get him for she can't make him mind. The owls seemed to have understood her request and were coming along and before anyone knew anything about it the child was carried off. The whole family went out when they heard no one crying and to their surprise, the child was gone. Just imagine how the parents felt! Word was sent through the village immediately announcing the trouble and nearly all the men even the women came out with their weapons to bring back the child. They searched all night and the next day till dark but all in vain. During the night they heard someone crying in the woods. Everyone rushed toward the place but nobody was to be found.

The next day the parents offered a reward of two fine ponies to anyone who found their child. Some boys went into the woods for game not intending to find the child, but they heard the same cry, which sent them to search. They heard the cry again in the hollow of an old oak. One of the boys climbed up and found that the child was there. They caught the owl in a true "cowboy fashion" and brought him to the ground. Of course the owl tried hard to get loose from the boy but was in the same fix as when a wild Texas steer is once caught by a skillful cowboy and there is no knowing as to its escape. The boys butchered the owl in such a manner as not to harm the child's life and succeeded in restoring the child in good condition.

The act of the owl has been one of the greatest if not the greatest event that ever happened on that river and therefore the Indians named it the Owl River. Some Indians even count their time from that period. If you should ask any of those old time Indians the year of their birth etc., they will answer you that they were born ten years or so before the owl carried that child away. Of course this may not be a true story but the Indians of that section of the country believe it to be a fact just as much as the people of Sleepy Hollow believed in the incidents said to have occurred in that spot years ago.[8]

Samuel Baskin (Santee Sioux)

See the Essays section for a profile of Samuel Baskin (born 1870).

Ite Waste, or Fair Face, 1895

Ite Waste was the name of a young Indian woman. Among the different tribes of Indians, she was considered as the prettiest woman that ever walked the earth. Many Indians had lost their lives and many had failed trying to get her. But one succeeded in getting her. His name was Swift Star. He had seen the woman and had promised to marry her if it took his life.

Star was a great leader of his people and was also the great medicine man. The time had come for him to marry Ite Waste. He took with him a pair of boots, or long legged moccasins, a table or mat such as Indians use to eat on, and a flute. After some weeks travelling, he came to a river and saw no way of crossing it. So he slipped on the moccasins and stepped across the wide river. The following day he came to a strange looking tipi not far from the road. A man came out and invited him to dinner. Star accepted the invitation. After dinner he was asked if he would like to see the place, and as he was being shown around, he was suddenly cast into a very deep and dark hole. After he came to his senses, he found himself among many Indians of his age who were half starved for want of food. Star then shook and put down his table and there was a long table set in the center of the hole with all the good things to eat that one could think of, steaming thereon.

He then asked all his starving comrades to dinner and they ate. After dinner he played on his flute and the music was so sweet and the Indians were so happy that they couldn't keep themselves from dancing. The owner of the tipi heard the music and dancing and wished to be invited to join in with the party. He was taken down very carefully while Star continued his music and at the same [time] he and his comrades rose until they came to the surface, but sad to relate, the man was left alone down in the hole.

Star then bid all his friends goodbye and went on travelling. Now after passing through many hardships and sorry days, he at last reached Ite Waste's home.

He had now gotten into a place where it was impossible to save his life, because there were three things to be performed by all seekers for the hand of Ite Waste and so far all others had failed.

The first thing was to level a hill with a small wooden spoon, the second was to chop a tree with a wooden axe, and the third was to bale a lake with a wooden spoon. One had to do all these before he could marry Ite Waste. Ite Waste loved this young man very much and had promised to do all in her power to help him.

After passing this examination, Ite Waste said to Swift Star, "Now, I do not know what father will have you do next in his attempt to take your life and I have only one way of saving your life and that is for you and me to steal away tonight." The following night they were ready to go, and before starting Ite Waste put a big handful of pop-corn around the fire. Then they both left the tipi very quietly and aimed for the land where the sun sets. All this happened in the early part of the evening and later in the evening the mother awoke and said to her husband, "Listen, it seems to me those young folks are not in." The husband listened just then several pop-corns popped that sounded very much like two persons talking and laughing. The husband said to his wife, "They are in, can't you hear them laughing?" Then once more they tried to go to sleep. Again [at] about midnight the mother got up and this time she went to the door and peeped in and was very much surprised to find the room empty.

She at once awoke and told her husband to get up and go and hunt the elopers. The husband got up and started hunting for them. Ite Waste and her lover were many miles away. When they were travelling she used to say to her lover, "If you see a small red cloud come sailing toward us that is a sign that father is after us and we are safe; but if you see a black cloud, mother is coming and we shall probably have to give up ourselves." Soon after they saw a reddish cloud coming. Ite Waste said, "That is my father and we are safe!" Then they both disguised themselves into crows and seated themselves on a limb of a tree. Father came up and stood gazing at these two crows and within himself said, "Oh, these are regular crows, I'll go home." So he about-faced and went home. When he got home, his wife was so anxious to hear the report that she asked if had seen anything of them. The husband said, "No, I didn't see a thing except two old crows sitting on a limb near the road." The woman said, "They are the ones! Why didn't you get them? I'll go this time." She then went and got some wild rice to take with her.

By this time Ite Waste and her lover were coming to a river and just as they got to the bank of the river, they saw a black cloud, which told them that the mother was coming. They again disguised themselves by turning themselves into ducks and swimming out. The mother came and stood on the bank and began to throw out rice into the water. When the drake saw the rice, he began to swim towards the shore, but the female kept him out of the mother's reach by keeping herself between the two until her mother wasted all the rice. Then the mother said, "Go, you are safe." Then she returned home.

The two young people are now on the other side of the river, free as birds. They went to a village and got married and are now living together as happy as could be after their great trouble.[9]

Stella Vanessa Bear (Arikara)

Stella Vanessa Bear (born ca. 1883) grew up on the Fort Berthold Reservation in North Dakota and attended Hampton before entering Carlisle in 1903. In Hampton's *Talks and Thoughts* and Carlisle's *Arrow*, *Indian Craftsman*, and *Red Man*, she published several stories and retold tales based on Arikara legends. After graduating from Hampton in 1910 she became field matron at the Cheyenne and Arapaho Agency in Cantonment, Oklahoma. She also worked as boys' matron at the Standing Rock Indian School in North Dakota. (*Carlisle Arrow*, 3 October 1913; Carlisle Indian School Digital Resource Center; Littlefield and Parins, *Biobibliography: Supplement*, 7–8, 172; *Red Man*, January 1911, 222)

An Indian Story, 1903

After having wandered over the lonely prairies all day in search of buffalo, some Indians came one night to a beautiful valley. Tired as they were they immediately began to pull the tent poles and other articles from the horses' backs and at once the women began putting up the tipis while the men went to water and picket the horses for the night. Supper was being prepared in the open air near the different tipis while the little dark-skinned boys and girls were playing a short distance from the camping place.

All at once a strange cry was heard far off in the distance; they were sure it was the cry of a human being, so the men watched in the stillness of the night, thinking it was one of their own tribe. They waited and watched but they were so tired that soon they went to sleep.

When all was quiet in the camp the man that had been heard crying crept slowly out from the long grass and went directly to the chief's tent. Lifting the mat door he walked in, and in a little while came out with one of the prettiest daughters the chief had. Alas, the poor Indian maiden did not know where she was being taken for she was fast asleep as she was carried out of the tent and taken to a cave about a mile from the camping place of her people.

This man I am telling you about is known as a cave dweller. Among my tribe it is supposed that during some outbreak they had with another tribe many people were scalped; they were ashamed to go among their tribe again thinking it a disgrace. They never returned but made homes in the high bluffs of the Missouri River or in the Bad Lands.

Next morning the chief was heard crying: "Have any of you seen my oldest daughter?" The people rushed out of their tents to see what was the matter and when they heard they readily guessed that the cave dweller had been there in the night. It was no use to look for the girl for if they had attempted to search they would never have found her. All the morning when they were getting ready to leave there was great wailing and when all was ready they went away sorrowful, especially the girl's relatives.

Every year when the Indians went on their usual hunt they passed this valley and recalled what had happened there. Several years after they came to the place and camped there and at night just as they were starting for bed the young Indian maid who had disappeared came back to them. No one knows how she came there or where she came from but there was great rejoicing over the tall, slender girl and a feast was made that night in honor of her return.[10]

How People First Came to the World, 1903

My people believe that we first lived beneath the earth in darkness and never knew that there was another world until a small ground mole dug its way up to the surface of the earth. When the ground mole looked out he saw the green land, its trees and the waters, and he immediately crept back down into the earth finding his way as best he could, for he had lost his eyesight as the sunlight was too bright for him.

When he got back to the other animals he told them what he had seen and that if they would help him in digging a hole they would all soon live in another world. So they all got together and began their work and did not stop until the hole was large enough for them to get through.

The next day they began to get ready for their journey, first all the creeping things crawled out and the other animals followed them. As they were passing out they saw a strange company among them and these were human beings. The animals were so frightened that they scattered in every direction, except the dog which stood by the hole wagging its tail as the people approached him. When they got near him he gave a strange cry. When this band of people heard a rumbling in the earth from which they had just come and when they looked at the hole they saw people like themselves coming forth, singing and laughing as they stepped upon the soil of the new world. For ten days the people did not stop coming out of the earth but finally they were checked when a large fat woman tried to get through. She got half way out but she could not go any further so she had to stay right there, which of course stopped the people from coming out any more.

After this sad accident the people journeyed toward the West until they came to some high mountains which they could not get across. They cried and prayed to the sun and while they were wailing a large eagle came and told them he would help them across. So the eagle flew over the mountains and they became like low prairie land and the people started to cross but some got left behind, for the mountains rose up again. Those who had gotten over went on until they came to a dense forest; they prayed as they did when they came to those high mountains. This time an owl came and relieved them of their sorrow by going through the trees and clearing a way for them but again the same thing happened, some were so slow in getting through that they were checked when the dense forest rose again.

They journeyed until they came to a large river and they had no idea how they were to get across, but a kind duck came to them and said that he would help them. So the little duck swam across and the waters parted. This time all the people got over safely and none were swallowed up by the waves.

This is the reason people are found in all parts of the world, because many were left behind as they were journeying to reach the West and never got there.[11]

An Enemy's Revenge, 1905

This is one of the tales that my grandmother used to tell us children in the long winter evenings around the fire.

One beautiful evening a party of Indian maids were playing near the edge of the woods, when suddenly a peculiar looking man sprang out and giving one loud whoop ran up to the girls and said in angry tones, "Many years ago, your people and my people had a fight, many lives were lost on both sides. I was there."

As he said this he removed the fox fur that was around his head and touching his hair he asked, "Do you see anything strange here?"

The youngest of the girls spoke up and said, "I see your scalp lock is gone."

By this time the girls were trembling with fear.

"Yes," he said. "It was taken by one of your people and now I am going to have my revenge."

When he said this the frightened girls scattered in different directions, he following after them. He soon overtook a pretty girl, the chief's only child. Instead of killing her he stuck his fist into her mouth to keep her cries from being heard and then carried her into a cave that was on a side of a high cliff.

The girls ran back to the camp and told what had happened.

Everything was in confusion. The young braves mounted their horses and were soon speeding towards the place where the girls had been. The women and even children were wailing and all that night not a soul slept except the little children.

Early in the morning the men returned from their hunt but had failed to find any trace of the girl.

Day after day the chief looked for his daughter but without success. He then gave up all hopes of ever finding her.

Ten years after the disappearance of the girl the people moved away from that place to a new hunting place. In the fall when they were on their way back they stopped at a beautiful ravine and camped there for a night.

That night when the campfires had gone out and the people were all in bed, a strange singing was heard near by. The men got up and watched but saw nothing and concluded that it must be the spirit of some dead person that haunted the ravine.

The next day the people did not go on with their journey for the horses needed a rest and it was agreed that all remain there another night.

That evening when the sun had gone down two figures were seen creeping through the tall prairie-grass, and the people noticed that one was that of a young woman. Two men armed with bows and arrows went through the ravine and came up on the other side. They cautiously crept up to the two figures that were hiding in the grass.

All at once one of the men shouted, "Chief Son-of-the-Star, your daughter is found!"

The people ran and when they saw the girl they cried with joy and brought her to the camp.

The man who was with her had disappeared as soon as the two men approached them. It was the man who had taken her away many years ago. He had brought the girl back only to see her tribe once more, for that night she passed into the happy hunting grounds above.[12]

Ghost Bride Pawnee Legend, 1910

The Pawnees were all ready to leave the village for a hunt, when a young woman suddenly died, so they had to get her ready for burial. She was dressed in her finest clothes and buried. A party of young men had been off on a visit and were on their way home. They knew nothing of the departure of the tribe and the death of the girl. As they traveled on they met the tribe and all joined them except one young man, who went back to the deserted village. As he was nearing the village he saw someone sitting on top of the lodge, and as he got nearer he saw it was the girl he loved. When she saw him she got down from the lodge and went inside. The young man began to wonder why she was alone. When he got close to her he spoke and said, "Why are you alone in this village?" She answered him: "They have gone off on a hunt. I was sulky with my relations so they left me behind." Then she told him that the ghosts were going to have a dance that night and that he must not be afraid. It was an old custom of the Pawnees. All was quiet in the village—until the ghosts began their dance. They went from lodge to lodge, singing, dancing, and hallooing, and soon they came to this young man's lodge. They danced around him and he was badly frightened. Sometimes they touched him. The next day he persuaded the girl to go with him and join the tribe on their hunt. They started off and the girl promised the young man that she should become his wife, but not until the proper time came. They overtook the tribe and were near the camp when the girl stopped and said: "Now we have arrived but you must go first to the village and prepare a place for me. Where I sleep let it be behind a curtain. For four days and four nights I must sleep behind curtains. Do not speak of me. Do not mention my name."

The young man left her and went into camp and told a woman to go out to a certain place and bring in a woman and she began to inquire who the woman was and to avoid speaking her name he told who were her father and mother. The woman in surprise said, "It cannot be that girl for she died some days before we started on a hunt." The woman went for the girl, but she had disappeared because the young man had disobeyed her and told who she was. If he had obeyed the girl would have lived upon earth the second time. That same night the young man died in sleep. Then the people believed that there must be a life after this one.[13]

Indian Legend—Creation of the World, 1910

There are many legends told of how this world was created and this is the story told by my tribe. We all once inhabited a region under the ground and lived in total darkness. One day the ground mole made his way up to the surface and discovered a new world. When he came in contact with the light he went blind and he returned to the people and told them what he had found, so the people got to work and dug the hole which the mole had made until it was large enough for a good sized person to pass through. After this task was completed the people began to pour out of the earth. They came out of this hole all day long and would have continued to come, but a very corpulent woman stopped up the passage, hindering the rest of the people from coming to the surface. They could not pull the woman out of the hole, so she died there. The people on reaching the surface did not know what to do, so they all started off on a journey and traveled until they came to a river. A bird flapped his wings and the waters parted and a good many of them succeeded in crossing, but the waters came together and the others could not get across. Those who crossed went on, leaving the others behind. Next they came to some high mountains; again the bird made the way easier for them in crossing the mountains, but some could not cross and they had to stay back. Finally they came to a forest and the bird showed them the way, but only a part of them were able to get through the dense forest. In this journey the people were all scattered and that is the reason why there are so many tribes and languages among the Indians.[14]

Anna Bender (White Earth Chippewa)

See the Essays section for a profile of Anna Bender (1885–1911).

Quital's First Hunt, 1904

In a little Ojibway camp near a beautiful little stream there lived a poor old woman with her grandson, whose name was Quital.

One day the boy's companions were going out to hunt buffaloes, but he could not go because he had only one poor pony while all his friends had a number of fine ones.

He felt very lonely and was almost ready to cry. His grandmother noticed this and was very sorry for him. She called him to her and said, "My grandson, you have always been a good boy to me; do now what I shall tell you. Take your pony down to the creek and give him a good washing. After that bring him to me." The boy did as his grandmother had said, and when he had returned she proceeded to paint the horse with bright colored Indian paints which she had made from some magic clay that she knew about, for she was a medicine woman and knew many strange secrets of this kind. When she had finished her work the poor little pony looked gorgeous indeed.

The other young men had started off sometime before, but the grandson, armed with his bow and arrows jumped into his saddle, and soon overtook the party that was on the trail of a herd of buffaloes, going at full speed. The brightly painted pony went even more swiftly and soon got ahead of all the others. This gave Quital a chance to shoot down a number of buffaloes before his companions came up. These he took home to his grandmother so that she had buffalo meat enough to last all the winter.

For this feat the boy was considered a great hero.[15]

The First Squirrel, 1904

Once there was a chief who was very sick and many thought he would die. The doctors and medicine men had done all in their power to restore him to health, but to no avail.

One day during this sad time an old man all dressed in red came into the camp, and went directly to the tent of the chief. He looked tired and hungry, but instead of receiving him hospitably and giving him a place to rest, as is the custom with all Indians, the chief's wife spoke unkindly to the man and sent him away unfed.

Now the chief had seven sons and when the youngest saw the old man going away tired and hungry he was sorry for him, and taking him aside gave him something to eat.

When he had finished eating the old man said to the boy, "My grandson, you have shown me a tender heart, and I will tell you this. I am a medicine man and came here to cure your father, but they have been unkind to me and I cannot do it. Look! Do you see yonder mountain? Beyond that is another and on the farther side of it stands a grove of trees. There I will meet you and show you where you can get some medicine to cure your father. You will meet difficulties on the way, but you must not stop to eat or to drink or to take part in any games or sports along the way."

When the youngest son heard all this he went in and told his father and expressed his desire to go for the medicine. But the chief preferred that his oldest and favorite son should be the one to cure him, so he sent for him and gave him the directions that had been given to the younger brother.

The young man started off on his journey and day by day the father awaited his return. After five days, when the son had not returned, the old chief sent out his second son, hoping that he would find his brother and both come back with the medicine, but five more days passed and he did not return. Then he sent the third son, and as he did not return he sent the fourth, and so on every five days until he had sent every one except the youngest. Then he bade the boy go and at least find his brothers.

The boy was anxious to go and started off at once. As he travelled on he came one day upon two of his brothers sitting down under a few sand cherry bushes eating the fruit. They tried to persuade him to stop and eat also, but he closed his ears and ran on.

When he had passed the first mountain he came upon two more of his brothers running races with some strange young men. They urged him to stay, promising to give him some of the beautiful blankets, buckskin clothes, and horses that they had; but again he stopped his ears and hurried on.

As he went on farther he came to a place where there was a table standing under the trees, and there he found two more of his brothers playing a game. They begged him to join them, and when he refused and went on, they ran after him, but soon got tired and went back.

After he had crossed the last mountain he came to a spring under a grove of trees. He was so tired and thirsty that he was going to lie down and drink, but just as he was about to take the water he heard a man's voice. He looked up to see who it was that had spoken to him and found beside him the red-robed medicine man. "This water," said the man, "contains mineral matter, and is not good for you, therefore do not drink."

The man then stooped down and taking up a little of the water, put into it a certain plant that grows in Montana and said, "This will cure your father. Take it to him."

The boy then took the medicine and carried it home to his father, and almost immediately the old chief began to get well. Then he said to the boy, "Go, my youngest son, and bring your brothers home to me."

Again the boy started out and found his brothers and tried to persuade them to go home with him, but they were enjoying themselves and would not listen to him, so he had to go home alone.

When the boy came back without his brothers the old chief was very angry because he thought his youngest son was deceiving him. He told him that he could not come home again until he could bring his brothers with him.

This made the boy very sad and he went out into the woods. He thought himself all alone, but all at once he found beside him his old friend the medicine man. He told him his trouble and the man was very sorry for him. He could not bring the brothers back, he said, but he could change him into anything that he would like to be.

The boy considered. He would not care to be a tree nor flower, he thought, but he would like to be some animal that could live like the birds in the beautiful trees. So the medicine man changed him into a pretty little animal that lives in the trees, that eats nice food, and can travel high up out of danger faster than any other. This is how there came to be squirrels.[16]

The Big Dipper, 1904

There was once a chief who had two daughters, the younger one of which he liked the best. One day they went out under the trees to work with porcupine quills. These were hanging on a tree. The older sister reached up for them, but the quills rose up out of her reach. She climbed the tree but still the quills went higher and higher, so presently she got tired and came down.

Then the younger one climbed the tree, but the porcupine quills acted in the same way. However she would not stop but kept on climbing. After awhile she went so high she came to another world and found that the chief there was the son of the Sun. She went on through the woods and came to a small tent where an old woman lived, and just at that time she was cooking dinner. The little girl went in but the old woman did not look up but kept on with her work. The girl did not say anything either. When the old woman got through she gave her a part of her dinner. After they had eaten, the girl helped her put away her cooking utensils and brought in some wood for her. This pleased the old woman and she told her she could sleep there that night, but that she must hide herself because the chief always went through every tent at night to see how his people were getting on, and might find her.

She did not know it, but the chief did see her and the next morning he called for her. He was pleased with her and told her she could stay there with his family. She was glad to do so, and after a while she became the chief's wife and had a little son. When the little boy was growing up her husband gave orders that she must never let him kill meadow larks, and she herself must never dig Indian turnips nor turn over round stones.

One day she took her little boy out to walk. He had his little bow and arrow, and all at once she found he had killed a meadow lark. Immediately all the rest of the birds began to sing, "This is not your home. This is not your home. Go back where you belong. Go back where you belong."

At another time the boy wanted some Indian turnips and she dug some for him. She had disobeyed her husband in two things so she thought she might as well finish up, so she turned over a round stone and under it she found a hole in the ground and through it she saw the earth that she had left long ago and the camp where she had lived when a little child.

This filled her with a great desire to come back to earth, but she wanted to bring her son with her. She asked her husband. He would not let his child go, but he ordered his men to get the sinews of buffaloes and to make a rope long enough to let her down to the earth. This they did and she was lowered to her old home. She found there instead of her family an old woman who was her step-mother. Her father had died and her step-mother treated her with great unkindness. One rainy day she sent her out to dig Indian turnips and told her she must also bring a rabbit home to her and must be back before sun down. She went but she could not find any rabbits and she had nothing to dig the turnips with so she sat down and cried.

There were seven brothers living near there and they were eating their supper. One of them said, "Be quiet, I hear a little girl crying somewhere." So they stopped and listened. One was kind hearted and said, "Let us go out and look for her," so they went out on a hill and the one who was good of sight pointed her out and another who could run fast went and asked her about her troubles. She told him about her step-mother and the task she had given her to do. He went back and told his brothers and they all started out to dig turnips and one of them killed a rabbit. Then he took the rabbit and turnips and brought them to the little girl and she took them back to her step-mother.

The next day she sent her out again, and the day after and each time she brought back the rabbit and turnips. One day she went out and never came back because the seven brothers had adopted her as their sister and she went to live with them. In someway her step-mother found out where she was and came there while the seven brothers were away. She asked the girl what she usually did when the brothers returned home and the girl replied that she went out to meet them and welcome them, but she did not tell her that she got their meals for them.

The step-mother then changed the girl into a dog while she put herself in her place. She went out to meet them and welcomed them home, but did not get their supper and they began to wonder why. The little dog jumped upon the brothers and tried to lick their hands, but the step-mother struck her and she cried like a person. The brothers thought this was strange so when the supposed girl had gone to sleep the brothers began to question the dog. Her step-mother had forbidden her to tell the brothers, but they threatened to kill her if she refused, so she told them. Then they called the woman and ordered her to change the dog back to a girl again. This they forced her to do and then sent her away. They did not like to live there any more because their place had been found out and they wished to live alone. Then the youngest said, "Let us be rock, hills, trees, etc.," but the oldest said, "No, let us be stars and place ourselves in the skies where we will live forever."

One of them could shoot very well so he took eight good arrows, and as he shot each one up into the sky a brother would go with it. When the sixth had gone up and had formed the outline of the dipper that we see in the sky every night he shot up one little arrow that took the girl, and then last of all went up himself. You will always see the little girl near the big dipper in the sky, near the seven kind brothers who had befriended her.[17]

William J. Owl (Eastern Band Cherokee)

William J. Owl (born ca. 1883) graduated from Carlisle in 1911. He was employed at the Cherokee Indian School in North Carolina in 1912. (Littlefield and Parins, *Biobibliography: Supplement*, 262)

The Beautiful Bird, 1910

The beautiful bird was in existence many, many moons ago, and at that time, the Cherokees claim he was the most beautiful of the fowls of the air, and that he was also the ruler of all the birds. He was adored for his good looks and praised for his courage.

The time came, however, when he began to exaggerate his authority in everything. At all feasts he was the first to be served, and no one could touch a bit of food without his presence and permission. He had been so rude that he had created an ill feeling in the hearts of all towards him. Finally they were unwilling to provide or contribute to his wants or needs.

The birds called a council to decide whether to banish him as their ruler or to put him out of existence. His ill behavior had impressed the hearts of all in such a way that they at once decided to get rid of him. Some thought it best to ostracize him entirely, while others thought it wiser and more of a punishment to degrade him by causing a change to come upon him, which would make life a burden to him the remainder of his days.

They arranged to have a great feast in his honor. The day was set and all preparations were made for the occasion. The eatables were set opposite the trap which was laid for him. The food was so arranged that in order to get anything to eat he must take it through the trap. Any time they wished they could spring the trap on him.

After a long and tiresome journey he arrived very hungry. He never once thought that a plot had been planned to punish him. He began eating his meal in the usual way and after he had nearly finished, the trap was sprung and the fun was on. He found his head was caught and he fought desperately for his release.

After a long and terrible struggle he succeeded in freeing himself, but only to be scorned and laughed at the remainder of his days, for in his desperate effort to free himself he had worn away all the beautiful feathers and plumes on his head and neck. He was so ashamed and humiliated, he tucked his head under his pinion only to find his wing feathers all worn away too. He demurely walked away never again to associate with the other birds.

When they realized the effect his conditions had upon him it was hard for them to decide what he should do to obtain a livelihood. They finally decided that he and all his descendants should forever lead the life of scavengers. This was considered the most degraded life any bird could lead. It would be necessary for him to be continually on the lookout for food, as there were just certain kinds of food which he could feed upon and only during a short time in the year.

After he was changed he became the turkey buzzard. His descendants are shy and always fly at considerable height. They are continually on the alert for carrion to feed upon. If a turkey buzzard is seen sailing around overhead it is a sure indication of a carcass in that locality.[18]

The Way the Opossum Derived His Name, 1912

Many, many winters ago, before the great snow, as the Indians termed the glacial period, the opossum derived his name from the tricks he played on the other animals.

He is a crafty looking little animal with a long tail, with which he can hang or suspend himself from a limb by winding it about the limb. He can climb trees and cling to the branches and the strongest winds cannot dislodge him.

Once upon a time there lived in his neighborhood a deer family with whom he became acquainted, because of Mr. Deer's beautiful daughter, and it was there that he met the panther, and because of the deer's daughter they became enemies. The panther was in the habit of making frequent calls at the deer's and the opossum met him there. The panther's jealousy became so great that he was led to try and kill the opossum.

When Mr. Deer learned of the rivalry between the two, he thought that he would settle the question, and do it in a quiet way, by keeping it a secret from the panther. So one day he told the opossum he would give him his daughter if he would ride the panther by his house, never thinking the opossum would have courage enough to attempt a task of that kind.

The opossum at once began planning for the ride. He knew the days and hours the panther made his calls at the deer's home. After thinking seriously he decided to meet the panther and have a talk with him; but when he saw the panther coming he decided to deceive the panther in such a way that probably he would have pity on him and help him.

While the panther was quite a distance away the opossum lay down in the path and began to roll over and over as if suffering from pain. When the panther came up he laughed and started on his way, for he was glad to see the opossum who was, as he believed, dying. After he had passed the opossum called to him for help, asking the panther to carry him home. The panther only laughed, but after a second thought he decided it would be a good scheme, for he could prove to the deer family that he was not an enemy to all the other animals as some had thought. The panther returned and took the opossum upon his back and started off to the home of the opossum for he was sure the opossum could not live.

In order to reach the home of the opossum they would have to pass the deer home and that was what both were anxious to do. Just as they came to the deer home all the deer family came out to see the opossum ride the panther. As they passed, they heard some of the deer remark about the courage of the little opossum. Upon hearing that the opossum sat up straight and began kicking the panther in the sides as if he were a horse, and then cried out, "See me ride the panther!" Upon bearing that, the panther became very angry and tried to catch the opossum, but he escaped in the branches of some trees nearby.

When the panther learned of the trick he was enraged and was more eager than before to kill the opossum, but he could not catch him because he could not climb a straight tree or one that had many limbs on it.

In those days the rain gods were not so numerous and water was scarce, there being only one pool from which the Indians and all animals received their water. The panther knew the opossum would have to have water to drink, for he could not live without it, so he went to the pool to lie in wait for him, for he was sure of getting him when he came for drink.

After a time the opossum became thirsty and knew that he would have to have water or else he would perish; so he began to plan another trick by which he might deceive the panther. One day he went down hoping to find the panther absent or asleep; but he was neither; so he was at a loss as to what he should do. As he was going down to the place he called home, he saw an Indian maiden coming toward him carrying a water pot. As he thought she was going for water, he stepped aside and awaited her return. She soon appeared, as she had only gone to a neighboring village for some maple syrup, which the Indians were accustomed to make.

While the maiden was gone the opossum planned a way to deceive her and thus get a drink; so when he saw her coming he lay down in the path and acted as if he were dead.

The maiden kicked him to one side as she passed him and went on. But when she was out of sight the opossum got up and took another path and so came in ahead of her and repeated the act, only to be kicked aside again, for the maid thought that two opossums did not amount to much as their meat was never eaten and their pelts were too small to make into robes, so she would not bother with them. The opossum did not give up, though his first two trials had been failures. He tried his trick again and this time he succeeded in deceiving her, for she thought that three opossums would be of some use; so she set her pitcher down beside him and went to search for the other opossums. While she was gone the opossum dipped his paws into the pitcher, and to his surprise he found that it contained syrup, and that he could not quench his thirst with it, so he started off very discouraged. When he walked off he stepped into some dried leaves, and the syrup caused them to stick to his feet, so he had another idea which would enable him to deceive the panther at the pool. The opossum went back and upset the pitcher and the syrup ran out, and he rolled in it until he was covered with it; then he went and rolled in the dried leaves until he was covered with them; then he headed for the pool and on his arrival he found the panther still waiting.

When he came up the panther asked who he was, and he told him that he was the porcupine, and that he had fallen from a tree and his quills had pierced the leaves and remained on him; so the panther let him help himself to the water and leave the pool unharmed.

After the opossum had gained a safe distance, he called to the panther and made known who he was. The panther did not chase him, but remained at his station, for he knew he would have to come again. The panther stayed at the pool until he was almost starved, in hopes of catching the opossum, but Mr. 'Possum never showed up, so the panther was forced to go in search of food.

While the opossum had a chance to drink water he drank all he could, then filled the pocket on his stomach with water, which would last a long time. The panther did not know that the opossum had a pocket or pouch in which he could carry things, so that was another way in which the opossum fooled the panther.

After the opossum had fooled the panther three times, the panther disappeared and was not seen for a long time, and then it was rumored that he had died in his den of starvation. All the animals had congregated about his den, but they were afraid to look in. After a few days the opossum came by and saw the other animals there and asked what was the trouble. They told him, so he went to the entrance and looked in and noticed that all seemed to be true; and then the opossum asked the crowd if the panther had kicked and breathed harshly when he died, but they did not know.

The opossum stated an instance when his grandmother died, how she had breathed and kicked, etc. Upon hearing this, the panther began to kick and groan. The opossum just laughed and said, "Dead panthers never kick or groan." The panther could not work the opossum's own tricks on him. The opossum derived his name because of his excellence at "playing 'possum."[19]

Emma La Vatta (Fort Hall Shoshoni)

Emma La Vatta (born ca. 1890) entered Carlisle in 1905 and graduated in 1911. After graduating she returned to Idaho, where in 1912 she sought a position as matron in the Indian School Service. (Littlefield and Parins, *Biobibliography: Supplement*, 242; Carlisle Indian School Digital Resource Center)

The Story of the Deerskin, 1910

Once upon a time a family of deer lived near a large river. The family was of the buck, doe, and three fawns. Whenever the doe went in search of food she always left the fawns at home and told them not to let any one in, no matter who came, because not very far from them, across the river, lived an old bear who might devour the young fawns. As the mother had said, the bear came and tried to get in, but they kept so still he went away thinking no one was at home.

Finally, one day he watched the doe go away and noticed the fawns were not with her, so as soon as she was out of sight the bear went over and pawed until he broke in and killed the three fawns. He then left.

When the doe returned and found her children dead she knew it was the bear's mischief and started to go to the bear's cave where she might kill him, but when she came to the river she saw she could not cross. As she stood there meditating what to do, two eagles, knowing her trouble, told her they would carry her across, but when they reached the middle of the river they dropped her and she was drowned. While all this was happening the buck was on the other side of the mountain and when he reached home he found the fawns dead and the doe gone, so he buried the fawns and went to find the doe. On reaching the river the same eagles offered

147

to assist him who had attempted to carry the doe across. This time they succeeded. When they reached the other side he found a large gathering of animals and the bear told him to stay inside of the cave and not to look out because they were going to have a war and he might be killed if he did not obey. When the war began, however, it was too much of a temptation, so he went out and was killed. The bear took the skin and stretched it over his door, so no one could look out when inside.

Usually you will find a deerskin stretched over the door of an Indian's wigwam.[20]

Why the Snake's Head Became Flat, 1911

Once upon a time there were two little boys who lived out on the western plains. Their names were Bow and Arrow. They were nearly the same size and enjoyed similar games and sports. They lived most of the time in the mountains where the game was plentiful and the streams full of trout. They naturally became skillful hunters and fishers. While they were away from home they depended upon whatever they could find, such as berries and roots, for food. The game they always took home for a great feast, which was spread in honor of their success. One day while they were out hunting they became hungry and there were no signs of vegetation near, so they thought probably if they went on the other side of the mountain they would find some berries, as they saw a great deal of shrubbery and trees. In order to make their way shorter they climbed around the mountain and found all the ripe berries they wanted; but while they were busily eating they heard a loud noise, and looking up the mountain side they saw a large stone which had broken loose from another rock rolling down the mountain side in their direction. They had moved out of the way and were standing on some rocks watching it when a large snake crept out from under the bushes, and the stone rolled over its head; and that is why the snake's head is flat.[21]

J. William Ettawageshik (Ottawa)

See the Essays section for a profile of J. William Ettawageshik (ca. 1889–1942).

The Maple Sugar Sand, 1911

It is more than a century ago since the territory about the Great Lakes was settled by the white people. Some times the Indians and the whites were on friendly terms and at other times they had trouble.

One day a white boy who lived some distance from an Indian village came to the camp of the Indians where he was kept as a prisoner. This was at a time when the Indians and whites were having trouble.

Every evening, about sunset, the Indians gave their prisoner some maple sugar, of which he was very fond. One day he was caught stealing some maple sugar, but the Indians did not reprove him for this act, but determined to punish him in an unusual way.

One of the Indians brought some sand to the camp from the lake shore. The sand along the lake shore resembles very closely pulverized maple sugar.

In the evening when it was time to give the prisoner his sugar, one of the Indians went to the sandpile and took a handful of sand; in the other hand he had sugar. On reaching the boy he gave him the sugar and kept the sand in his hand. After watching the boy devour the sugar, all the Indians with the exception of one went into their different wigwams to retire for the night.

After everything was quiet the boy thought he would help himself to the sugar, so he took a good handful of the sand, which so closely resembled sugar that he did not notice the difference, and put it into his mouth. He was badly fooled and had some difficulty in getting the sand out of his teeth. The Indian who was placed as a sentinel awoke the others to enjoy the joke which had been perpetrated on the boy who was so fond of maple sugar. Needless to say, he never again stole maple sugar from the Indians.[22]

Caleb Carter (Nez Percé)

See the Essays section for a profile of Caleb Carter (born 1888).

The Coyote and the Wind, 1913

The coyote, once upon a time, made himself a dwelling place out of tall bunch grass. It was in late fall, and the wind would always blow it apart. This made the coyote very angry, so one day he devised a snare in which to trap the offender. As he was fixing up the snare he thought to himself, "I will fix him!"

The next morning he set out to see if he had caught the wind. Upon arriving he beheld a man with big ears and of great stature. "Well," he said, "so you are the person that has been tearing my wigwam up, eh?" With that he pulled his ears right and left, kicked him on the nose, and slapped him till he had him begging for mercy.

The coyote then made him promise that he would never blow such cold, stormy winds again. But the coyote doubted his word, and again he had him begging. When the coyote would get tired, he rested. All this time the wind was making all kinds of promises, so at last the coyote let him go with the understanding that he would kill him on his next offense. So to this day the winds on the west side of the Rockies are warm and known as the "Chinook winds."[23]

The Feast of the Animals, 1913

Having been brought up by my grandmother, whom I always regarded as my mother until I attained the age of nine or ten years, I used to listen with great interest to some of the legends she related to me. Here is one which tells how some of the wild animals received their present forms and characteristics:

Long before the human race came to dwell upon this world, there existed a race of beings now known as bears, wolves, etc. They all spoke the same language, and therefore they understood each other. The time had come when all had to assume their present state, so a great feast was prepared. At this feast each had to select his own name, a name by which he would be identified by the human beings, also to choose what his chief prey would be and in what parts of the country he would be found.

The coyote was always regarded as an announcer and chief. He was the wisest of the race and had power even surpassing the best of the magicians. After everything was ready, the coyote announced in a loud voice that all animals should be seated, and after a brief speech the feast commenced. At this feast their fates were decided. The sucker having no spoon, mistook a stick with fire on the end for a common piece of wood and burnt his lips, so that to this day he is obliged to suck his food. The shiner, another fish, was crowded almost out of the feast and he became flat, as he is to this day. Still another fish, another form of sucker, used a flint for a spoon and cut his lips.

After the feast all were gathered together. The eagle said his dwelling place would be among the mountains and deer and other wild game his prey. His feathers would supply the warrior's warbonnet and his name would be Eagle. Bears came in turn. They, too, announced their names and the habits by which they were to be identified. During all this the coyote was jealous, because someone mentioned the very name he wished to choose. So it happened that the names, appearance, and habits of all the animals were changed.

While various ones were announcing their names, the coyote's curiosity was aroused by a feathered being, whom he admired very much. Every now and then he would breathe a sigh of relief and stretch out his huge wings and fold them again, and sit back at ease. He, the coyote, wondered what this fellow would choose as a mode of living. After every one except this feathered being and the coyote had gotten through, the coyote arose and told the people that his occupation would be to look for mice as prey, also for various shrubs, berries, and perhaps some eggs and young animals, and his name would be changed from that of "Spielie" to the one by which he is known at home to this day.

When everybody was about ready to go and take up his abode, this much admired feathered being got up, and said, "After listening to all that each one has had to say, I have decided that my name, here-after, shall be Buzzard, and I shall look for nothing but the rotten carcasses of various game that my brothers, the eagles and the con-dors, shall have left." The coyote jumped up and said, "Here, I have been looking you over and admiring your physical development; you don't mean to say that you are not going to exercise the same!" With that he slapped him right and left, so that to this day we see the buzzard soaring around and around above a dead horse or cow.

After this, all departed for their various quarters. The coyote stayed at home while his friends, the foxes, wolves, bears, cougars, and deer, all made for the woods among the mountains. All the fish abandoned their human characteristics and dived into the streams. The mountain goat and the big horn made for the cliffs among the lofty mountains. The lobster was puzzled as to his future location and forgot to leave his limbs behind as he dived into the water.

This is why the Indians believe that by fasting they can obtain wisdom through these animals from the "mysterious unknown." They claim they do or rather did understand these various animals even so far as to hold conversation with them; but modern Indians regard that belief as ridiculous, because they never had the experi-ence of the power attained through animals.[24]

Part Two

Writings by Late Nineteenth-
and Early Twentieth-Century
Native American Public Intellectuals

Francis La Flesche (Omaha)

Francis La Flesche (1857–1932) was born on the Omaha Reservation in Nebraska. He attended the Presbyterian Mission School on the Omaha Reservation from 1865 until 1869. In the late 1870s he acted as interpreter and informant for ethnologist James Owen Dorsey. He also interpreted for Alice C. Fletcher, who studied the Omaha tribe and with whom he collaborated to collect Omaha and Sioux artifacts for Harvard's Peabody Museum. He was an ethnologist for the Bureau of American Ethnology from 1910 until his retirement in 1929. In 1911 he joined the Society of American Indians and published *The Omaha Tribe*, which he co-wrote with Fletcher. La Flesche also studied the Osages, and published some of his findings in *The Osage Tribe* in the Annual Reports of the Bureau of American Ethnology between 1922 and 1930. In addition to his ethnographic works, he published *The Middle Five*, an autobiographical account of his experiences at the Presbyterian Mission School in 1900, as well as essays and short stories in boarding school newspapers. (Littlefield and Parins, *Biobibliography: Supplement*, 240; Peyer, *American Indian Nonfiction*, 292–93; Peyer, *Singing Spirit*, 67–68)

Address to Carlisle Students, 1886

The Indian problem, as it is generally called, can never be fully solved by the white people. Its solution rests mainly with the Indians themselves. The law that governs individuals is applicable to nations. Man's salvation is an individual responsibility for which he alone is answerable, and the salvation of a nation depends on its own life struggles and not upon outside influences, however strong they may be.

The Indians can no longer support themselves by hunting. The white man has driven the game where no Indian can follow. The annual supplies of food and clothing furnished the Indians by the government, mainly in pay for the purchase of lands, are fast becoming exhausted, and many of the Indian tribes have not enough lands remaining to exchange for further annuities. They cannot expect to live always at the expense of the government, neither can they depend on the charity of the white people who have their own poor to take care of, besides, there must ever be an end to charity, however deserving the object or however philanthropic the benefactors. The time is coming when all the support this government is giving the Indians will cease and when they will be expected to take care of themselves whether they desire to do so or not.

Prior to the advent of the white man upon this continent, and until this country was covered by his settlements, the Indian men and women were not idlers or dependents; they labored for their food and clothing and supported their families honestly, but their life was one of hardship, mingled with much of savagery. It was a life unfitted for advancement in thought, in industries, and in all that goes to make up civilized living. No better way lay before our forefathers, and we must not blame them but a better way lies before us, and we should be justly blamed by God and by man, did we not advance toward the higher life opened to us and try to help forward in that life the weaker ones of our race.

Upon us, therefore, who have received some education, devolves the duty of thoughtfully considering our problem and of helping in its solution.

In view of the fact that the past conditions which surrounded the Indian, and helped to make him what he was, are gone, it is clear, that if the Indian is to live, he must take his place among civilized men. To reach that end it is necessary that he have, first, education; second, training in industries; third, he must rise to the fullness of his manhood by claiming for himself the rights of citizenship.

What are the means open to use for an education? They are many, my friends, and let us never forget that we owe this to the Christian men and women who have labored long in our behalf, under circumstances full of privations and frequently in peril, and through whose influence the government has been induced to deal generously toward us in this respect. It is true that the Indians have been slow to appreciate the fact that it requires time and study to obtain a good education, but now, we see it, and it becomes the duty of us who have learned to explain to our parents and friends at home that it takes time to secure an education and to master a trade, so that they may not be disappointed when we decide to stay for a term of years where we can receive the thorough training we need. The doors of the schools, established on the reservations and in some of the eastern states by the churches and the government, are open to us and we must avail ourselves of the opportunities that are thus offered us for education. We must study hard and always bear in mind that time and constant practice make perfect. We must show our willingness to learn and to remain in school until we have mastered the English language which will enable us to make ourselves better understood by the white people who do not yet know our capabilities. We must also try to perfect ourselves in our trades or professions, if we take up any, so that we can have an equal chance with the white people to make a living.

On the other hand our white friends must be patient with us if we do not learn as fast as they expect us to, and remember, that they were born and brought up in the midst of civilization and inherit their mental capabilities, and the power of observation which enables them to comprehend quickly, from ancestors who had been studying for hundreds of years. They must also remember that the Indians have always been hunters and that even today they know but very little, if anything, about literature, and that the English language is a hard language for a foreigner to learn. I have known educated white men to live among Indians, and for more than ten years make a careful study of the Indian language and yet they could not learn to speak perfectly notwithstanding the comparative simplicity of the language. If it takes more than ten years for an educated white man to learn to speak an Indian language perfectly, it is expecting too much to think that an Indian student, within four or five years can learn to speak and write the more complicated English language. We must, therefore, suggest to our white friends, when they are considering the advantages which accrue to the Indian from education that it is also necessary to take cognizance of the difficulties that lie in the way of its attainment. Language is a great barrier between the Indians and the white people and between the different Indian tribes, and this barrier must be broken down so that the two races and the various tribes may understand one another in every particular. It will be impossible for the older people to learn to speak the English language but the younger people can and must acquire English and not hold back because their fathers are unequal to the task. The ability to speak English is one of the essentials to the welfare and advancement of the Indians.

While the young people are thus gaining a knowledge of books and being trained in industries, the older people should be taught the use of agricultural implements and how to till the soil in order to secure their living. They will thus learn by their own experience that work is both honorable and profitable, rather than degrading and profitless, as so many have been accustomed to think. They will, however, need to be constantly reminded that the wealth of the white man represents tireless and persistent labor, both mental and physical, and also the careful expenditure of the profits of work, in a thoughtful consideration of the future.

Much depends upon the development of the manhood of the Indians to make them useful members of society. The question is, how is their manhood to be reached? How is it to be awakened?

The answer is simple. Treat them as men, give them the same opportunities for experience, the same laws, and the same changes as are permitted white men.

Treat them no longer as children, feeding and clothing them. Give each man the ownership of his farm and home, and whatever is justly due from the sale of extra lands, either from past negotiations or provisions, to be made in future; pay him in money as you would a white man and throw him upon his own responsibility. If there are some who will spend their money foolishly they will do better the next time after having felt want; or if there are those who will spend it wisely it will lead to further success. Believe me, if you treat the Indians as men, they will respond to you as men, and will endeavor to work with you in the upbuilding of our common country.

In speaking to you, I have dwelt upon the importance of education, of acquiring the English language because it seems to me to be the key to the solution of many of our difficulties. English opens up to us not only the means of communication with the white people by word of mouth, but it enables us to study their history and see the causes which led to the advancement. We learn from their history how diligently the men who have accomplished great deeds have worked, holding to their purpose for years, seemingly unmindful of discouragements and temporary defeats. We learn that nothing is accomplished that is worthy and lasting, that does not take time and persistent energy. We learn that the great force of the world is the mind of man. By that power man has crossed that seas, measured the stars, made the lightning do his bidding, and belted the earth with his iron road. It is mind, the cultivated, trained mind of the white man that has made the wealth and prosperity of this land of our forefathers. We Indians have minds. Shall they remain dull and untrained? No! We intend to strive for education, for the training of all our faculties, for our civil rights, that we may act our part in the labors that engage the civilized man.[1]

The Laughing Bird, the Wren: An Indian Legend, 1900

Ja-bae-ka came in with a big armful of wood, threw it down with a crash, stamped his feet and gave his blanket a few vigorous flaps to shake off the snow. The squint eyed little chap was always willing to go after water, or wood or to run on any other errand; and when a thing of that kind was to be done, the dozen boys, who were chums and went together, always looked to him first.

A dozen hands were stretched to place the wood on the fire, and a number of mouths were blowing upon it. Soon the flames leaped upward with a roaring, cracking noise, and the sparks chased each other in a lively fashion up through the round opening at the top of the dome shaped roof on the earth lodge. The light threw a ruddy glare upon our youthful faces and our shadows danced in a fantastic manner against the somber walls of the large, circular room.

"Wha! Goo-da-ga!" exclaimed a black eyed youngster, as he gave a whack with the back of his hand to the little spotted dog that came smelling and sniffing in front of our venerable story teller, who sat filling his pipe and staring into the flames to refresh his memory. The little dog gave a yelp and quickly disappeared under one of the willow compartments in the back part. Even little dogs were required to show respect to storytellers.

The old man lifted his small pipe, stem upward, toward the sky and muttered a few words; then every boy quickly bent forward, each one eager to be first to hold the brand for the story teller to light his pipe. After taking a few whiffs, the venerable man began, and all of us youngsters fell to an attentive silence.

"Of all the living things brought into existence by the breath of Wá-kon-da," remarked the old man by way of introduction, "none but the birds possess the wonderful power of leaving the earth, lifting themselves into the air and moving at will in the midst of the restless winds."

"Once in the progress of time, so the story tellers say, there came out of the ever silent depths of the blue, far above the reach of earthly sounds, a mysterious voice commanding the feathered creatures of the earth to gather at a certain place, where, on an appointed day, they were to display their power of flight."

"In obedience to this command all the birds hastened toward the chosen spot, some flying in flocks; some speeding along in lines; others soaring alone; each according to the habit of its kind. From the lakes, the rivers and the marshes came the geese, the ducks, the gulls and all the birds that find their food in the waters; out of the black forests emerged the vultures, the hawks, the owls, the crows and the magpies; from the sand hills came the cranes whose loud calls, resembling the cry of a warrior, could be heard from river to river; from the sandy banks of the streams and from the rocky cliffs came the swallows, the messengers of cloud and storm; from the 'Four Winds,' from any and every direction came birds large and small with plumage of varied hue, each one intent on having a share in the coming contest.

"The shadow of night passed westward over the hills and valleys and 'the great star' appeared, heralding the grey dawn of the appointed day. When the first rays of the sun shot upward myriads of voices were lifted to give to the great day a joyous welcome. Then, as though touched by a common impulse, every wing in that vast multitude was stretched and each bird, uttering its mystic cry, put forth its strength and rose for the momentous struggle. As the thousands upon thousands of wings whipped the air an awe inspiring sound, like an angry tempest plunging through a forest of gigantic pines, vibrated over the land and the earth became darkened by countless shadows as the confused mass of birds sped swiftly toward the sky.

"On the limb of a dead oak sat an eagle smoothing the feathers of his wings with his hooked beak, as though indifferent to the struggles that were going on about him. Among the whitened branches of the same tree a little brown bird moved about in a restless manner, at times almost touching the eagle but unnoticed by him. At length the huge bird spread his great wings, gave a powerful spring and mounted the air with wild cries. The lifeless tree quivered from the shock and from its branches the decaying bark fell piece by piece to the ground. With a few vigorous strokes the eagle gained his poise and was soon soaring upward with increasing speed in ever widening circles, seemingly without effort and as though borne aloft by the wind alone.

"At the moment the eagle had lifted his wings for flight the little brown bird had darted under one of them, fixed its tiny claws in the feathers, and buried itself in the soft down close to the body of the mighty bird. There it clung safe from the violence of the wind, while the eagle, all unconscious of his burden, swept onward. He passed the meadow lark already descending to the earth, having given up the race, but none the less happy and filling the air with the sweetest of melodies. The curfew, the thrush, the robin and other small birds were also fluttering earthward each singing its own song, content with this power although outflown in the race by the larger birds.

"The eagle with the little brown bird under his wing quickly passed the slow moving crow and the raven; overtook the swift hawk; further on he swept by the forked-tail kite, who among all the winged creatures is unequaled in grace and beauty; then he distanced the crane; and at last he passed the buzzard, the grandfather of all birds. Still the eagle went on, rising higher and higher, until the trees, then the hills, and at last the high mountains flattened to a level and the earth itself began to grow dim.

"The struggle was over, no living thing met the eye of the weary eagle as he gazed into the empty space around him. All at once he felt a strange stir under his wing, as with a sudden whirr out flew the little brown bird from its cover filling the air with a mischievous song as it darted about, then, laughing as it sped upward, it soared away into the sunlight leaving the astonished eagle far below.

"For the merry wit by which the little brown bird won the honors of that great day, it was given the name, Kí-ha-ha-ja, laughing bird.

"You have all heard the laughter of that little bird. He builds his nest in hollow trees and when the leaves are out in the spring he fills the woods with delightful sounds. No bird is happier than he. Shaeton."

"Woo-hoo!" we all exclaimed in chorus. "What a beautiful story."

"But it's so short, Grandfather," said Ne-né-ba, who was always wanting more, "tell us another one."

"Yes!" we all echoed, "tell us another one, Grandfather."

"No, little ones, go now to your homes," replied the aged man, "and dream of that tiny, laughing bird, who cheated the great eagle out of his victory."

At last we reluctantly arose, took our leave of the old man and made for the doorway, leaving him sitting there cleaning his pipe, his face radiant with a kindly smile. As we passed through the long entranceway of the lodge we pushed each other and scuffled with boyish laughter, and when we came out into the open air, we drew our blankets over our heads and raced for our own lodges through the falling snow.[2]

The Past Life of the Plains Indians, 1905

There were two lines of industry by which the tribes of the plains secured their living before the coming of the white people among them. One was by cultivating maize, beans, and squash, and the other was by hunting.

The task of preparing the soil and the planting of the seeds fell to the women, for in those days there was continual warfare between the various tribes, and the men were obliged to give their entire attention to the protection of the villages and the fields against war parties. Oftentimes, when unguarded, the women and the boys, while putting the ground in readiness for planting, or while tending the growing crops, were surprised by scalp-hunting parties and put to death.

The only implement used in cultivating the soil was the hoe, which was usually made out of the shoulder blade of the elk and sometimes out of flint or other hard stone. With this rude implement a woman was always able to raise enough corn, beans, and squash to feed her family the entire year. The boys, who assisted in the planting and harvesting, prided themselves upon the size of the fields, or upon the neatness with which the growing crops were kept. A boy would sometimes boast to another, "My field is so large I can't shoot an arrow across it, standing on the edge."

Most of the tribes believed that the corn was a special gift from the Great Spirit so that the planting or gathering of it was attended by rites and ceremonies expressive of their gratitude or their craving for the blessing of the Mysterious One. Among the Omahas it was the duty of the field owner, when the corn was harvested, to find one red ear and one perfect white ear and present them to the priest having charge of the rites pertaining to the planting of the maize.

In the month of May, when the prairie grasses shoot out their blades and drink the dew, and the meadow lark calls to its mate, the priest, in official attire, visits every lodge and tent and leaves four grains each of the red and white corn. Then the women, who are the owners of the fields, having chosen and improved the lands, lead their sons and daughters out to prepare the soil for planting. On the way out there is much merriment, particularly by the younger people, and the maidens chase each other with noisy laughter and wrestle among the wild flowers. Two boys fight over the possession of a hoe, the brother of one comes to his aid, the cousin of the other takes a hand, and then follows a general scrimmage among the future warriors. Fists, toes, and elbows do considerable damage all around. If one can imagine the appearance of a football team after a hard scrimmage without the protection of padded breeches and heavy sweaters, he could get a pretty fair idea as to how the brown-skinned combatants look when the fight is over.

Arrived at the fields, the dry weeds and the old stalks are gathered in a heap, the smoldering punk is drawn from the buffalo horn and applied to the pile, a snapping blaze arises, and the smoke ascends to the sky, leaving behind a few scattering ashes. The work goes on and in a day or two the fields are covered by hundreds of little mounds with flat faces looking up at the sun, ready to receive the seeds and the rain to make them grow. Willow poles are brought by the boys and planted in the center of the bean mounds for the vines to climb on; the corn and squash mounds need none. The work of the human hands is done for a time, but the work of nature goes on, the rain moistens the earth, and the sun warms the faces of the little mounds, and by the time the moon comes to life again the kernels of corn have sent up shoots like "rabbit ears," the vines of the squash have begun to creep, and those of the beans to climb.

Again there is a busy stir of women and boys in the fields, and every noxious weed is removed from the tiny hills and the intervening spaces between, and the work of the first cultivation is done. About the middle of June there is a second and final cleaning up of the weeds and a feast is given by the field owners to the priests of the Thunder Clan who pray to the ruler of insects for protection of the crops against beetles and other pests that destroy the growing plants. The fields are not visited again until after the return of the people from the summer buffalo hunt.

To civilized man, hunting means the going out into the wilds armed with long-range guns of the best make and shooting at wild animals from a safe distance. It suggests to him no hardship, but recreation and fun. It does not mean to him labor and industry. He stalks the game, shoots it with considerable accuracy, and frequently leaves the carcass to be devoured by wolves, or to rot in the sun. However, he carefully preserves and hangs over the mantel of his elegant house the head and horns of the buffalo and elk, or the grinning heads of bears and wolves, as trophies of the hunt, and writes thrilling tales of his adventures. From this standpoint the white man has judged the red man and regards him as a worthless being.

To the Indian, hunting had a very different meaning. It meant danger and hardship; danger from hostile tribes that might be hunting upon the same ground; from the close range made necessary by his primitive weapons; and hardship from the difficulties attending the transportation of the animals he killed; but it all meant food, clothing, and shelter.

After the second weeding of the fields, already spoken of, the village becomes a scene of great activity, for it is then that the preparation for the summer buffalo hunt begins. The skin tents are mended, dog harnesses repaired, and all the things not to be taken are stored away in the caches. Then one morning the sun rises to find a great caravan moving over the grassy prairies toward the land of buffaloes. The older men, the women, the boys, and the dogs carry the provisions, tents, and tent poles, while the fleet-footed young men, unburdened, guard the front, flanks, and rear against surprise from hostile tribes. The young women, armed with sharpened poles, scatter over the hills to dig the prairie turnip to add to the subsistence supplies. With one or two dexterous thrusts in the ground with a sharp pole, the diggers pry up the brown turnips, drop them into a bag, and move quickly on, chatting gaily over some humorous event or the latest gossip. The young men on their line of march often secure quantities of small game, such as prairie chickens, rabbits, turkeys, and sometimes deer, and thus add much to the family food supplies.

After a few days' journey, signs of buffalo are discovered, and one morning, when the dawn approaches, the chiefs assemble to hold a council. Then, as the sun peeps over the eastern hills, the tribal herald appears in front of the sacred tent, wherein the chiefs sit, and calls in a loud voice: "*E-ba-hom-be mon-zhon in-dhe-ga-thon ga ta ya thin ho*!" He is calling by name the sons of the chiefs and prominent men to go and seek for a herd, for this is one of the few occasions when a man is called by his name. Far at the other side of the camp a young man rushes out of a tent and with swift strides he runs to the herald and enters the sacred tent. The old man calls again and from another quarter comes a man, his feet scarce touching the ground, and he also enters the tent. The herald continues to call until ten or more runners have come. The hurrying of the young men to the sacred tent was an expression of their willingness to serve their people. Upon the entrance of the last man a lighted pipe is offered the first runner and as he places the stem to his lips a priest slowly recites the solemn oath administered to runners to refrain from mischievously deceiving the chiefs and the people, and to report truthfully all the things they see on their journey. Each man draws four whiffs and then passes the pipe quickly to the other and the recital of the oath ends with the last puff. Then the young men hastily leave the tent by twos and go out of camp in every direction.

The herald again appears and calls: "*Ca-hae-thum-ba wa-tha non shae ta ya thin ho*!" This time those who are summoned are warriors, men who have distinguished themselves in battle and have won public honors by valorous deeds. They approach the sacred tent with stately tread, and enter. The lighted pipe is offered them and as it passes from hand to hand the priest recites the oath administered to officers appointed to enforce order among the people during the actual hunt. By the act of smoking the sacred pipe each man pledges his honor to favor neither kith nor kin in the performance of his duty, and to punish alike all who willfully and maliciously stampede a herd consecrated to the use of the people; and further, to punish his own or any other chief who presumes upon his authority and chases a herd on his own account and for his own benefit.

The council is over and the chiefs and officers walk toward their tents. This is the signal to break camp; down comes every tent and soon the caravan is again on the march, this time in a compact body. No one is allowed to leave without permission. The officers are in charge and woe betide the man who steals away and hunts buffalo all by himself. Many are the hard blows he will receive if caught, and when he has recovered his senses he will find his tent and all its contents reduced to ashes. If he resists the officers, his very life will be in danger.

As the sun approaches the zenith there is a sudden halt and everybody gazes forward along the horizon. Far off in the distance two small figures like exclamation points move swiftly from side to side and then disappear. They are two of the runners returning and signaling their success in finding a herd. There is a hum of joy, the caravan moves on and again comes to a stop.

With labored strides the two runners approach and stand before the herald and assembled chiefs. The first, with heaving chest, and husky voice says to the herald in guarded words: "I believe I saw a herd"; and the other, "I saw no better than my companion, but at the head of yonder stream I thought I saw a herd of buffalo, numbering something like two hundred." The herald repeats the report to the chiefs, then a voice arises and everybody listens. It is the herald announcing the order of the chiefs: "You are to move on to the nearest creek, leave the women to pitch camp, and go on to the chase."

The people hurry on to the nearest creek, the men throw down their burdens hastily, string their bows, and away they go at a rapid trot. Four times the chiefs order a halt so that the priests may make smoke offerings to the four winds, where the gods are supposed to dwell, and ask for success in the dangerous enterprise. After the fourth offering the hunters approach the buffalo from the leeward as near as possible without frightening them, and then under the management of the officers string out to make a wide circle around them. The ring is hurriedly closed at the windward, a signal is given, and every man rushes forward with wild shouts. It is a large herd numbering nearer to five thousand than two hundred. Startled and bewildered by the shouts, the leader of the herd dashes forward at a brisk gallop, followed by the rest. Their course is deflected by the line of shouting men, there is no way out, and the whole herd runs in a circle ever faster and faster and the men, drawing closer, begin to shoot with their flint-pointed arrows. The clash of horns, the clatter of hoofs, and the heavy tramping of many feet upon the ground make a sound like the rumbling of thunder and the dust raised pierces the sky. The hunters continue to shoot; they are so close to the fleeing beasts that they almost touch them with the points of their arrows. Many of them use heavy lances with great effect. Suddenly the leader of the buffaloes makes a plunge at the line of men; it gives way and what is left of the maddened herd disappears over the hills, leaving a trail of dust. As the clouds of dust clear away hundreds of dead buffaloes are seen upon the ground.

The "surround" has been a success. The excitement of the chase is over and every man proceeds to identify, by his arrow marks, the animals he has shot. An angry altercation arises over a fat cow and two men are about to come to blows. A warrior official who happens to be near goes up to them and settles the dispute by claiming the animal as fee for the service of the officers. Meanwhile the unpleasant and difficult task of butchering has begun, every man attending to his own animal. Those who were so unfortunate as not to shoot any assist in the work and get a portion of the meat. It is not easy to cut meat and unjoint bones, even with the sharpest of flint knives.

By the time the butchering is done the boys arrive with the dogs and travois. These are loaded to their fullest capacity and every man and boy carries his portion, for nothing but the bones, hoofs, and horns are thrown away. The leg bones are cracked and the marrow is taken for use as food, and the brains are preserved for tanning purposes. Soon the hunters, with the boys and dogs, are on the march homeward, a distance of some six or seven miles, each bending under a heavy load. The greater part of the burden is on the men for each one carries from three hundred to four hundred pounds.

Almost dead with exhaustion from the day's excitement and labor, the men and boys enter the camp long after dark and soon seek their beds to rest. When they arise in the morning they find the meat cut into thin slices and hanging upon scaffoldings of poles, and the hides tightly stretched and pegged to the ground, skin side up, ready for the sun and the wind to dry. Some willing hands have worked hard all night long by the dim firelight, the older women perhaps.

By the middle of the day the prairie winds and the heat of the midsummer sun have done their work and both meat and hides have become dry and hard as wood. Then the strong young women appear; they unpeg the hides, turn them hair side up and begin the

Francis La Flesche   171

task of shaving the skins down to a certain thickness. This process removes the hair, reduces the weight of the rawhides, and renders them pliable for packing purposes. For this work a small adze-like, bone-handled, flint-bladed implement is used and requires skill for its manipulation.

Usually, when the conditions are favorable, this work is finished by sunset and the day following is spent in packing for the removal of the camp to another herd. Three more chases conclude the formal buffalo hunt and the caravan turns homeward, more heavily laden than when starting out. After the fourth "surround" any man who has not been able to secure enough meat and skins for his own needs is at liberty to follow the game on his own account. The purpose of the summer buffalo hunt is to secure a season's supply of three necessary articles; namely, skins for tenting and moccasins, sinew to sew with, and meat for food.

When within one or two days' journey from the village many of the young men get together and start for home, and they return to meet the people with the report that the fields are rich with young corn, beans, and squashes. They bring with them many roasting ears and there is great rejoicing over the prospects of a plentiful harvest.

When the people reach home they put the lodges in order and then enjoy a few days' rest. Then the women again visit the fields and the work of preparing the green corn for winter use is begun. Long shallow ditches are made in the ground and filled with dry wood which is set on fire. In the meantime the young maidens are busy picking the tenderest corn, and, if faithful to duty, soon return with bags filled with the long ears. Some linger to listen to the old, old story of love that began with the growth of the human race. A mother, impatient at the tardiness of her daughter, calls: "Ta-dae-win, why are you so slow?" "I'm coming!" answers a girlish voice from the farther end of the field, but she does not come. Again the mother calls: "The fire is ready, why don't you hurry?" "I'm coming!" shouts the maiden. There is a rustling of the leaves of the stalks, and she does really come; she starts to tell a tale of excuse, but the mother quickly empties the bag, giving no heed to the story, and begins to remove the outer layers of husk from the ears. Then she places them in a row on the live coals in the ditch and turns them over with a stick. When the thin layers of husk are scorched, the woman with her stick deftly tosses the ears out of the ditch. In the meantime the daughter continues her task with more or less delay, until a sufficient quantity of corn is gathered for the day's work. After the roasting of all the ears the scorched husks are removed and the grains of corn are separated from the cob by the use of the sharp-edged shell of the fresh-water mussel. The grain is then spread on skins and put out in the sun to dry. The corn prepared in this manner is called sweet corn by the Indians. Enough is cured in this way to last the family a whole season.

In the fall of the year the fields are visited for the fourth and last time. Again the maidens are busy, this time gathering the ripened corn. Occasionally the plaintive notes of a flute come from the woods, indicating the presence of a lover, but the work goes on. The mothers sit by the piles of corn and remove the outer husks, turn the inner layers back over the butt ends of the ears, and braid them. In this way twenty or thirty ears are fastened together and hung upon pole scaffolds to dry in the sun. After the corn is gathered the squashes are brought in and the skins pared carefully; then the fruit is cut into long thin strips which are also hung upon poles in the sun. When these strips are partially dried they are woven together like a mat a yard square and hung up again to dry. In color and texture the dry squash is not unlike the dried apple. Lastly the beans are gathered, threshed, and winnowed, and the harvesting of the crops is completed.

When the harvesting is finished the hunters go to the woods to hunt deer, for at about that time this game seeks the forests for shelter from the severity of the winter. Out of the skin of the deer, leggings and jackets are made by the women for the men and boys, and dresses for the women and girls. The deer skin is always preferred for clothing because it is more pliable than that of the other larger animals and much time is spent by the hunters in securing it. The sinew is also much desired by the women for fine sewing and embroidery such as porcupine quill work. The hunting of the deer lasts till about the middle of the winter. The elk has also been useful to the Indians but it did not take so important a part in their life as the deer and buffalo. The early winter months was the time to hunt the buffalo for robes, for then the hair is always in good condition.

The hunting of the buffalo has always been attended with elaborate religious ceremonies, both on the way out to the hunting grounds and on returning, for it was believed that the buffalo was a special gift from the Great Spirit. The corn was the sacred seed and was always planted and gathered with solemn rites.

When the hunting season is over, which is about the middle of the winter, the men spend the time making new bows, arrows, and lances, and repairing the old ones. The boys are then taught, not only how to make the bow and arrow, but are also instructed about the moons (months) in which the wood should be cut, for when cut in the wrong season it will split in drying. They are also taught the kinds of wood to use for the bow and the arrow. In making the arrow three small undulating grooves are cut on the shaft, running down to the head from the lower end of the feathers. This has attracted the attention of some of the ethnologists, who gave the matter considerable study and wisely concluded that the little lines were made for the blood to run through, or that they represented lightning. An old Omaha who had the reputation of being very skillful in cutting the grooves in arrow shafts was called by the chief to do that work for him on some arrows he was making. The chief himself was a fine arrow-maker but he recognized the skill of the old man in this particular line. While the work was in progress, the chief's son, who had reached the inquisitive age, and was looking on with wide-eyed interest, suddenly asked, "Venerable man, why are you making those crooked lines?" The chief gave a hearty laugh and said, "Father, tell him, for he will be making arrows himself some day, and he should know." "Every sapling," answered the old man, "out of which the arrow is made has some defect, however faultless it might appear to be. The good arrow-maker takes a great deal of pains to smooth out and straighten the imperfections by oiling and heating. But the wood, in time, will spring back because of its inherent defects, unless these grooves are cut in the shaft soon after seasoning and straightening."

Besides this work, the men made shields, war-clubs, glue, blades and handles of the skin-scrapers, wooden and horn spoons, wooden bowls and mortars and pestles, all of which required a great deal of time and labor because of the crudeness of the tools used for making them. The women were also quite skillful in making spoons, bowls, mortars, and pestles. The boys spent most of the winter days in hunting small game, such as rabbits and raccoons, and in this way helped to supply the family with fresh meat. The women occupied themselves during the long winter months in dressing skins, and making tents and articles of clothing for the family. At the same time they taught their daughters how to dress skins and make tents and clothing, as well as how to cook.

In common with the rest of the human race, the plains Indians had their religion, their social customs, their joys, and their sorrows, but this brief sketch of one phase of their life will give an idea as to how they secured their living before they came in contact with the white race.[3]

One Touch of Nature, 1913

The hunting of black bear was a sport much loved by the Osage Indians in the days before the coming of the white settlers into the country west of the Mississippi. It afforded them not only the thrill and excitement of the chase, of which every hunter is fond, but it also added largely to the animal food supply upon which the Indians depended for their living.

Many strange and interesting tales are told to this day of black bear hunting but of those that I have heard not one is so human as the following, which was an actual occurrence.

One day a man noted for his skill in hunting went out in search of black bear that he might add to the food supply of his home. Being familiar with the haunts and the habits of the animal the hunter soon found signs, and as he cautiously looked about he saw a female bear in a large tree busily gnawing at a hole in the trunk. The man quickly raised his gun and took aim but he was suddenly seized with an irresistible desire to see what the creature was doing.

After scratching and biting at the edge of the hole for some little time the bear thrust in her paw and in a moment quickly withdrew it. She put something into her mouth and smacked her lips with apparent delight and satisfaction. Then she suddenly scrambled down to the ground and with an ambling gait disappeared in a low bush.

The hunter brought the butt of his gun to the ground and waited to see if the bear would return. He had not long to wait, for she soon reappeared with two cubs on her back. On arriving at the foot of the tree the bear shook the cubs down, then seizing the larger one with both her paws she put him up against the trunk of the tree as high as she could reach. The youngster seemed to understand what was expected of him, for he went up the tree with the agility of a cat and took a seat on a limb close to the hole. Then the mother picked up the younger one and held him against the tree. He clutched the bark tightly but, whether out of mischief, deliberate disobedience, or lack of common bear sense, he would not move. After waiting a few moments the mother lifted a paw and gave the little imp a whacking spank, which, perhaps, was not the first he had ever had, then up he went in as lively a manner as had his brother and took a seat close beside him. The mother followed and with eager haste thrust her paw into the bee-hole, for such it was, and drew out a piece of honey. She carefully removed the bits of bark and slivers sticking to it and then gave it to the oldest cub. He quickly seized it with both paws and began eating it, twisting his little head to one side and then to the other, and smacking his lips with genuine delight. The mother brought out another piece of the honey and offered it to the younger cub. The foolish little fellow looked at it first with one eye and then the other, then slowly he stretched out both paws to take the honey with the tips of his claws and dropped it. With a start he looked down and watched intently the spot where the honey struck as though wondering why it should fall. A change of expression came over the face of the mother, which the older cub could not have failed to understand as indicating disgust and displeasure, and which might be followed by some act of discipline. Then again the bear thrust her paw into the hole and brought out a choice bit. With a look of motherly forbearance she held it out to the little one. As before he looked at it a long time with one eye and then with the other, smelled of it and then cautiously lifted his paws, distending his claws as he did so, to take it gently, but the honey dropped to the ground. The look of affectionate patience in the mother's face turned into one of anger, she lifted her paw and gave the foolish little one a whack over the ear. He lost his balance and down he went sprawling to the ground.

Just at this moment the hunter stepped on a dry twig which snapped loudly as it broke, the mother bear took alarm and down she scrambled to the ground, followed by the older cub and then all three quickly disappeared among the bushes near by.

At dusk when the evening fires were lighted the hunter came home. He entered his wigwam and put his gun in its accustomed place, then took his seat by the fireside. The wife gave him a look of silent inquiry as she paused in her work of cooking the supper, which he solemnly answered by saying, "I am not going to shoot bears any more; they are human beings like ourselves."[4]

Carlos Montezuma (Yavapai)

Carlos Montezuma, or Wassaja (Signaling, ca. 1866–1923), was born in Arizona. As a young child, he was captured by the Pimas and sold to a photographer. He attended public schools in Chicago and New York and earned a degree in medicine from the Chicago Medical College in 1889. He worked as agency physician in the Indian Service; from 1894 to 1896 he served as resident physician at Carlisle. He later returned to Chicago, where he worked as a private physician. For a brief period he was engaged to Gertrude Bonnin.

Montezuma was one of six founding members of the Society of American Indians (SAI) and published numerous essays in its magazine. He founded his own monthly newsletter, *Wassaja: Freedom's Signal for the Indians*, in April 1916 after growing dissatisfied with the accommodationist stance of the SAI's magazine under the editorship of Arthur C. Parker. Montezuma used *Wassaja* as a medium for launching his critique of the Bureau of Indian Affairs. As Montezuma explains in the first issue, *Wassaja's* "sole purpose is Freedom for the Indians throughout the abolishment of the Indian Bureau." (Littlefield and Parins, *Biobibliography: Supplement* 255; Peyer, *American Indian Nonfiction*, 341–42; *Wassaja*, April 1916, 1)

An Apache, to the Students of Carlisle Indian School, 1887

I have been thinking what would be best to write that might be a help and encouragement to you in your studies this year.[1] I have concluded to relate to you briefly my early schooling and graduation to the degree of Bachelor of Science.

Now, imagine a small Apache boy in the wilds of Arizona, just as happy as a bird, free from every thought of danger.

How little did I think one night would separate me from my

mother, father, sisters, and brother to live among strangers and be no more free! How little did I realize that this horrid prison life was but the stepping-stone to a better and nobler aim! A brighter morning dawned at last! So with you all.

In the year 1871 I was taken from the most warlike tribe in America and placed in the midst of civilization in Chicago. My greatest wish was to understand the paper talking, as it was interpreted to me. I often saw boys and girls go to and from the schoolhouse. I had no idea that they all had to be taught, but I had a little suspicious idea of the house. One morning, in April, the boy with whom I had associated persuaded me to come into the schoolyard to play marbles by saying that "I could win piles of marbles if I did!" So I consented.

The bell rang for the school to begin. I went in and took a seat. The teacher came forward and asked me if I wanted to attend school. I could not speak English; all I could say was "yes."

Of course, I naturally said yes to every question. I was taken up to the principal. Here I was questioned and given a small note. This note specified what books I was to get. I left the school feeling as big as ever, and took the note to my guardian. He gave me a few pieces of money to purchase what was necessary. This was the beginning of my education.

At this time I knew not my A, B, C's. I could not count nor understand letters. It was but a few months before I could repeat the Lord's prayer, sing "Precious Jewels" with the scholars, say my A, B, C's, and count to one hundred, besides write and describe different objects.

I learned as fast as any of the whites, for the reason that the teacher delighted to instruct me.

I left this school and went to another one. Here was the best teacher I ever had in a public school. This lady seemed to comprehend the nature of my circumstances and aided me all she could. I made good advancement in my first reader by taking my books home at night, so that I could be instructed there also.

Most of the reading I committed to memory.

On account of ill health I left this city and went into the country where for two years I walked two and a half miles to school, and worked to earn my board. This was when I was only nine years of age.

In the spring of 1877, I went to Brooklyn to school. I was by this time sufficiently advanced to study grammar, arithmetic, and history. At this school I always stood at the head of my class. I did this by staying at home nights to study; not by standing at corners as did some of the white children.

In the fall of 1877, I returned to Urbana, Ill., where I was assisted in my studies with the view of preparing me for the State University. Inside of one year I passed an examination in geometry, algebra, philosophy, bookkeeping, botany, composition, and physiology.

I made my way in College by paying and by working for my board.

In summer I worked on a farm. This I continued for four years, when I graduated with the degree of Bachelor of Science in the School of Chemistry.

During these years I never have doubted that the great problem of the Indian question is capable of solution if the advantages which were open to me could be extended to all Indian youth.

So with you all. Take care! You are being watched, and time will prove whether you are worthy of being protected and educated.[2]

The Indian Problem from an Indian's Standpoint, 1898

The reports of the Commissioners of Indian Affairs, Indian Agents, school officials, and the missionaries usually create the impression that the Indians are all improving.

An anxious friend of a patient inquired of the doctor as he passed from his morning call:

"How is the patient?"

"Improving," was the reply.

Next day she asked again:

"How is the patient this morning, Doctor?"

"Improving," he said.

And several times again she inquired with the same answer.

Some days after her last inquiry, she heard of the patient's death. One of her friends asked her:

"What did the patient die with?"

She replied:

"I guess she died with 'improvement.'"

It is high time that a red flag or some other danger signal be hung up on the present Indian policy or the Indians will all die with "improvement."

The Indians of today are not the Indians of the past. They have been cut loose from the advantages of barbarism and thus far have not profited by civilization. This makes the Indians of the present more degraded than their forefathers ever were.

I go back to my childhood and behold coming forth from his wigwam, the stoic warrior of mountain, plain, and forest. He was the child of nature and a true American. Erect in form and strong in presence, his head was carried high, was mantled with long black hair, and decorated with the feathers of the bird that soars above the storm. These were the tokens of strength, prosperity, and happiness. The brow told of purpose, of conscience, or independence, or liberty; the penetrating eye measured the depth of human nature and spoke louder than words. The massive jaw and the clear-cut, firm lips told of natural strength and character; the beads that ornamented his proud neck, placed there by the hand of a woman, were tokens of her pure devotion and love for him when far away.

This man took in the pure breath of heaven and defied the germ of disease. A strong and steady arm drew the bowstring and brought in the wild game for food and clothing. The girded loin sustained hunger, thirst, and fatigue from early dawn into darkness of midnight. Strong and elastic limbs and fleet moccasined feet, which distance never tired, overmatched the panting deer.

But the times have changed, and the Indian has changed with them. The picture fades away; the warrior sings the last chant, droops the high bow, abandons personal hope, and gazes with yearning heart into the face of his children.

What about the Indian boy and girl? The little warrior and his sister?

If brought out under the broad daylight of your civilization they might in a higher way outstrip their grandfather and escape the deadly fate of their father.

Do you know that your whole effort has been and now is crowding them into depths of a state worse than barbarism?

If you go on and hold down the latent power of the young Indian in the poisonous tank of your present Indian system the new picture will present a form that once glowed with health, scarred by disease; the once open face and piercing eye will be filled with suspicion and fear; clear cut feature is no longer there; the hands that pulled the bow are weakened by misuse and poisoned by vice.

Nature's child has fallen.

From generation to generation you have played upon our ignorance and superstition; you have blinded us. You have made us believe that you were helping us to your ways, but instead of that you are degrading us lower and lower by keeping us as outlawed Indians, and dumping upon us the evils, not the good of your ways.

We Indians are struggling in the dark to find a way out.

I have faced your civilized and uncivilized Indian in his own home, have investigated the Indian school system on and off the reservation, and above all have I passed from the Apache grass hut through the different stages of development among enlightened people.

Now I say more and more every year, I know that you are short-sighted in dealing with the Indian. Your mistakes have made him what he is today.

My convictions come from intense interest, from personal observation. I have put all my thought into it. Most people have a wrong idea of the reservation; it is not an earthly paradise, nor a land of milk and honey, where the pipe of peace is continually smoked. It is a demoralized prison; a barrier against enlightenment, a promoter of idleness, beggary, gambling, pauperism, ruin, and death. It is a battlefield on which ignorance and superstition are massed against a thin skirmish line sent out from civilization.

What rational officer would place a few inferior soldiers against an overwhelming number of his foes?

What right has civilization to do just that in its effort or pretense to deal with the Indian question?

Do you hold a dog to freeze it to death and place yourself in the same atmosphere? You will freeze before the dog will.

Five or ten Government employees at an agency or on a reservation can never elevate its thousands of Indians; on the contrary, you send teachers to elevate the Indians and in a few years these teachers become Indians in habits and thought.

Would you isolate your children on a barren soil?

Would you surround them with ignorance and superstition?

Would you put them among idlers, beggars, paupers, and cowboys?

Would you put around them the bowie-knife, the revolver, and the bayonet?

Would you deliberately place them away from any civilization whatever?

If you did all this, would you expect them to be cultured, refined, intelligent, humane, and honest?

Would you expect to make them industrious and self-supporting citizens?

No, you would place them in the midst of the most refined, cultured, and educated communities, among English speaking people, where they could come face to face with all the phases of civilized life, so that they might utilize and improve all their faculties. You would do this not merely for five years, but for all of their lifetime, and even then if they turned out well you would have a sense of relief.

You are blinded and ignorant in the enjoyment of your civilized life.

In the midst of your refinement and education you are without a trace of an idea of the real facts about the Indian question. You need to have the real conditions forcibly brought to you before you can realize your duty.

What about the Indian on his fifty-two reservations?

"But 'tis in vain, the wretch is drenched too deep.

His soul is stupid and his heart asleep.

Fattened in vice, so callous and so gross.

He sins and sees not, senseless of his loss.

Down goes the wretch at once, unskilled to swim.

Helpless to bubble up and reach the water's brim."

Shame! upon a Nation to have these fifty-two dark spots in the map, after God has given us four hundred years to wipe them out!

Yes, the Indians are more degraded than they were when Columbus discovered America.

Do you know why?

It is because you have constantly thrown us back upon ourselves, hiding us in the darkness of our ignorance and superstition, because you have sent in more vice than virtue, and you have taken out more virtue than vice.

You have given the Indians schools on the reservations, and your churches endeavor to Christianize them in their wigwams; the Government tenderly feeds and clothes them; but, in their ignorant, stupid condition; cut off from the light of the world, they will remain Indians for ages to come or disappear through the ravages of idleness and vice. A higher race contributes to these sad conditions.

Some one has said: "Civilized nations have often become savage when left to themselves; savages left to themselves have never become civilized."

Goldsmith says: "People seldom improve when they have no other models but themselves to copy after."

It is not enough to make visits like swallows to civilization; that will never do.

Long range education away from civilization is an utter failure.

Five years of schooling is not education for the Indian boy any more than for the white boy. It is a mere white-wash education. The boy and girl go home and back to barbarism.

To accomplish the elevation of the Indian, compulsory education will be necessary. This education should not be on reservations nor near them, but in your public schools. If the choice of my life had been left to my mother and father or myself, I would not be here. Ignorance and the very depths of barbarism would have been my fate.

You are sympathetic and philanthropic; but your sympathy and philanthropy when exerted to the secluding of the Indians on the reservations are misplaced. It is unjust, it is inhuman; it is criminal to stun the Indian from his birth to his death.

Would you give a child a few hundred dollars a year to do with as it pleases?

The Indians in their present state have become children. The intention of the people and the Government towards the Indian is good, but you cannot cancel your obligation by giving him large money annuities. You feed able-bodied men and women; you take away the need of personal effort; you hold them in idleness; you encourage barbarism. Against these methods and this treatment, I protest.

You may care for the weak and helpless but do not make strong men idle.

Good people wish the Indians were like themselves but think it cruel to change their relations and habits at once.

There is a story that goes this way:

There was a saint who had a dog; the dog had too long a tail. He concluded to cut the poor unfortunate's tail off little by little so as not to hurt the dear dog too much.

In much this way we are treating the Indians. Let us stop this destructive policy. Let us cut the Gordian knot by the quickest way possible. Delay is ruin to my race.

Does anyone say that this race is not endowed by nature with some great qualities which the Caucasian would do well to preserve? Yes, more to imitate?

Do I hear any one say that the Indian has no fine qualities worth preserving? Do I hear this from anyone? If I do, my words are not for him.

Why do you not wipe out these dark reservations? Let the Indian earn his living in God's appointed way, "by the sweat of his brow."

This is the only way to liberty, manhood, and citizenship.

Some of these Indians when brought into competition with white men will die, you say.

True, but that is what they are doing now.

But you say: They are wards of the nation and we must deal honorably and justly with them.

What you say is true, and you mean well, but to hear you speak of dealing honestly and justly with the Indian makes an Indian smile.

You ask what shall be done with the reservations which the nation holds in trust for the Indian?

I answer, sell them to bonafide settlers.

What shall be done with the money?

Use it and more if necessary for the education of every Indian child or youth.

Where and how would you educate them?

Away with the reservation schools! Send all children to the most civilized communities, not in large masses, but scatter them in small classes over the United States and place them in the public schools. Let them be brought up in and become citizens of the various states.

But this would be cruel to take little children from their parents and natural protectors.

True, I know about that because it happened to me.

But you ask: What right have we to take away a child from its Indian parents?

I answer: It is done every day by the courts in the cases of white children whose parents are incapable of taking care of them. You can never civilize the Indian until you place him while yet young (and the younger the better) in direct relations with good civilization. When you do this with judgment, you will succeed and make him a useful citizen of the Republic.

You have compromised and compromised with the Indians, fed and clothed them as children and have kept them pent up away from civilization. You know the results.

By leaving the education of the papooses to their ignorant and superstitious parents, you have encouraged the blind to lead the blind. The system is worse than a failure. And worst of all you have done this carelessly and not without good motives.

As an Indian, I thank God for helping hands that led me step by step, perhaps not far, but at least to where I am now. Had it not been for this, my fate would have been that of my people. The Indian children when transplanted must have friends who will give them advice, support, and encouragement. This will help them on over the difficulties. Small difficulties will seem to them like mountains.

The reservation can never furnish the necessary conditions. The cure must come from association with enlightened Christian people.

"Out of geographical barbarism into geographical civilization and citizenship" is the true war cry for the Indian of today.

It is entirely practical to distribute all Indian children among your families. This has been done with great success.

Four hundred and some odd thousand emigrants land upon your shores annually; in a few years they and their descendants are absorbed and lost sight of. This is because their children have the benefits of the public schools.

I wish that I could collect all the Indian children, load them in ships at San Francisco, circle them around Cape Horn, pass them through Castle Garden, put them under the same individual care that the children of foreign emigrants have in your public schools, and when they are matured and moderately educated let them do what other men and women do—take care of themselves.

This would solve the Indian question and would rescue a splendid race from vice, disease, pauperism, and death. The benefit would not be all for the Indian. There is something in his character which the interloping white man can always assimilate with profit.[3]

Civilized Arrow Shots from an Apache Indian, 1902

AWAY WITH INDIANS! THEY CANNOT BE CIVILIZED!

So says the frontiersman.

My words are not for this man.

He does not justify all there is in civilization.

The Indian is human; if cheated, wronged and misused, he will justly resent it, the same as the white man.

I deny that the Indian is more of a savage than the white man.

I deny that the scalping knife and the tomahawk are more significant of great savagery than the sword and gattling gun of the pale face.

Can the Indian produce such destructive and cruel implements of warfare as the monstrous canon and that death-dealing explosive, the Lydite?

Yet this same man will use every means to influence the Government to appropriate large sums of money for the reservations in his state or territory, as if he were actually the redman's almoner.

The white man looks after his own interest. Why not allow the Indian to do the same thing?

The Sympathetic Plea

"POOR THINGS! DO NOT CHANGE THEIR CUSTOM ALL AT ONCE. BRING THEM INTO CIVILIZATION BY GRADUAL PROCESS."

This sounds very much like the saint who cut his dog's tail off little by little so as not to hurt the dear dog too much. This kind and gentle ideal is a sham.

Four hundred years of gradual taking away his savagery and giving him your civilization have elapsed, and what are they?

A caged being, worse than his forefather ever dreamt of.

Idler, beggar, gambler, pauper, ruined!

Let us stop this destructive process by the quickest way possible. For the sake of their future, the Indian heart of today must be broken.

The Church

"TO CHRISTIANIZE THE INDIANS WE MUST SECLUDE THEM BY THEMSELVES AWAY FROM THE VICES OF CIVILIZATION AND SEND MISSIONARIES TO THEM."

A prominent divine has said: "If I were the devil and wished to do the most devilish thing, I would not destroy the churches, but I would corrupt them."

The reservation is a devilish method of Christianizing my people.

I believe in missions.

Not one missionary to thousands of Indians, but thousands of missionaries to one Indian, which they would get if brought into the midst of civilization.

The Educator's View

"BUILD MORE SCHOOLS ON RESERVATIONS, SO THAT THE INDIAN PUPILS MAY BE AN OBJECT LESSON FOR THEIR PARENTS, TO CONVINCE THEM OF THE PRACTICALITY OF EDUCATION."

I say very few Indian schools are needed in the United States.

Or, rather no Indian school is necessary, when the public school, the anchor of our educational system is available.

To me to deprive the Indian children of this anchorage is an insult.

You may as well say, "you are an inferior race of children, we do not want you in our public schools."

In Indian schools, Indians teach Indians.

When you allow their ignorant parents to decide for their children's welfare, you only encourage the blind to lead the blind, and Indians will remain Indians for ages to come.

If the public school is good enough for all other races, why not for the true American children?

The Sentimentalist

"IT IS CRUEL TO SNATCH THE INDIAN PAPOOSE AWAY FROM THE MOTHER'S BOSOM AND TRANSPORT IT TO A DISTANT SCHOOL. IT SHATTERS PATERNAL RELATION."

How inconsistent you are!

For your children's education you will sacrifice their absence from home ties, you will send them across the water.

What for?

So as to give them the best schooling.

And yet you weep and stand in the way of the Indians' children when a few are passing you to go to the Eastern schools.

The Indian children of today are in a stage of crisis.

Why not treat them as you do your own children?

Stop this exceptional policy.

When you have done that, you have done your duty.

Rumors from the Indian Service

"WE OUGHT NOT SEND INDIAN CHILDREN EAST TO EDUCATE THEM; THE CLIMATE WILL KILL THEM."

When all other arguments have been exhausted to keep Indians Indians, then the weather comes in very appropriately.

The Indian seems to be almost persuaded.

"Climate will kill your children. Climate will kill your children," comes like a message of death to this superstitious race.

The time has come when the Indian must take his chances with the white man.

How little do the eastern people take into consideration the vicissitudes and dangerous regions of our globe when their pockets and education are involved.

It is as reasonable to implore the Yankee to stay where he was born as to tell the Indian pupils not to go where they can get the best education and thus accomplish the most for themselves.

But the statement is not true. Death in greater proportion than at the remote school comes to the Indian on his reservation in all its lines of disease, simply because on the reservation he is not and cannot be as well protected or helped when attacked.

The Showman and the Anthropologist

"LEAVE THE INDIANS ALONE. IT IS BEAUTIFUL TO PRESERVE THE TRUE CHILDREN OF NATURE AS OBJECT LESSONS TO STUDY."

By blinding the Indians, Buffalo Bill has wrongly educated the public.

To leave the Indians alone as curiosities and studies may be well enough for the showman and the anthropologist.

But what about the Indian?

The standard of a splendid race is degraded by it.

He deserves a better fate than to be redecked with savage attire, only to be ridiculed and jeered at for mercenary and scientific purposes.

Do away with your ignorance of the Indian.

Help him to escape the deadly fate of the reservation system.

Learn of him, as he will of you.

Then you will develop the man and not the savage, the citizen and not the pauper.

This is my cry to all the world for my people.[4]

The Indian Dance, 1902

Thirty years ago among the primitive Indians, I participated in Indian dances.

Taken captive by another tribe then, it fell to my lot to be an object for a dance.

Twenty years later as Government physician I witnessed many dances in as many tribes, from the East to the West coast.

Therefore, I write reality and facts, not from romancing and imaginations.

The primitive Indian dance was a religious rite—the highest social and spiritual function.

It was the token of good friendship, a gathering for peace and happiness.

It united mind to mind, and heart to heart.

It was to show their gratitude to nature, and sing peace to the world.

It was where the sick were cared for.

The maid and her lover were given in marriage.

Here the competitions for prizes were carried on, and a general feast was enjoyed by all.

Spiritually, the medicine man preached the highest morals that a human heart could give to its beloved ones.

The dance camp was broken up, the participants strengthened in mind, body, and soul.

Reservation Indians are not the primitive Indians.

They are corrupted and blinded to the noblest ideals of their forefathers.

They are graduates of the school whose teachers have been the cowboys, soldiers, and the worse element of frontier life.

There is something radically wrong in the present Indian dances.

The Indian, being brought up from childhood in this poisonous atmosphere, gets the idea it is not wrong, just as a saloon keeper thinks his business is legitimate.

The child of nature does not know the end of his folly.

The aged may enjoy the occasion, but they do it at the expense of their children who will unavoidably suffer.

It kills time and the Indian.

It generally takes days to prepare for the Fandango.

To dance it, requires several days and nights.

It consumes that many precious days to recuperate from the effects of the debauchery.

At this time the unusual excessive smoking and exposure produces sickness.

The mortality is greater.

If the object of dancing were only to dance to commemorate the old days, I would be the last loyal Indian to speak against it.

Not so!

It is a general holiday for all sorts of vice.

Indians are in the gambling stage, which whites have forced upon them as a pre-requisite to civilization—a danger line that the Indians cannot see.

In the darkness of the night, secreted behind a bush, a stone, or a wigwam are two young souls.

Some affection may be there, but passion predominates.

The Gospel is dead.

Satan has fully sway.

Early dawn finds the Indian rolled up in a branded U.S.I.D. blanket, fast asleep until noon.

Afternoon, in the tents or under the shade of trees scattered here and there in the camp are groups of ten or more women and men playing the devil's Bible of civilization—cards.

Quarter, half, and one dollar coins flitter and glitter from one hand to another.

If money is scarce, saddles, blankets, or anything equivalent to the stake are wagered.

About four o'clock the horse race!

All horses take part whether the cayuses can run or not. As the saying is, "they are bound to be in it."

Then on this nature's level track, no livelier or more enthusiastic participants ever gathered on Harlem Track.

Carlos Montezuma   193

With every race there is a roar, a cry of victory and exchange of money.

From all appearances one would exclaim, "Surely, the Indians are fast getting into civilization."

Shame on such civilization!

It is demoralizing and fatal for the future generations of the Indians.

I speak with emphasis, as most of our educated Indians do, and declare that the Indian dance today does gross injustice to the character of our people.

It conveys to the public, wrong impressions!

The outburst of savagery, the painted face, the feathered hair, the tomahawk, the scalping knife, the hideous war-whoops, the mutilated body, and eating fat dogs.

It separates the Indian and leaves him an Indian—a foreigner within his own country, which is an undeserved fate; but the inevitable result of the shortsightedness of our boasted civilization.

To us Indians it does not pay.

We must seize on to and hold fast to the standard which we have attained in so brief a period of time.

If we have to work our own way into civilization let it be in the broad and honorable field of competition, right among the enlightened masses, and not by ourselves in the darkness of our ignorance on a reservation.

Amid all these perplexing questions that pertain to the welfare of our people, let the divine utterance be our guide:

"Whatsoever things are true, whatsoever things are honest, whatsoever things are just, whatsoever things are pure, whatsoever things are lovely, whatsoever things are of good report; if there be any virtue, and if there be any praise, think on these things."[5]

Flash Lights on the Indian Question, 1902

History seems to convey that America and the Indian were lost and Columbus discovered them. Since then the Indian has met so many "entreating friends," that much like the poor gold-brick farmer, he is bewildered and at a loss to know what to do. Thus comes the Indian Question.

The Indian Question is a question because we have sidetracked the Indian from the main road to freedom, manhood, and citizenship.

The question today is not what we must do for the Indian, but what the Indian must do for himself as an individual not collectively.

It seems strange we can cheat the Indians but cannot educate them.

To rob a race of their land is bad, but to rob, imprison, and stunt that race morally, physically, and intellectually, what is it?

There was a time when Government bullets killed the Indians. Now it is the Government red tape.

If one one-hundredth of the amount taken to kill the Indians had been used to educate them among the masses of the people of the United States, the Indian question would have been settled long ago.

Civilization ought to develop the good qualities in the Indian and make the Indian a man, and not a better Indian; he is "Injun" enough, already.

Shame on the athlete, who by reason of his strength, tramples on the weak! Our duty is to help our brother man up to our standard of strength. This applies to the Government in its relations to the Indians.

Any methods (it makes no difference how good the intentions might have been or from what source they may have originated) which come between the Indian and civilization are hindrances, and will keep the Indian in the background of progress, a worthless expense and helpless.

Gradual processes of civilizing the Indians might do, if they were to live as long as Methuselah and the white man's greed could be suppressed for the same length of time.

Reservation is "hell," a poisonous tank where vice and corruption predominate and all Indians are corralled and stamped U.S.I.D. The United States Indian Agent is a little god that has more sovereignty over his subjects than the President of the United States or the Sultan of Zulu.

The reservation system is a civilized bluff, a painted tissue paper partition that debars the Indian from his natural rights. Why has this been done?

The Government method of treating the Indian is contrary to the constitution of our country, which grants every one the right to life, liberty, and the pursuit of happiness.

One hundred and sixty acres and money annuities do not and will never equip the untutored Indian to compete with the outside world any more than such gifts to a child.

"Mother, may I go out to swim?"

"Yes, my darling daughter:

Hang your clothes on a hickory limb,

But don't go near the water,"

Yes, poor Brother in Red!

Be civilized!

But don't come near civilization!

The sanction is there, but the opportunity is denied.

Let the same agencies which aid the white man be applied to the Redman. Why not?

To Christianize the Indians, one missionary to thousands of Indians is not enough. Rather let there be thousands of missionaries to one Indian, as is the case when they go out into civilization.

Five years of schooling is not education for the Indian boy any more than for the white boy. Distant schooling, away from civilization, is worse than a failure. Teachers are Indianized before they civilize the Indians.

Six hours inside of a school house on a barren soil and eighteen hours in an Indian camp never has and never will civilize the Indian boy or girl.

Of the two schools, Indian school and public school, the public school is better for the Indian as well as for the other races.

The marked difference between an eastern school and a reservation school is in one the papoose gets ideas of things outside of the reservation, and in the other, no ideas of these things.

Give the Indian a chance where the chances are best—in the heart of civilized light—the sooner the better.

It is absurd to judge the Indian as savage. Our civilized savagery is more brutal and destructive than the Indians.

Misrepresent the Indian and you will cause him to be misunderstood. That is what Buffalo Bill and many Indian novels do.

In the large cities of the United Sates the Indian is so scarce that when seen he is branded as a foreigner. What an audacity!

We claim the Indians are human, yet we treat them as though they were incapable of yielding to human treatment.

White people's frequent question: "Are the Indians capable of grasping our ways?" Such ignorance is inexcusable.

Say "Indian" to your children; they shudder and run as though they heard and saw a rattlesnake. They imagine a savage monster that roams over the plains and through the forest.

Present an educated Indian, cultured and refined, and the white man experiences a sad disappointment, because this Indian gentleman is not painted and feathered from scalp-lock to moccasin.

We may appropriate great sums of money; we may send teachers and missionaries to the reservations; he is still a reservation Indian, a ward of the Government. To change him get him out bodily. Let him sink deep into civilization and become a very part of our civilization.

You may corral cattle, you may push the button to move your machinery; but the Indian is a man. He will not be subservient to your whims. He will and must have his rights.

In order to make the Indian children like your own children, you must treat them like your own children. Stop this exceptional business, because they are Indians. It is destructive and fatal. When the Indian is once among civilized people, to return to the reservation is to fall back on the blanket. Indians, "Get you out!"

Be out and out for your manhood and womanhood, and stay out!
It is all outs.

I speak out of my good heart.[6]

How America Has Betrayed the Indian, 1903

On this most interesting occasion in Chicago's remarkable history it is well to pause and consider the great question of the true brotherhood of man.

The Indians have attracted a great deal of attention. I hope it has been a right education for the public, but I fear you went there to see the feathers.

You went there to see the painted face.

You went there to see the savage dance, to hear the war whoops; in other words, you went there to see the real Indian with all of his paraphernalia—a mere curiosity and "nothing more."

To me it represented cheated possibilities, imprisoned and stifled latent powers; representatives of a race that have been crippled and deluded with misapplied methods.

If the Indians had only to review a path of progress as Chicago is doing, then there would be cause for rejoicing in the reunion of the descendants of the tribes who first occupied the site of Chicago.

Then there would be a deep significance in the mock war dance; then the shriek and loud war whoops would put the Indians of 1803 to shame, and the powwows would be supplemented with a barbecue in token of prosperity and justice to the Indians.

But, alas! such is not the situation.

The Indian has not made any progress.

He is the real Indian plus the vices of civilization that make him worse than his progenitor.

You have abused your mission, and in the light of your promises and power to do, you have been weighed in the balance and found wanting.

And, taking advantage of his ignorance, you have left him where his last state is little better than his first.

The great hindrance to the right road for the Indians comes from the sentimentalists and literature on the Indian question.

The one thought it was too cruel to change their condition all at once and the other teaches that the Indian has ways of his own better for him than civilization's.

Reservations are prisons, the fiendish device of so-called civilization for the Indians; while the prisoner is kept in his cell, the mere placing of furniture therein and supplying him with necessary food and raiment leave him none the less a prisoner still.

No! You must first get him out of his prison cell.

Make him know that he is a free man and then surround him with good environments.

The law of nature is expansion and growth. The first step towards civilization of the Indian is to place him geographically so that he can commingle with the conquering race, in the same manner and to the same extent that natives of foreign countries have become a part of the people in general in our country.

Would anybody deny that whatever progress the negro has made has been due to the extent to which he has associated with those by whom he was once held as a chattel?

Indian schools for Indians are roundabout ways to dodge the public school systems and to encourage the Indian children to remain Indians as long as possible.

Carlisle school is an Indian school, but the commander at that institution has been and is an unceasing advocate of the public schools for the interest of his children.

It is as incongruous for the government to maintain Indian schools for Indians as it would be German schools for Germans.

Why should it be tolerated exclusively for the Indian?

I would not object to remain as an Indian and live as an Indian for ages to come were you to agree to take my ways and let me lead the trail of life. But when you monopolize all and leave me nothing I object.

On the reservation, its limited sphere, we roamed at will, thinking all would be well because the white man said so. Have you not cheated us out of our birthright?

Maybe you have intoxicated us to sleep, and, Rip Van Winkle like, we came back after many years and see the real as though after a dream.

I see your houses, tall as the mountains.

With the speed of the wind you fly over our forefathers' hunting grounds with your iron horses.

For riches you dig into the earth.

Your canoe on the lake is wonderful.

Your talks go miles and miles, and you have gathered the mysterious lightning to give you light.

All these are things our medicine man could not do.

Now we see why you have been so good to us.

During all these years you have been toiling selfishly at everything with the light of the civilization of the past and you may well be jubilant at our expense. Tell me, is it not worse than robbery to make us blind and then take everything we possess?

O! for a hundred years to go back and see as we do today.

We would warn our children here never to lose sight of the white man.

We would urge them to go side by side with the white papooses and outstrip them if they can.

Ah! if we are hindrances to our children, the hope of our race, we shall stand aside and let them take everything of your Christian civilization.

We will have no fear because they will do their duty to honor their people and country. Does not the Great Spirit say today, as of old, "Let my people go?"[7]

Charles Alexander Eastman (Santee Sioux)

Charles Alexander Eastman, or Ohiyesa (The Winner, 1858–1939), was born near Redwood Falls, Minnesota. His father was Sioux, and his mother, the daughter of a well-known army officer and grand-daughter of Chief Cloud Man of the Sioux, died shortly after his birth. Eastman lived on the Santee Sioux (Dakota) reservation in Minnesota until, at the age of four, he fled with his grandmother and uncle to Canada following the Great Sioux Uprising of 1862. There he was raised by his grandmother and trained by his uncle to assume the life of a Dakota hunter and warrior. Meanwhile, Eastman's father, Jacob, whom the family presumed dead as a result of the Mankato mass execution, was imprisoned. While in prison Jacob adopted the markers of civilization—he wore white man's clothing, converted to Christianity, and learned English—and decided that his son should "learn this new way" of life. When Eastman was fifteen his father reappeared to take him to a tribal settlement in Flandreau, South Dakota. Jacob convinced Charles to attend the Santee Normal Training School. After leaving the boarding school Eastman continued his education at Beloit College, Knox College, Kimball Union Academy, Dartmouth College, and Boston University Medical School, where he became one of the first licensed Native American physicians.

In November 1890 Eastman became the government physician at the Pine Ridge reservation in South Dakota. Eastman cared for those Lakota who were injured during the massacre at Wounded Knee. In 1893, after resigning his post, he moved to St. Paul and launched his literary career by publishing in *St. Nicholas: An Illustrated Magazine for Young Folks*. That same year he delivered a speech, "Sioux Mythology," at the World Columbian Exposition. Soon thereafter

Eastman became a representative of the International Committee of the YMCA and served as their field secretary. He also worked briefly as an outing agent at the Carlisle Indian Industrial School, became a spokesman for the Boy Scouts, and was a founding member and officer of the Society of American Indians.

During a literary career that spanned almost thirty years, Eastman wrote ten books and published widely in periodicals. His nonfiction prose appeared in national magazines like *St. Nicholas* and *Harper's*. He also published in venues geared toward those interested in Indian reform, namely, Carlisle's school newspapers and the SAI's magazine, the *Quarterly Journal* (later the *American Indian Magazine*). None of Eastman's writings reprinted here appear in Michael Oren Fitzgerald's 2007 edited collection, *The Essential Charles Eastman (Ohiyesa): Light on the Indian World*. (Eastman, *Indian Boyhood*, 246; Littlefield and Parins, *Biobibliography: Supplement*, 206; Peyer, *American Indian Nonfiction*, 368–71)

An Indian Collegian's Speech, 1888

At a recent meeting of the Jamaica Plains Indian Association, the most novel attraction was the speech of C. A. Eastman, a full-blooded Sioux Indian, graduate of Dartmouth, and now a medical student at Boston University. He is described as "a young man of fine physique, with the admirable air of reserved force characteristic of his people." This was but his second attempt to speak in public, and he held his audience in close attention. He said:—

I will speak of my father, rather than myself, for he has been of more importance to my race, and is to me the model of a strong and good character. He was once a warrior, who painted his face and scalped his enemies; but after the great Sioux war of twenty years ago, he was imprisoned for four years in Davenport, Iowa; and there he embraced Christianity, through the influence of the missionaries, Williamson and Riggs, who taught him to read the Bible in the Indian language and to write. My father surrendered himself voluntarily to this imprisonment because his near relatives were either there or probably dead in the war.

As a baby, I found myself in my grandmother's care in the British dominions, and I grew up under the impression that the whites had killed my father and brothers, and my great desire was to "get at" one of these fellows and be even with him. When I was five years old, a tall Indian in citizen's dress appeared before me, saying he was my father and had come hundreds of miles from his Dakota home to take me back with him and make a Christian man of me. I wondered what that might be. Every morning my father read his Bible, and my grandmother adopted his belief; but my uncle would have none of it. As I was generally off roaming, I heard little of all this discussion, and so I well remember the impression my father's prayers first made upon me. It was at our first camping-ground by a beautiful lake, at sunrise on our way back to Dakota. The water-fowl were about and the birds went singing through the air, but far sweeter to me was my father's voice as he sang "Ortonville." I asked who this Jesus was that he sang about. He replied that it was a man from above, through whose influence he had come to make a man of me.

When my father was released from prison he was determined not to be confined on a reservation, so he went to Yankton to cut wood for the Missouri steamers, eventually hoping to take up land for a farm of his own. He was joined by twenty others and they took homesteads at Flandreau and sold ponies to obtain oxen.

Thus I found him established when I came back with him, but nothing could overcome my terror of my white neighbors, who would come in to exchange work; I would run in the barn. My father was anxious we should know the English language, and would always speak the few words he knew to spur us on. My older brother, a graduate of Beloit College, now teaches in Mr. Alfred Riggs' Indian Normal School at Santee, Nebraska.

It is true my people love the chase far better than manual labor, and it is also true that the United States' promises have been rotten for one hundred years back. I wanted to picture my good father to you tonight to prove that if Indians have land assured to them they will work, and I want to add that one hundred Indian families on the Big Sioux River have just eagerly cast their Republican vote.[1]

Address at Carlisle Commencement, 1899

It seems to be characteristic of the white people, at least those on the frontier, that when one of them is cornered and at a disadvantage he is apt to use profuse profane language; and it is also characteristic of the old Indian warrior when one is forced to a corner and taken advantage of he will probably give a war whoop. But, as I am not given to either of these characteristics, I have to suppress my feelings after the Major [Richard Henry Pratt] has called me out, especially when I look at the good speakers here ready to address you tonight, and I will simply say a very few words. When one of the Senators, on visiting Congress the other day, asked me whether I was an "anti-scalper," I happened at the time to be following a lobbyist into his room who was an anti-scalper.

I said, "Most assuredly I am an anti-scalper," and when I first took that position some twenty-five years ago, I took my blanket and my bag and started from Sioux Falls, in South Dakota, to the Santee Agency up above Yankton on the Missouri River, some one hundred and thirty miles, on foot in search of education. In those days, this school having been established only about twenty years ago—the Government was not so generous to the Indian, and the Government was not so sympathetic as it has been since furnishing education, and I had to hunt for my education over the prairie. That accounts for my not being here at the Carlisle School.

But I want to say that the Sioux is not going to be left behind because he once evidenced roughness, atrociousness and barbarous qualities. Now my friend here, the physician, medicine man, or whatever you may call him thinks that the Apaches were beneath all civilization, and all that, but the Sioux were equally as bad when on the war path, yet they had those redeeming qualities that all races have. God has made them emotional, religious, and with proper training and under favorable environments they can develop those talents and those pure thoughts that are common to all men, and they will prove to be just as trustworthy, good people as any race.

I have found in the last few years of my traveling among the Indians a boy or girl here and there who had been instructed here, true to the principles that the Major and his corps of good teachers had instilled into their hearts and inculcated in their minds from the day of their arrival here until the day they left, and although sometimes at a disadvantage with no encouragement, and sometimes surrounded by unfortunate circumstances, they stick to the instruction that the Major gave them—"Stick to the truth,"—and today many of them are becoming self-supporting men and women.

There are times when I sit down by the camp fire that my heart swells. There are times when girls come to me and ask me for advice what they shall do under certain circumstances, and tell me a pathetic story. I say:

"What did Major Pratt tell you?"

She would reply that he told me to be truthful, be steady, persistent, stick to a position and push right on; live an honest life. And I say to her, "That is right."

There is not a person living but has their storms; but has their hard weather to go through; but has to pass through deep rivers; but has to ascend rough mountains, and those who are not able to do these things had better never have lived. The survival of the fittest is almost as the Bible among all races, and in order to be equal to the great privilege of citizenship of these United States, we must use our own muscle, use our own mind and put our shoulder to our responsibilities wherever we are, whether among Indians or among white people.

Charles Alexander Eastman   205

There is but one Heaven over us and one earth under us. Heaven gave us light and Heaven gave us rain, and gave us all the food necessary for us so that we were well provided for before the white man put his foot upon this country. We didn't lie idle: we chased our game from early morning to late at night, and we never stopped until we carried our game back to the tepees or wigwams to feed our wives and children. It is exactly the same thing today; we are in very different circumstances, but we must not lie idle. We must strive to overcome the prejudices that exist against us.

You must not think that our ancestors were indolent, thoughtless, aimless, without ability and purpose, that our people don't have just as high aims and ability as you white people have today. Sometimes I think that our people have purer aims, when I see the aims of a great many office seekers that you have here who seek by mercenary means to bring about their purposes. I think our aims are freer from mercenary motives and no office seeking can change it.

I want to say to you that what this school is doing and has done we Indians will never realize, and when the Major is gone I hope and pray, that the seed which he has sowed may develop one hundred fold, and that those who have been taught here may develop into leaders among our people. God has produced some of the greatest men in the history of the world out of the poorest parentage; men who founded great nations; men who overcame difficulties; and I still longingly hope that some of these dark faces over here, young men and young women, may look to that and may have purer and higher ideals and press steadily onward and upward, that we may some day take a distinctive part in the great civilization of this western nation.[2]

The Making of a Prophet, 1899

"Ogalallas, pray to the Great Mystery! An Evil Spirit is enveloped in yonder cloud." The speaker was a "Medicine Man" of savage repute, and the cloud to which he pointed was at the least an unusual sight. It had all the appearance of a cyclone, and it was swiftly approaching their encampment.

The warning was quickly heard, and the Ogalalla camp became a scene of turmoil. The people ran hither and thither, scarcely knowing which way to turn; some leading a child by the hand while another was carried on the back. Dogs were baying and ponies neighing shrilly as they wildly galloped along.

In the midst of it all an old retired brave with scarcely a garment upon his body, which was painted black, was seen calmly riding around the inside circle of the rows of teepees, singing a "Strong heart" chant. There was something solemn and mysterious about his conduct, yet there was no time for conjecture or questions. He paid not the least heed to the general terror of the camp. If someone there had reflected even for half a minute he would have clearly understood the old man's action, for the Indian customs are familiar to all the people. But see what those old "Medicine Men" are doing on the outskirts of the camp. Each one is holding a huge, filled pipe with the mouthpiece foremost pointing heavenward. Some are singing Medicine songs, others are crying in a sing-song fashion, and still others are devoutly praying to the "Great Mystery" to turn aside the course of the "drunken Thunder Bird," which is apparently about to devour them with all their possessions.

Most of the Ogalallas were acquainted with the occasional advent of the drunken Thunder Bird or cyclone.

The Bird's wings, it is supposed, scarcely cover a mile laterally, and its course is an occasional downward sweep for a few miles and then upward. So they all ran for the line of safety.

But fortunately the winged inebriate took its upward flight before reaching the camp, therefore they received only the heavy rain and hail. What a triumph for the "Medicine Men!" They were considered from that hour to be among the greatest of their class.

Some say to this day that one of those priests can cause a hurricane to deviate from its course!

Charles Alexander Eastman   207

As the storm departed with a rattle of thunder like artillery after a heavy engagement, quiet succeeded. All the fleeing Ogalallas now returned. The men resumed their usual indifferent and stoical expression, which the Indian habitually assumes to conceal his real susceptibility. In fact, their calm was so completely restored that a stranger would not have guessed that there had been any excitement or disturbance in the camp but a few minutes before.

The "Medicine Men" had not been alone in seeking succor from Him who holds the lariat of the powers of the universe, for there were many who, though excitedly fleeing to be sure, were casting anxious glances heavenward, and were not unmindful of the fact that their God not only loves to give and to pity, but appreciates gifts himself, even though in the form of promises.

Feasts, Sun dances, and tobacco were the usual inducements presented to him. There was an old woman whose chief possessions were two litters of dogs. In the confusion it was impossible for her to carry them all; so finally, despairing and distracted, she seized two of the fat pups and held them aloft, while she excitedly entreated the "Great Mystery" this: "Be kind to me and mine, O Great Mystery! I give thee these two pups for thy feast!"

The topic of conversation throughout the village of tents was the narrow escape. What became of the old man who rode around the camp during the excitement? was the thought that came back like a flash, and closely following it another "Poor Black Pipe!"

The old man's conduct needed no explanation now; but during the excitement everybody had only thought of the end of the world—his world, at the sight of the approaching hurricane.

In the sunshine of rejoicing over their escape, poor Black Pipe, the brave, was once more forgotten. He was then standing upon the highest butte in all that region, praying assiduously to the "Great Mystery" for a sign.

If the old man, his aged father, had been observed in his movements, he would have been seen to leave the camp as soon as the heavy storm subsided, when his pony carried him as fast as he could toward the highest butte. But he did not actually reach it. He paused at the foot of a lesser hill just below the other.

Breathlessly he climbed it and looked toward the summit of the high butte. He distinguished a form; though motionless it was still standing. Devoutly and with arms outstretched toward the blue sky he sang the praises of the "Great Mystery."

Briefly, Black Pipe was a young brave of a suitable age, who was possessed of a burning ambition. Though quite young, he had already achieved for himself a reputation, according to the savage way of thinking. He had determined to seek some sign of the "Great Mystery." If successful, his aim would be accomplished. He would then become a "Medicine Man" as well as a true brave.

Hence, he had taken all the preliminary steps with much deliberation. He had given a pony for the advice of one "Medicine Man," and a blanket, which was then a rarity, to another for a similar service. At last, he had made a sweat or bath-house, which is really the altar of the "Medicine Man," and invited a few of the noted ones. He had not spared any of his savage wealth in offerings. Therefore he was confident of success. Black Pipe was advised to fast and sojourn upon the highest butte for three days and three nights, singing, praying, and weeping. The songs were rude chants of exultation and praise to his God. In the first part of the prayer he enumerated to the Supreme Being his sacrifices and gifts ever since he could remember; that he had been an obedient and faithful son; in fine, he was deserving favor and mercy.

The weeping purported to be the last argument in his cause. It was an act of submission, and intended to solicit sympathy and pity, as a child begs of his father.

When the disturbance occurred below at the camp, the young man had been already two days and two nights upon the butte. Though exhausted and weak, he was an anxious spectator of the approaching cyclone. The animals and birds had apparently interested themselves in his solitary and helpless state, and did not fail to observe him from a respectful distance. Besides these unrequested offices, the wolves had evidently held, during the two nights, some sort of a meeting, at which they did not hesitate to make themselves heard all over the neighboring region. These things were not pleasant in the least for Black Pipe.

He had noticed, at a glance, when he took a bird's eye view of the country about him in his first appearance, that there were two large eagles who had their young birds perched upon an inaccessible butte near by. Yet he had entertained no thoughts of interference from that quarter. But as the Sun hurried over the prairie of the heavens, he had evidences of ill will on the part of his neighbors. Mr. Eagle would obviously start off on his hunting excursion in an opposite direction, but always turned up from some other quarter in Black Pipe's vicinity. His suspicions were verified during the second day. As he was weakened perceptibly by lack of sustenance and loss of sleep, though his spirit was willing his body had to stoop towards the ground for rest. But no sooner was this done than he heard a noise like the sighing of the wind through a pine tree, only it became stronger every second; therefore he lifted his weary head reluctantly to ascertain the cause of the disturbance. Lo, down came his neighbor, the eagle, as if he were shot from the mouth of a cannon!

At the first sight Black Pipe hoped for a messenger from the "Great Mystery," but as the eagle descended his fearful mission became too clear. He sprang upon his feet with all the energy he could muster, and shook irreverently the sacred calumet over his head. The bird swung upward within twenty feet of the brave's head, with the air of saying "There! I fooled you. I did not intend to touch you."

The second night of his fasting was a trying one, for he felt as if the wrathy thunder bird would hurl him headlong over the precipice. The night was dark. He could not detect any object a few paces away from him, except when the great bird winked and sent forth zigzag flashes of fire. Thought he, "Thunder Bird has come to earth to punish some evil-doer!"

He continued his program during a wakeful and restless night. A brilliant flash of lightening exhibited before him a stranger, who greeted him with double rows of white teeth, and a pair of eyes of flaming fire, the effect intensified by the leisurely swaying of a snaky tail. A mountain lion! It was a vision of a second but never left the memory of the beholder. Another flash and peal—the visitor had departed.

On the following morning Black Pipe again gave way to physical weakness, and was asleep most of the forenoon in a sitting posture, with the calumet in his hand. When he awoke, the deliciously cool air and long sleep together had restored his senses. The atmosphere was clear. The sky above him was a spotless blue canopy. The Black Hills loomed up against the ocean-like sky. The "Bad Lands" lay around him. It seemed to his simple mind that the Thunder Bird had once, in some remote time, searched for the evil spirit who was hidden under these hills, and had thus torn up the land; but to a civilized eye, the country would have appeared like the debris of an ancient city destroyed by an earthquake. Pillars were still preserved here; columns and walls there; and yonder monuments and pyramids. Between these were heaped masses of ruins indescribable.

Suddenly in the western sky a black speck appeared. It continually developed until it assumed immense proportions and gradually advanced southeastward. It was a peculiar coneshaped cloud; part gray and part black. The clouds around it seemed to be in a turmoil. "Ah!" said Black Pipe to himself, "the drunken Thunder Bird who occasionally visits these hills is coming, I must pray." In a few minutes the cloud had passed and Black Pipe noticed that a rider came swiftly away from the camp and disappeared at the foot of the hill below him. Then he saw a man appear on the summit and stand there as if in prayer.

Charles Alexander Eastman   211

But all at once he felt chills and heat alternately, accompanied by a severe headache, and a feeling of utter weakness. Alas; the world around him was gradually fading away from his sight! At last, he thought he saw again the same landscape, and the Ogalalla camp lying below him. The people moved about like ants and the teepees appeared like ant hills.

But he was impressed with the added beauties of the scene. Upon the green prairies he saw vast herds of buffaloes. On the buttes adjacent to the one upon which he stood, were terraces like balconies high up on the sides, with perpendicular precipices above and below, on the edge of which were cedar trees and pines growing almost upon nothing. Under these were the daring Rocky Mountain sheep, quietly chewing their cud. Upon the ridges back of him were herds of elk, while lower down among the pine groves he saw the black-tailed deer lying in the shade. Just above him, among the rough banks, was digging the bear. As the young man looked about him with delight, he heard a voice:

"My son, I have heard thy prayers. Thou are a brave. I shall make thee also a Medicine Man. The Great Mystery has given me this power. I understand the mysteries of the roots and herbs. But thou must be strictly obedient to my rules. Thou shalt always keep my claws around thy neck for a token. Thou shalt sing my songs."

When the speaker ceased, Black Pipe timidly turned his head to see who was addressing him. Behold, an old grizzly was sitting upon his haunches a few paces away. He bowed his head with a "how," acknowledging these commands, and the old bear walked slowly away. Black Pipe resumed his former position but he was addressed again, in an unknown yet perfectly intelligible tongue.

"Brave, do not fear. Thou shalt be given the strongest of hearts henceforth.

"Behold me! I am no longer allowed by the Great Mystery to live in the world but with my contemporaries I a[m] returned to stone. Throughout these Bad Lands thou wilt find us. Our bodies have been turned to stones and commanded to remain thus until the end of time. Yet I have in possession some wisdom and knowledge, with which the Creator endowed me. I am now commanded by him to impart it to thee. I was originally given the power to see the heavens and earth, and know the events of the future, though I may be buried in the bottom of the lake or river. I was made to live longest of any animal, and my heart will beat even when it is taken from my body.

"Thou shalt be a prophet and live to a great age. Behold me!"

Black Pipe again turned to regard the speaker and, lo, a tortoise! A huge petrified tortoise, half buried in the smooth wall of a butte opposite him!

Just then, a great war party of the Crow Indians appeared suddenly in the neighborhood, and he was already discovered!

They attacked him upon their ponies, shouted wildly and surrounded him. In his brave defense he brought himself to his senses, and it was another bright morning, and the Crow Indian war party turned out to be a multitude of vulture[s] flying in circles over his head.

He sprang up quickly, and having smoked the pipe that he had held three days and three nights for the "Great Mystery," he descended the butte with all the assurance of a great "Medicine Man" and a prophet. He found a new white teepee had been pitched just outside of the camp to receive him, and that he was now considered a full-fledged leader in his new profession.[3]

Notes of a Trip to the Southwest, 1900

You ask me how I like Arizona. I say it is too hot and dry. As the old Pima chief, Antonio says, nothing will grow there unless it is heat-proof. It was ninety degrees above on March 31st, and kept it up during the three days I was in the Sacaton region. I can't say that

I like Arizona for her climate, her giant cactus, Gila monsters and centipedes. Yet nearly all the white people I met were there for their health. It is a good incubator in which to protect exhausted lives.

You ask further how the Pima and Papago Indians are getting on. I say very badly indeed. The Pimas are very good people—willing to work and help themselves but they have been deprived of everything—even the natural courses of their streams have been diverted. The Gila River runs dry. No water for stock; none for their gardens; nor even for daily household use in some places! They live in what was once a beautiful valley, but now it is the valley of death.

I never saw more gentle and genial Indians in my life than these people, and I have seen many. Yet I cannot see but that starvation stares them in the face. Everywhere my eye meets the same mummified and half-starved faces. I looked into the clear sky of that region and could not help saying: Where are you, Charity? Can not these miserable people appeal to you?

The Pimas ask no charity after the usual fashion. They seek only such assistance as will be for their own lasting good. They want a reservoir large enough to irrigate their valley. They have already dug ditches on a small scale about their gardens hoping to catch every drop if it should rain. A bill has been introduced in Congress for the building of such a reservoir, at a cost of a million and a half. There can be no better and more humanitarian legislation than this. It will not only make these people self-supporting, but it will also help many poor whites in their vicinity to gain a livelihood.

"And what did you see in the Osage country?" I saw there conditions directly opposite to those described above. If you were to ask me where the Indian customs linger longest, I would say, among the Osages and Sac and Fox at Tama City, Iowa. Nowhere in all my travels have I ever met an Indian woman in full Indian costume, and talking excellent English, except at this agency. The Indian woman referred to had with her an adopted daughter, who is a full blooded white girl. She also was attired in the native dress of the Osages. Both the white girl and her adopted Osage mother said that they had been educated at the Catholic mission school. I do not blame the school. I think the church has done what it can for these people. It is the conditions and environment that have kept them from progress.

The Osages possess a competency second to none. They are in fact a rich corporation. They have $8,500,000 invested at 5% interest and a country good enough for any one. They have lived in close touch with civilization for forty years—longer than most Indian tribes; yet I have seen more real Indians there than almost anywhere else. I was told that there was very little work done by them. A custom exists among them that is very much like that of an English prince— they draw a fine annual income from the Government and get into debt to everyone at the same time.[4]

An Indian Festival, 1900

It was mid-summer—the Indians' festival time, when the medicine men fulfilled their promise of the year before to make a "sun-dance," a "fox-dance," or any other kind of dance that has an intertribal significance. The Ogallalas, the Brules, the Hunkpapahs and the Minne-conwojus were encamped together. It was an imposing village of white teepees that had sprung up in one afternoon upon one of the broad bottom lands of the Cheyenne, overshadowed by the high peaks of the majestic Pahah-sapah (Black Hills).

The village was in four distinct circles or rings, according to custom. When separate, each tribe usually has a council teepee within the circle, from which all the unwritten codes of the tribe are made and enforced. But at such a reunion as this, one or another of the four tribes is selected to maintain their joint government during the festivals. If all these bands have been successful in war and the chase, the occasion is a happy one. Many a new reputation or chief is announced with extravagant savage pomp and ceremony. Children of noted chiefs or warriors are named publicly, a custom by which the poor and old profit, for at such times the parents of the newly named child give a great feast, and distribute presents in the form of ponies, blankets, and garments of every description. Likewise many widows and widowers, or other respectable mourners, publicly announce that they will again paint their faces and cease to mourn; but not until they have made a great feast, and their good and loving relatives have given away ponies and other savage wealth in honor of the event.

Following a two-days' sun dance one morning, a half century or more ago, the criers went the rounds of the circular village extending the cordial invitation of Grey Eagle to a feast at which his only son, Lame Deer, would have his ears pierced. The crier further announced as an extraordinary inducement that the chief would give away three ponies, one of them his favorite war-horse.

"Ugh!" exclaimed a warrior, "that pony saved his scalp in many a battle, especially when the Sapah-wichasha (Utes) pursued us over vast plains—will he part with him? That pony is an honor and ornament to him. He has been struck and wounded nine times, and is entitled to eagle feathers both in his dock and mane, besides the usual war-paint for ponies, according to the custom."

"How," interrupted another, "It is in his mind to show his love for the boy—his only son."

"Listen! The crier of the Ogallalas, upon his white pony, has entered our circle. Let us hear what he has to announce." The speaker was a Minneconwoju woman, who was standing upon a buffalo skin, in the act of scraping off the hair. The fog-horn voice of the crier fairly re-echoed from hill to hill as he proceeded in this manner:

"Hear ye, Minneconwoju people! Your friend, Fire Lightning, the Ogallala chief, invites you to his feast in honor of his son's first act of note. Hear ye, Minneconwoju people, Fire Lightning, according to the custom of his family, will give away ten spotted ponies! Let all come to the feast! Let all the pretty maidens and great braves come and witness the great chief's act of strong heart."

It was to be a gala day for the Sioux upon the Cheyenne in that moon of Wee-pah-zoo-ka! (June berries.) Every maiden of any pretensions to beauty was intent upon surpassing her competitors in extravagance of attire. Many used the placid waters of a pond near by for their looking glass, many grouped together painted each other in turn. As for the young men, their toilet was made in similar fashion; with few exceptions they say in groups of six to ten, while one small hand mirror or perhaps only part of one did service for all.

The young maidens used generally but two colors—red and yellow; the young braves used anything for variety and always endeavored to out-do each other. In consequence of this singular taste, their faces looked not unlike the colors of a crazy quilt. Really handsome, however, were their blankets and buckskin shirts, embroidered with porcupine and set with elk's teeth, and with profuse fringes down the seams. Their long braids of hair were wound with otter skin and heavily scented. The aboriginal dude was the most picturesque of them all!

The day was half over and all had completed their painting— even the antiquated women had smeared their wrinkled faces with a dull red, and the old men surpassed them by generously painting their hair as well. But the young people upon calico ponies, with gorgeous bridles and blankets—they really were objects of interest!

It was accorded to Fire Lightning to have his event come off first. All entered the Ogallala circle. The chieftain stepped into the ring with native dignity and addressed his audience thus:

"Ye people of the different bands of the Dakotas, hearken: My second son has just returned from a successful war-path. The war-chief reports that his conduct upon the battlefield was worthy of his ancestors. I beg the people to join with me in celebrating the beginning of his public career. It is my purpose to give him a new name with your approval." ("How! how! how!" was the response from all sides.) "I name him Red Cloud. Remember at the eve of day the red clouds appear in the west to denote the promise of a bright day to follow."

At this point he turned to the herald; the latter announced that the ten horses with fine aboriginal saddles would be brought into the circle by young Red Cloud.

"He looks very young. I do not believe he is over fifteen winters," whispered a pretty maiden of chieftain's blood to her girl companion.

"But they say that he is seventeen, and hunts the buffalo with a skill of an old hunter," replied the other.

The old women and men struggled feverishly for a good position, for it was understood that Red Cloud would distribute these ponies among the poor and old, which he did gracefully and kindly. From that day the young brave was considered a man.

Now came Grey Eagle's feast. He had announced that his boy, Lame Deer, would have his ears pierced. An Indian is not happy unless he wears earrings, and it was the fashion that the ear-piercing should be done publicly and some savage wealth change hands because that also shows the social position of the parents.

As had been heralded, Grey Eagle gave away three ponies; among them his own war-horse. Few warriors can part with their favorite pony.

An old medicine man was appointed to pierce the little boy's ears. He did not use an awl or a needle, but a very sharp-pointed knife. The boy was now called upon to display his courage. He simply tightened his lips and his eyes were fixed upon the blue sky. He uttered no cry. (This was the same chief who grew up to fight General Miles on the Little Big Horn the winter following the Custer battle, and was killed.) He was a small but bright-looking boy with long black hair, and wore upon his head a warrior's son's eagle feather.

Grey Eagle was a man of intense feeling, yet he possessed a great deal of humor. He rose and addressed the throng: "I have invited you to partake of my meat. I will now tie a leather cord to the mane of each pony. A duplicate is to be thrown up into the air, and who-ever catches it will be entitled to keep the pony that wears the cord."

This unexpected proposition took the general fancy. Of course, every one would like to see one of the cords fall into their hands.

The big Indian drum was sounded and savage music rent the air. A strong brave sent the cords over the heads of the crowd, one at a time. The result was a general turmoil.

Everybody rushed toward the flying object—a confusion of up-raised arms and swinging lariats! Old warriors were as free to give excited war whoops as any of the younger men, while women with their characteristic screams augmented the already intolerable noise.

The first cord was knocked about over their heads until it fell into the hand of a warrior. The disappointed contestants greeted its fall with a tremendous yell. All were on the utmost look-out as the next was thrown high into the air. Savage excitement neared its height and many were injured in the fray. At this instant the crier shouted above the din:

"The last cord will now be sent up!"

"Ugh! ugh!" exclaimed many a young brave, "I must catch this cord, or I am no athlete."

Then came a terrific clash of bows, clubs, and nude bodies. The struggle, though a playful one, seemed desperate. The cord was kept on the jump from man to man, until finally it went under their feet. This change of position was even more dangerous to the contestants but no one heeded the danger.

At last a tremendous whoop went up. The crowd parted and a brave came out with the last cord in his hand. He did not resemble a human being so much as a buffalo bill or a black bear. The dust, the disarrangement of his massive hair, and the demoralization of his painted face made him anything but pleasing to behold. But as he approached there was satisfaction written on his hideous coun-tenance, for he had won the prize![5]

Charles Alexander Eastman   219

A True Story with Several Morals, 1900

Not many weeks ago some of the Oklahoma Poncas went to South Dakota to visit their friends and relatives at Niobrara. Of course everybody was delighted. All the stories of old days were told in turn and the pipe of peace and the pipe apiece were filled and refilled.

But there came a time when the stories and provisions were exhausted and the young men strayed off to a neighboring town, in search of food and amusement.

One of them spied a strange thing. He saw a white farmer who had just sold some vegetables walk up to a slot machine and drop a dollar into it.

"Ugh!" said the Indian, when he saw a keg of beer roll out.

A council was held immediately. A collection was taken up among the Indians and the nickels and dimes resulting changed for a silver dollar. The keg of beer rolled out and was soon upon pony's back, travelling toward the Indian village.

After it reached there, all the old stories were told over again, but this time with an accompaniment of songs, wailing, and shooting.

When quiet was restored at last, one young Indian lay dead. The murderer was sitting by in deep meditation.

"Ugh! I will go with him, before his spirit has gone too far. No white hangsman shall avenge his blood. I will go to his aged mother and will give her the gun that killed him, to kill me with it."

He went; and the old woman did not argue the matter with him but immediately took the gun and shot him dead. If all the white murderers should follow this Indian's example, they would save much time and money for their trial and execution.[6]

Indian Traits, 1903

It is natural that the subject of the Indian should be of the deepest interest to me. It is natural for me to cling to the early training that I received—training that was instilled into the very fibre of my being—training that this civilization of steam, machinery, and electricity cannot wipe out. There is a cry that sometimes comes to my soul: "O let me go back to my childhood and primitive man and the love of Mother Nature!"

God made the Indian a part of Nature and made him to understand the Great Mystery as the Power of the universe. The Indian in the days that are past, in this beautiful country, had everything that a wild man could wish for. The Great Mystery was so generous to him that he made no effort other than to keep to the nomadic life and follow the profession of the chase. The climate was always congenial to him, whether in the blizzards of the Dakotas or the hot suns of Arizona. He saw God in His handiwork; the lofty peaks, the mighty river, the rushing falls, the proud oaks and pines spoke of His power. At times you would see the Indian youth standing upon a precipice commanding a most impressive view, in the act of offering his silent prayer to the Unknown God—the Great Mystery. He never expected to see his God and never expected to talk with Him except through Nature. Daily he sought for a sign.

The Indian hunter never set out in the morning until he had first raised his hand and offered his filled pipe, silently recognizing Him who controls all things, even the fortunes of the chase. He then chased the deer all day and came back to his tent at night satisfied, whatever the result of his day's labor. He must often endure the severest exertion to supply food for his children. The Indian did not shirk that tremendous duty which presses upon us all—the duty of providing for his family.

Now what was it that made the Indian peculiarly interesting to all who study primitive man? Was it not a certain native power of faithfulness, as displayed in close observation and patience in practice? His eye swept the ground, and the moment he saw a footprint he knew whether it was that of a deer or a moose, a bear or a buffalo. He knew whether that track was made an hour ago or the day before yesterday, and he knew approximately where the animal was.

He had been thoroughly taught. As a boy he had made that footprint with his own fingers in the sand or the mud until he knew it. And from that time on he continued to observe until the language of the footprints was as clear to him as hand-writing. This is an education. It is a profession.

At night the father comes home with a detailed account of his day's experiences. The child sits there with his mouth and eyes wide open, and eagerly catches everything that is said. Afterward the old grandfather, or grandmother perhaps, tells one of the old legends, or a personal experience that was something like that of the father, perhaps something humorous. If there was anything new in the day's experience they would note and discuss it. So the boy learned his lessons. His teacher was not a brilliant young lady. It was a wrinkled, wise old woman who was his teacher. Beyond all this the child was so impressed with the Great Mystery taught from childhood that he listened for its voice everywhere. He could not get away from that thought. Sometimes in the night, when he was older, he would go away from the camp and visit alone the summit of the highest hill. There he would sit looking out and meditating upon a mighty Power.

Indian customs, it has been said, are atrocious, barbarous, in the wild life. This is true of all the primitive races and it is true in civilization. I cannot see that war is beneficent at any stage of man's progress. When I read that one iron-clad man-of-war blows up another, drowning many like rats or mutilating them beyond all recognition, then I say: "O civilization, where is your blush? Where is your shame?" It is true that the Indians fight sometimes, but I see those things wherever man exists. I will speak now of that side of war which the Indian supposed to be instituted by the Great Mystery to test and to develop man's higher nature. Many people suppose that an Indian warrior in his war-paint and scalp-belt must necessarily have butchered many of his fellow-creatures. As a matter of fact, he may not have killed a single man all his life long. Some men go into battle armed with a stone war-club and quiver full of arrows; some carry only a staff. When an enemy falls they rush forward and touch the body, simply to show their bravery. This act entitles a man to wear an eagle feather. There are, it is true, treacherous and cruel men among the Indians. There are also many such in every city.

In order to be a really great man the Indian must be a feast-maker. There was no such thing as money in our life—one of the most powerful things to influence men, both for good and evil. In those days fine muscles were demanded—wonderful endurance, which it took much practice and self-denial to gain. In order to be a feast-maker it was necessary to be a fine hunter, and in order to be a fine hunter it was necessary to have a fine body. And you know it takes a good deal of moral fibre to make and to keep a fine body! We did not have sleepless nights in those days, and we did not need to have our food digested before we took it! In order to be a warrior or a chief, a man's nervous system must be kept near to perfection up to the age of sixty-five. Among the Sioux tribe personal worth was the first thing required in choosing a chief. Only a man of spotless character could attain that high position. That was the way *then*. There is a great difference now. Indians of no standing have been made chiefs by the American press. A number of such chiefs are not recognized by their own tribes.

But we have lost a good deal. We don't blame civilization. We had to rough it with the bad element upon the frontier before civilization really came. Some of these frontiersmen are good men—men who make civilization march along. But there is a class of people who come among us for another purpose. They ruin the innocent and childlike races of this continent, and through contact with them we have lost much in the way of honesty and upright living. The Indians are not natural lawbreakers. They had unwritten codes of law that none could break.

Among many the Indian is misunderstood as to his home life; it is claimed that the women have to do all of the work. But the tepee has few rooms to sweep and tend and no windows nor bric-a-brac to wash and dust. The woman has the whole management and care of the home and she does her womanly duty faithfully and gladly. The man is not idle. He must go out and follow the hunt to provide food. It may take him the whole day to find it. Many times there is danger from an enemy—he must defend the home. But unless engaged in either of these ways the Indian stays at home. He goes out to council meeting. Besides his council, or his club, he has no outside demands. He has perfect confidence in his wife. He comes home perhaps after hunting all day in the rain. His wife will be so kind as to take off his wet moccasins and put on dry ones, provide his food, set it before him, and he is perfectly happy. After supper he has a little smoke and recounts the experiences of the day. The old men tell stories and legends and they all laugh and enjoy themselves.

What about the sons and daughters? In those days it was not considered good taste for a young man to go away from home for his pleasure. All the laughing was done in the family circle. The daughter had even more restrictions. That old grandmother was a severe chaperone. When the girl got to be about fifteen years old the grandmother took her in hand, and a young man couldn't get a peep at her even through a hole in a blanket!

All of these things were customary fifty or more years ago. Our old rules of conduct have broken down through contact with civilization. Even in my own time a good many of the Indian customs had fallen into disuse.

The child was trained before it was born, and when it was born it was taken out under the branches to hear the birds and become Nature-born. We were taught to think quickly. We attained accuracy by the coordination of the muscles and the eye. Keenness, swiftness, strength—that was part of us. You say this was intuitive, but it was not. It was taught us from the cradle. These things made the Indian love his family and his country, and made of him a strong, devoted warrior to defend his people.[7]

The Indian's View of the Indian in Literature, 1903

The Indians in general are not readers. Of the great mass of that which has been written about them, they know little or nothing. Here and there a book or a magazine article falls into the hands of one who can read and is translated to the old people, bringing a smile of contempt upon their faces. The pictures drawn therein are altogether foreign to their real life and mode of thought. Nor is it strange that this should be so. By their long-established habit of reticence and reserve, they have never been ready to show their inmost thoughts to the casual visitor. It is their pride to discern the characters of others before letting their own be understood.

Many of the forces which most strongly influence the minds of other men do not exist for the Indian. His strongest impulses to action came to him in the field, either of hunting or war. These motives cannot be learned by the stranger, as he lounges among the sluggish and apathetic reservation Indians. Neither can you obtain such knowledge through the illiterate interpreter, who is not at all able to portray character as the Indian himself might reveal it, in vivid descriptions of his own experiences in battle or the chase. The mirthful, humorous side of his temperament cannot possibly be known except by an intimate. It is never shown to the chance comer; one must live with him in his own home until all strangeness is worn away.

It is true that something of the red man's nature may appear through his modern and freer way of living, but that also is modified by his recent adoption of the "white man's way." These new manners, not being fully assimilated to his native ideas and practice, too often serve to make him appear ridiculous.

The mind of the Indian nowadays is further hampered by the authority held over him upon the reservations. He is no longer free and spontaneous in expressing his thoughts, but rather feels obliged to say in a general way what he thinks will be pleasing to the white people. Even when questioned concerning old stories and customs, he commonly tones them down and introduces later ideas which he imagines will be more acceptable.

Occasionally, when greatly provoked, he may speak freely, but then it is apt to be more in the white man's way than the old Indian fashion, which was dignified even in anger. Such occasions used to be rather to his advantage than otherwise, as his noblest eloquence and most admirable self-control were displayed under trying circumstances. It is quite the contrary now that the old barriers of speech are broken down. His simplicity of expression, which was original and peculiar to him, is fast disappearing. The great orators are nearly all gone. Even the old chiefs nowadays have heard so much of the official talk of Government agents and commissioners that they unconsciously drop into the hackneyed commonplaces of speech.

The writer of today goes to the reservation to study his red men. Because he still sees an Indian here and there wearing long hair and a blanket, it does not follow that such a one still practices the typical customs of his race. One man alone cannot effectively hold the beliefs and unwritten codes of hundreds of years, in etiquette and ethics and religion. The poor Indian merely clings to his blanket as the last remnant, the shell of his old life: the soul of it is gone.

Here and there one adheres to the dance and pounds the "Omaha" drum. What of it? He has already forgotten many of the old songs which formerly expressed the greater part of their social and religious life. The Omaha dance, which is generally kept up at the present time for amusement alone, is a very simple affair. It is really a modern innovation. All dances had once a religious significance, a higher purpose than mere entertainment.

The truth is that no one, writing from present-day observation, can portray the typical aborigine of this country. He has forever departed. Those who went among the wild tribes fifty or more years ago may have had some glimpses of his real nature, although tremendously handicapped, as a rule, by being unable to address him in his own language. You must know his language to understand him. Much of his eloquence is in idiom and inflection impossible to translate. His flights of rhetoric at times would not fall short of Choate's or Webster's, if interpreted with sympathy and intelligence.

In current fiction the Indian is introduced only as sensational effect is wanted, and is described as unstable, faithless, and venomous. He is represented as frightful and repulsive, and compared to the tiger and the snake. The writer is not seriously considering him as a man; he only seeks a sensation and therefore intensifies the traits of bloodthirstiness and cruelty which he perhaps imagines him to possess. The effect is altogether bad, for the general reader is fortified in a heartless prejudice, and it is really a gross injustice, though it may be without intention.

Let us consider for a moment the American classics, Longfellow's *Hiawatha*, Cooper's *Last of the Mohicans*, and Helen Hunt Jackson's *Ramona*. Here some of the deeper qualities of the Indian are brought to light. Alessandro's patience and self-control in desperate straits are truly characteristic. Cooper went a little further in word-painting, and possibly took advantage of the general ignorance of his subject to give his brush free play. However, Uncas is not untrue to his race. Indeed, he is one of the best types of the Indian existing in our literature.

In *Hiawatha*, the poet was mysteriously able to collect the gems of native American legend, poetry, and song into a harmonious whole, expressed with the simplicity of truth. I think the work will survive as the poetic interpretation of the Indian mind, although it is yet inadequate, regarded as a study of his life and character.

In American history, the red man has never been presented in a true light. His defense of his country and his people has been miscalled murderous and treacherous. From his standpoint it was the highest patriotism. His courage and devotion led him to face forces utterly disproportioned to his own and he was often victorious against great odds. Yet he has been deprived of his victory upon the records of history as written by the white man. Whenever he surpassed his trained opponent in strategy and generalship, and annihilated his foes, the battle is described as a massacre!

However, it has been admitted by competent authorities, outside of written history, that many of these leaders of the plains and the woods were great generals and statesmen, to be compared with those of any nation. King Philip, in his war against the colonies, had no adequate force to carry through what he had undertaken, yet he attacked them at nearly every point, and seriously threatened their very existence. Chief Joseph of the Nez Perces, in Montana, Washington and Idaho, Crazy Horse, Gall, Red Cloud, Sitting Bull and Spotted Tail in Montana and the Dakotas, were leaders in modern times.

As a statesman, Pontiac showed a high order of diplomacy when he united the various tribes of the Middle States and organized a simultaneous attack on all the forts along the Great Lakes. Had he succeeded in his determined effort to destroy Forts Detroit and Niagara, he might have checked the westward progress of civilization for at least a generation. Certainly he stands equal with Tecumseh and the others I have mentioned in military affairs. In oratory, Red Jacket, Logan, Strike-the-Ree, Six, Osceola, Grass, White Ghost are some of the greatest names.

There is one important truth which has been generally ignored by our historians. The red man is peaceful by nature and from choice. He is a devoted husband and father, a very agreeable host, and he never forgets a friend. The provocations which turned him to severity in war have not been fairly set forth. It is a fact which ought to be universally known that the wild tribes were invariably friendly and hospitable until they had been deceived and injured by the white man. The barbarities dwelt upon in all the text-books studied in our schools, as if they were habitual and characteristic, were in reality the acts of men driven to desperation by such provocations on the part of their enemies as have led to similar atrocities by the soldiers of all civilized nations, down to the present day.

The Indian's side of any controversy between him and the white man has never really been presented at all. History has necessarily been written from the white man's standpoint, and largely from the reports of commanding officers, naturally anxious to secure full credit for their gallantry or to conceal any weakness.

Take as an illustration the so-called "battle" of Wounded Knee. A ring was formed about the Indians, and after disarming most of them one man resisted and the troops began firing toward the center, killing nearly all the Indians and necessarily many of their own men. The soldiers then followed up fleeing women and children and shot them down in cold blood. This is not called a massacre in the official reports. The press of the country did not call it a massacre. On the other hand, General Custer was in pursuit of certain bands of Sioux. He followed their trail two days, and finally overtook and surprised them upon the Little Big Horn. The warriors met him in force and he was beaten at his own game. It was a brilliant victory for the Indians, whom Custer had taken at a disadvantage in the midst of their women and children. This battle goes down in history as the "Custer Massacre."

Of the modern school of American ethnology Dr. George Bird Grinnell, Mr. James Mooney and the late Frank Cushing are leading representatives. Cushing studied the Zunis alone, and of their customs and religion he had a more intimate knowledge than any other white man has been able to gain. Mr. Mooney's work is preserved mainly in scientific collections, where it is inaccessible to the general reader, and the same is true of other scientific workers. Dr. Grinnell has had rare opportunities to come into close touch with the Indians of several tribes, in the days of their wild life as well as in their semi-civilized state. He has done, perhaps, more than anyone else to popularize the subject, and in his versions of old legends and folk-tales he preserves admirably the native simplicity of expression. His sincere love for the Indian character is the secret of his success. A popular author, new in the Indian field, is Hamlin Garland. His sympathy with the red man is unmistakable, and he paints him in such a way as to win the sympathy of the reader.

To sum up, however, the Indian who is loyal to his race and familiar with its history, cannot but feel that his people have been unfairly treated in literature as in Governmental affairs. He has not been called to an equality with other men, but rather arbitrarily assigned to a part which he had no inclination to play, and left under the stigma of an imaginary character. Our writers, with few exceptions, seem to forget that he is a man, endowed with the faculties and virtues common to all men, except degenerates. The original American was an unspoiled man, and a fairly well-balanced character. In the white man's books, either his faults are exaggerated or his good points sentimentalized.

The life of the red man, simple as it was, had many interesting phases, and its competent expression might prove a valuable contribution to the human story. The record of Indian wars and their cruelties should be kept entirely distinct from the portrayal of his national and domestic life. His conception of the "Great Mystery," which was really the basis of all his development, his songs, music, and native literatures are as yet almost unknown, except for the good beginning made in this field by Miss Alice Fletcher and Dr. Grinnell. Miss Fletcher, in her recent book, *Indian Story and Song*, has revealed some of the secret motives and deeper feelings of the Indian as expressed in music. Yet, upon the whole, the Indian's story has been written only from the outside, and he is yet to appear as his own interpreter.[8]

Life and Handicrafts of the Northern Ojibwas, 1911

Among the forest Indians of the Northwest they are still some few who maintain themselves in the old-fashioned way, living in birch-bark houses during most of the year. Their home is the lake regions of northern Minnesota and the Province of Ontario. This country is so interlaced with watery highways that the primitive [bark] canoe is the main carrier. The horse is scarcely used, but in winter the dog-sled replaces the canoe. Each family roves about within an area of perhaps a hundred miles.

These people actually live by hunting and fishing, wild rice and berry gathering, and no country be more perfectly adapted to such a life. Each season of the year has its characteristic occupation. In the early fall they fish with nets at the outlets of the large lakes or in the narrows between their countless islands, sometimes spearing the sturgeon and other fish by torchlight. The flesh is cut into thin strips and smoked or sun-dried. At this time they also shoot many ducks and cure them in the same way for winter use.

A little later, they separate into small groups of one or two families each and scatter for the winter fur-hunt. Moose and caribou may also be hunted in winter; but if food is scarce they may fall back upon fishing through the ice. In the spring they deliver their furs at the nearest post of the Hudson's Bay Company, although sometimes agents from the posts gather up the furs by dog-team, thus saving the Indian the long journey. This is the time for maple-sugar making, and delicious sugar is made with the primitive utensils, mostly of birch bark, and packed away in birchen boxes of a peculiar shape called "mococks." In April large groups of from ten to thirty families gather at some waterfall near the mouth of a river for the spawning season, and again large quantities of fish are caught and cured.

From this time to the middle of July, as they plant no gardens, the people come together on their "sacred grounds," and there conduct the ancient rites and festivities. This is the play time of the year—the time for courtship, dances, and feasts, as well as ceremonies of a distinctively religious nature.

In July they begin stripping the birch and white-cedar bark for canoes and basket-making, gathering pine roots also for the same purpose. The bark is baled and kept flat under large stones, to be used when needed. The pliable cedar bark is utilized in mats, as well as for binding and stripping the canoes; the framework and paddles of the canoe are made of its wood. During the latter part of this month bulrushes are gathered, dried, and pressed for use in making mats. After this comes the blueberry picking, an occupation which again scatters the Indians pretty widely in small groups throughout the country. The dried berries are put away in coarse stacks woven of grass rushes.

By the first of August, the people begin to seek out the wild-rice fields, where the precious cereal grows most abundantly about the outlets and swampy bays of these northern lakes. The harvesting of this natural crop is an interesting and important feature of their lives. A large field having been located, certain portions of it are pre-empted by different families, and men and women go out by pairs in a canoe [to] tie the straw in bundles to ripen. A month later, they again enter the field and beat out the grain with a club while holding it over the canoe with a hooked stick. In this manner the light craft moves slowly in water several feet deep, while only the black heads of the harvesters are visible through the thick straw.

After the field is cleared and the canoe emptied on shore, a hole is dug, or a natural water-worn rock filled half full with rice and covered with rawhide. Then the young men dance bare foot upon it until husked in its winnowed skins or flat baskets, thoroughly dried, and finally packed in rush sacks or skins, sometimes in whole fawn skins. This nutritious food is mainly used in the form of a soup or stew with wild duck and other game. Last come the cranberry picking and the fall fishing, when the cycle is complete.

Some of these Ojibwas have log cabins of their own construction, with mud chimneys, but few care to live in them except during the coldest part of the winter, preferring teepees covered with birch bark in overlapping strips, and supported by poles arranged in the shape of a cone. Their craftsmanship is as simple as it is ingenious, and nearly everything they use is made by themselves, lovingly, and with patient skill. Years ago all their fish-nets were of the wild hemp, but now they use twine bought at the trading-posts. I saw the women at work making them in different sizes for catching different kinds of fish. Two light, thin cedar strips are used for netting, one about two inches square, the other from five to eight inches long with a rounded point, slit to form a tongue. When thirty yards or so are made, it is weighted with stones, and strips of cedar wood are tied to the upper edge as floaters. These white floaters are noticeable along the shallows and wooded shores of the lakes, and in the early morning it is common to see the women, together or singly, lifting their nets and taking the catch into the canoes.

The canoe is begun by pegging out an outline upon the ground, after which the cedar framework is built up, and the bark sewed firmly into place and thoroughly calked with boiling pitch. Baskets are made of sweet grass, rushes, split roots, and strips of bark, the larger and coarser ones being uses for carrying fish, game, wild rice, berries, and even babies. The regular cradle has a pliable cedar board for a back, while the front is of tanned skins securely laced and provided with straps for carrying.

Skins are tanned and dressed by the women with their primitive instruments, scraped with the shin-bone of a deer, and softened by rubbing with liver and brains. These are skillfully made up into garments and especially moccasins, of which those made of moose-hide are the best and most durable. They are ornamented chiefly with beads, the more difficult and characteristic work in porcupine quills, flattened and dyed, having fallen largely into disuse. Sometimes the entire skin of a fawn or other small animal is tanned with the hair on, cutting it as little as possible, sewing and stuffing it so as to present an almost life-like appearance. Stuffed birds, skins of skunk, ermine, and other ornamental furs, bear-paws, horns of different animals, plumes of heron and eagle, are curiously combined in the characteristic warbonnets or head-dresses of the chiefs, some of which have been preserved through more than one generation.

The drum for the "sacred dance" is a hollowed log of bass-wood over which a wet moose-hide is tightly stretched by means of a ring and which, when struck, gives forth a weird and hallow resonance. There are also rattles made of bone with supposed sacred or mystic properties. Rough dishes in many shapes and sizes are made of the ever useful birch bark, and more durable ones of the flat horns of the moose. Spoons are carved of cedar wood. I found very few old pipes, such as there were being small and of black stone.

To me these last of the hunting Indians seemed happy and contented, and for a few short weeks I lived over with them my boyhood days, unexpectedly finding a little bit of the past in the midst of our noisy and strenuous today.[9]

"My People": The Indians' Contribution to the Art of America, 1914

In his sense of the aesthetic, which is closely akin to religious feeling, the American Indian stands alone. In accord with his nature and beliefs, he does not pretend to imitate the inimitable, or to reproduce exactly the work of the Great Artist. That which is beautiful must not be trafficked with, but must be reverenced and adored only. It must appear in speech and action.

The symmetrical and graceful body must express something of it. Beauty, in our eyes, is always fresh and living, even as God Himself dresses the world anew at each season of the year.

It may be "artistic" to imitate Nature and even try to improve upon her, but we Indians think it very tiresome, especially as one considers the material side of the work—the pigment, the brush, the canvas! There is no mystery left; all is presented. Still worse is the commercialization of art. The rudely carved totem pole may appear grotesque to the white man, but it is the sincere expression of the faith and personality of the Indian craftsman, and has never been sold or bartered until it reached civilization.

Here we see the root of the red man's failure to approach even distantly the artistic standard of the civilized world. It lies not in the lack of creative imagination—for in this quality he is truly the artist—it lies rather in his point of view. I once showed a party of Sioux chiefs the sights of Washington, and endeavored to impress them with the wonderful achievements of civilization. After visiting the Capitol and other famous buildings, we passed through the Corcoran art gallery, where I tried to explain how the white man valued this or that painting as a work of genius, and a masterpiece of art.

"Ah!" exclaimed an old man, "such is the strange philosophy of the white man! He hews down the forest that has stood for centuries in its pride and grandeur, tears up the bosom of mother earth, and causes the silvery water-courses to waste and vanish away. He ruthlessly disfigures God's own pictures and monuments, and then daubs a flat surface with many colors, and praises his work as a masterpiece!"

This is the spirit of the original American. He holds Nature to be the measure of consummate beauty, and its destruction, sacrilege. I have seen, in our midsummer celebrations, cool arbors built of fresh-cut branches for council and dance halls, while those who attended decked themselves with leafy boughs, carrying shields and fans of the same, and even wreaths for their horses' necks. But, strange to say, they seldom made free use of flowers. I once asked the reason of this.

"Why," said one, "the flowers are for our souls to enjoy; not for our bodies to wear. Leave them alone and they will live out their lives and reproduce themselves as the Great Gardener intended. He planted them; we must not pluck them."

Indian bead-work in leaf and flower designs is generally modern. The old patterns are mainly geometrical figures, which are decorative and emblematic rather than imitative. Shafts of light and shadow, alternating or dove-tailed, represent life, its joys and sorrows. The world is conceived of as rectangular and flat, and is represented by a square. The sky is concave—a hollow sphere. A drawing of the horizon line colored pale yellow stands for dawn; colored red, for sunset. Day is blue, and night black spangled with stars. Lightning, rain, wind, water, mountains and many other natural features or elements are symbolized, rather than copied literally upon many sorts of Indian handiwork. Animal figures are drawn in such a manner as to give expression to the type or spirit of the animal rather than its body, emphasizing the head with the horns, or any distinguishing feature. These designs have a religious significance and furnish the individual with his personal and clan emblem, or coat of arms.

Symbolic decorations are used on blankets, baskets, pottery, and garments of ceremony to be worn at rituals and public functions. Sometimes a man's teepee is decorated in accordance with the standing of the owner. Weapons of war, pipes and calumets are adorned with emblems; but not the everyday weapons used in hunting. The war steed is decorated equally with his rider, and sometimes wears the feathers that signify degrees of honor.

Woman and Her Craftsmanship

In his weaving, painting, and embroidery of beads and quills, the red man has shown a marked color sense, and his blending of brilliant hues is subtle and Oriental in effect. The women did most of this work, and displayed rare ingenuity in the selection of native materials and dyes. A variety of beautiful grasses, roots, and barks was used for basket weaving by the different tribes, and some used gorgeous feathers for ornamentation. Each article was perfectly adapted in style, size and form to its intended use.

Pottery was made by the women of the Southwest for household furniture and utensils, and their vessels, burned in crude furnaces, were often gracefully shaped and exquisitely decorated. The designs were both imprinted on the soft clay, and modeled in relief. The nomadic tribes of the plains could not well carry these fragile wares with them on their wanderings, and, accordingly, their dishes were mainly of bark and wood, the latter sometimes carved. Spoons were prettily made of translucent horn. They were fond of painting their rawhide cases in brilliant colors. The most famous blankets are made by the Navajos upon rude hand-looms, and are wonderfully fine in weave, colors, and design. This native skill, combined with love of the work and perfect sincerity—the qualities which still make the Indian women's blanket, or basket, or bowl, or moccasins, of the old type, so highly prized—are among the precious things lost or sacrificed to the advance of an alien civilization. Cheap machine-made garments and utensils, without beauty or durability, have crowded out the old; and where the women still ply their ancient crafts, they do it now for money, not for love, and in most cases use modern materials and patterns, even imported yarns and poor dyes! Genuine curios or antiques are already becoming very rare, except in museums, and sometimes command fabulous prices.

As the older generation passes, there is danger of losing altogether the secret of Indian art and craftsmanship.

Modern Indian Art

Struck by this danger, and realizing the innate charm of the work and its adaptability to modern demands, a few enthusiasts have made of late years an effort to preserve and extend it, both in order that a distinctive and vitally American art form may not disappear, and also to preserve so excellent a means of self-support for the Indian women. Depots or stores have been established for the purpose of encouraging such manufactures and of finding a market for them, not so much from commercial as from artistic and philanthropic motives. The best known, perhaps, is the Mohonk Lodge, Colony, Oklahoma, founded under the auspices of the Mohonk Indian Conference, where all work is guaranteed of genuine Indian make, and, as far as possible, of native material and design. Such articles as bags, belts, and moccasins are, however, made in modern form so as to be appropriate for wear by the modern woman. Miss Josephine Foard assisted the women of the Laguna pueblo to glaze their wares, thereby rendering them more salable; and the Indian Industries League, with headquarters in Boston, works along similar lines.

The Indian Bureau reports that over six hundred thousand dollars' worth of Navajo blankets were made during the last year, and that prizes will be awarded this fall for the best blanket made of native wool. At Pima, fifteen thousand dollars' worth of baskets and five thousand dollars' worth of pottery were made and sold, and a less amount was produced at several other agencies.

Another modern development, significant of the growing appreciation of what is real and valuable in primitive culture, is the instruction in the Government schools in the traditional arts and crafts of their people. As schooling is compulsory between the ages of six and sixteen years, and as from the more distant boarding-schools the pupils are not even allowed to go home for the summer vacation, most of them would without this instruction grow up in ignorance of their natural heritage, in legend, music, and art forms as well as practical handicrafts. The greatest difficulty in the way is finding competent and sympathetic teachers.

At Carlisle there are and have been for some years two striking exemplars of the native talent and modern culture of their race, in joint charge of the department of Indian art. Angel DeCora, a Winnebago girl, who was graduated from the Hampton school and from the art department of Smith College, was a pupil of Howard Pyle, and herself made a distinctive success, having illustrated several books and articles on Indian subjects. Some of her work appeared in *Harper's Magazine* and other prominent periodicals. She had a studio in New York City for several years, until invited to teach art at the Carlisle school, where she has been ever since.

A few years ago, she married William Dietz, Lone Star, who is half Sioux. He is a fine manly fellow, who was for years a great football player, as well as an accomplished artist. The couple have not only the artistic and poetic temperament in full measure, but they have the pioneer spirit, and aspire to do much for their race. The effective cover designs and other art work of the Carlisle school magazine, the *Red Man*, are the work of Mr. and Mrs. Dietz, who are successfully developing native talent in the production of attractive and salable rugs, blankets and silver jewelry. Besides this, they are seeking to discover latent artistic gifts among the Indian students, in order that they may be fully trained and utilized in the direction of pure or applied art. It is admitted that the average Indian child far surpasses the average white child in this direction. The Indian did not paint Nature, not because he did not feel it, but because it was sacred to him. He so loved the reality that he could not venture upon the imitation. It is now time to unfold the resources of his genius, locked up for untold ages by the usages and philosophy of his people. They held it sacrilege to reproduce the exact likeness of the human form or face. This is the reason that early attempts to paint the natives were attended with difficulty.

Music, Dancing, Dramatic Art

A form of self-expression which has always been characteristic of my race is found in their music. In music is the very soul of the Indian; yet the civilized nations have but recently discovered that such a thing exists! His chants are simple, expressive and haunting in quality, and voice his inmost feeling, grave or gay, in every emotion and situation in life. They vary with tribes and even with individuals. A man often composes his own song, which belongs to him and is deeply imbued with his personality. These songs are frequently without words, the meaning being too profound for words; they are direct emanations of the human spirit. If words are used, they are few and symbolic in character. There is no definite harmony in the songs—only rhythm and melody; and there are striking variations of time and intonation which render them difficult to the "civilized" ear.

Nevertheless, within the last few years, there has been a serious effort to collect these folk-songs of the woods and plains, by means of notation and the phonograph, and in some cases there has also been an attempt to harmonize and popularize them. Miss Alice C. Fletcher, the distinguished ethnologist and student of early American culture, was a pioneer in this field, in which she was assisted by Prof. J. C. Filmore, who is no longer living. Frederick Burton died several years ago, immediately after the publication of his interesting work on the music of the Ojibway, which is fully illustrated with songs collected, and in some instances harmonized, by himself. Miss Natalie Curtis has devoted much intelligent, patient study to the songs of the tribes, especially of the Pueblos, and later comers in this field are Farwell, Troyer, Lieurance and Cadman, the last of whom uses the native airs as a motive for more elaborated songs. His "Land of the Sky Blue Water" is charming, and already very popular. Harold A. Loring, of North Dakota, has recently harmonized some of the songs of the Sioux.

Several singers of Indian blood are giving public recitals of this appealing and mysterious music of their race. There has even been an attempt to teach it to our schoolchildren, and Geoffrey O'Hara, a young composer of New York City, made a beginning in this direction under the auspices of the Indian Bureau. Native melodies have also been adapted and popularized for band and orchestra by native musicians, of whom the best known are Dennison Wheelock and his brother James Wheelock, Oneidas, and graduates of Carlisle. When we recall that, as recently as twenty years ago, all native art was severely discountenanced and discouraged, if not actually forbidden in Government schools and often by missionaries as well, the present awakening is matter for mutual congratulations.

Many Americans have derived their only personal knowledge of Indians from the circus tent and the sawdust arena. The Red Man is a born actor, a dancer and rider of surpassing agility, but he needs the great out-of-doors for his stage. In pageantry, and especially equestrian pageantry, he is most effective. His extraordinarily picturesque costume, and the realistic manner in which he illustrates and reproduces the life of the early frontier, have made of him a great romantic and popular attraction, not only here but in Europe. Several white men have taken advantage of this fact to make their fortunes, of whom the most enterprising and successful was Col. William Cody, better known as "Buffalo Bill."

The Indians engaged to appear in his and other shows have been paid moderate salaries and usually well treated, though cases have arisen in which they have been stranded at long distances from home. As they cannot be taken from the reservation without the consent of the authorities, repeated efforts have been made by missionaries and others to have such permission refused on the ground of moral harm to the participants in these sham battles and dances. Undoubtedly, they see a good deal of the seamy side of civilization; but on the other hand, their travels have proved of educational value, and in some instances opened their eyes to good effect to the superior power of the White Man. Sitting Bull and other noted chiefs have, at one time or another, been connected with Indian shows.

A pageant-play, adapted by Frederick Burton from Longfellow's poem of "Hiawatha" was given successfully for several years by native Ojibway actors; and individuals of Indian blood have appeared on the stage in minor parts, and more prominently in motion pictures, where they are often engaged to represent tribal customs and historical events.

Useful Arts and Inventions

Among native inventions which have been of conspicuous use and value to the dispossessors of the Indian, we recall at once the bark canoe, the snowshoe, the moccasin, (called the most perfect footwear ever invented), the game of lacrosse and probably other games, and the conical teepee which served as a model for the Sibley army tent. Pemmican, a condensed food made of pounded dried meat combined with melted fat and dried fruits, has been largely utilized by recent polar explorers.

The art of sugar making from the sap of the hard or sugar maple was first taught by the aborigines to the white settlers. In my day, the Sioux used also the box elder for sugar making, and from the birch and ash they made a dark-colored sugar that was used by them as a carrier in medicine. However, none of these yield as freely as the maple. The Ojibways of Minnesota still make and sell delicious maple sugar, put up in "mococks," or birch bark packages. Their wild rice, a native grain of remarkable fine flavor and nutritious qualities, is also in a small way an article of commerce. It really ought to be grown on a large scale and popularized as a package cereal, and a large fortune doubtless awaits the lucky exploiter of this distinctive "breakfast" food.

In agriculture, the achievements of the Indian have probably been underestimated, although it is well known that the Indian corn was the mother of all the choice varieties which today form an important source of food supply to the civilized world. Indian women cultivated maize with primitive implements, and prepared it for food in many attractive forms, including hominy and succotash, of which the names, as well as the dishes themselves, are borrowed from the Red Man, who has not always been rewarded in kind for his goodly gifts. In eighteen hundred and thirty, the American Fur Company established a distillery at the mouth of the Yellowstone River, and made alcohol from the corn raised by Gros Ventre women, with which they demoralized the men of the Dakotas, Montana, and British Columbia. Besides maize and tobacco, some tribes, especially in the South, grew native cotton and a variety of fruits and vegetables. The buckskin clothing of my race was exceedingly practical as well as handsome, and has been adapted to the use of hunters, explorers, and frontiersmen down to the present day.[10]

Angel De Cora (Winnebago)

Angel De Cora (1871–1919) was born on the Winnebago reservation in Nebraska. She attended a reservation school for four years before entering Hampton in 1883. She stayed at Hampton for five years, returned to Nebraska for a brief period, and then went back to Hampton. She was editor of *Talks and Thoughts* from 1890 to 1891. After graduating from Hampton in 1891, she briefly attended a private school in Massachusetts and then went on to study art at Smith College, Drexel Institute, and the Cowles Art School. In 1899 she published two illustrated short stories in *Harper's Monthly*, "The Sick Child" and "Gray Wolf's Daughter." From 1899 until 1906 she maintained studios in Boston and then New York City. During this time she illustrated several books, including Francis La Flesche's *The Middle Five* (1900) and Zitkala-Ša's *Old Indian Legends* (1901). Commissioner of Indian Affairs Francis E. Leupp appointed De Cora instructor of Indian arts at Carlisle in 1906. She held the position until 1915, during which time she worked to cultivate and preserve her students' artistic talents and promoted the value of Indian art to American culture. She published autobiographical sketches and essays on the contributions of Indian art to American art in the *Southern Workman* and the *Red Man*. She also lectured on Indian Affairs and was an active member of the Society of American Indians.

De Cora died from pneumonia in 1919. After hearing of her untimely death, Gertrude Bonnin paid tribute to her friend and fellow activist in her Summer 1919 editorial in the *American Indian Magazine*. Bonnin explained that De Cora's commitment to the work of the SAI was so strong that in her will she bequeathed $3,000 to the SAI. Bonnin writes, "The gift is a sacred trust! Such faith in her own race inspires us to our uttermost effort. Angel De Cora Dietz, living and dying, has left us a noble example of devotion to our people. (Gere, "Art of Survivance," 649–84; Littlefield and Parins, *Biobibliography: Supplement*, 199; Peyer, *American Indian Nonfiction*, 325–27; Peyer, *Singing Spirit*, 43–44; Bonnin, Editorial, 62)

My People, 1897

A great many have heard of Winnebago Indians, but very few have taken the trouble to study the character of the tribe. Many have passed through the reservation and their remarks are anything but flattering. The Winnebagoes were moved to their present home in the northeastern part of Nebraska in 1863 during the Sioux trouble. Since then very little has been done towards the civilization of the tribe,—that is, civilization in its truest meaning. Most of the Indians are farmers and live in frame houses. They use the English language to quite an extent, but their morals are bad. They have adopted all the vices of their white neighbors and these, added to their own, give the tribe a name not altogether enviable.

The sacredness of home life is but little appreciated now, although in the past it was one of their virtues. The old people tell of the strict ways in which they were brought up, and speak sorrowfully of the present. I do not think that the influence of the old people is so bad as some people say it is. The morality of the place is determined by the young people. They have thrown off all that reverence for age that used to be so noticeable a feature. They want to live in the "white man's way" as they call it; and are willing to give the last penny they have in order to have a carriage, and other luxuries that do not help them very much. As a rule they are careful about their personal appearance, but here and there may be a family which does not take very much interest in anything beside the food it eats. I have said that most of them live in frame houses, but not more than two families in the whole community know how to beautify their homes and make them attractive. They may keep their homes perfectly clean, but they do not know anything of the use of flowers about the house and yard. As to the food and the cooking of it, the rapid decrease of the population tells that story better than I can. Surely a field matron is much needed.

The rough class of white people around the Indians do a great deal of harm to the Indians by selling liquor to them. It is true that the law forbids the selling of whiskey to Indians, but they avoid it by a system of what is called the "underground saloons." A few years ago a half-breed was found keeping one of these saloons; the law laid a slight punishment upon him, but it is doubtful whether it stopped him. One day a white man, while driving past some Indians, got one of his horses in the mire. Naturally they helped him out of his trouble. He expressed his gratitude by smuggling whiskey from the nearest town to these thirsty souls.

There is an old religious dance called the "Medicine Dance," which in its day was really pure and helpful, but is now only an excuse for all sorts of most degrading amusements. This dance always comes off on Sundays, and men and women who take part in it usually manage to drink a great deal. Perhaps some people might feel shocked at the thought of women drinking with men, but, since the old days of the subjugation of woman have passed away, she is on an equality with the man, and sometimes she carries herself even lower than a man would. Such women cannot be expected to be very good mothers and there are enough sad examples to show what this kind of motherhood is doing for the present generation. The girls are given away in marriage when they are scarcely in their teens, and those who have minds of their own generally follow the example of their parents by running off with some ruffian. The same parents encourage their children to drink, for to them it stands for manliness. At no time does a woman feel her importance more than when she is supporting her staggering, bleared-eyed heir away from the crowd at some feast or dance. It is one of the most pitiful things to hear parents tell of making their little children drunk, but that is not uncommon among my people. Of course with such, marriage can be but loosely held, and although they are often married by proper form, they leave each other as soon as they are tired of living together. Is it then any wonder that girls who have been to school, after going back home, "go back to the blanket?" While I do not try to justify them, I can but feel that they are not so much to blame as those who have better surroundings and better developed consciences. This is the sort of life that is waiting for us Winnebagoes, and whether we want to or not, it is our duty to do what we can for our people.

> "Shall we whose souls are lighted
> With wisdom from on high,
> Shall we, to men benighted
> The lamp of life deny?"

Let us, who are members of this unfortunate tribe, strive to prepare ourselves to elevate our people into a higher civilization. The responsibility is ours.[1]

Native Indian Art, 1907

The time has not been long enough since the subject was put into practice to show some of the possibilities of adapting Indian art to modern usages.[2]

Indians, like any other race in its primitive state, are gifted in original ideas of ornamentation. The pictorial talent is common to all young Indians.

The method of educating the Indian in the past was to attempt to transform him into a brown Caucasian within the space of five years or little more. The educators made every effort to convince the Indian that any custom or habit that was not familiar to the white man showed savagery and degradation. A general attempt was made to bring him "up to date." The Indian, who is so bound up in tribal laws and customs, knew not where to make the distinction, nor what of his natural instincts to discard, and the consequence was that he either became superficial and arrogant and denied his race, or he grew dispirited and silent.

In my one year's work with the Indians at Carlisle I am convinced that the young Indians of the present day are still gifted in the pictorial art.

Heretofore, the Indian pupil has been put through the same public school course as the white child, with no regard for his hereditary difference of mind and habit of life; yet, though the only art instruction is the white man's art, the Indian, even here, does as well and often better than the white child, for his accurate eye and skillful hand serve him well in anything that requires delicacy of handiwork.

In exhibitions of Indian schoolwork, generally, the only trace of Indian one sees are some of the signatures denoting clannish names. In looking over my pupils' native design work, I cannot help calling to mind the Indian woman, untaught and unhampered by white man's ideas of art, making beautiful and intricate designs on her pottery, baskets, and beaded articles, which show the inborn talent. She sits in the open, drawing her inspiration from the broad aspects of Nature. Her zig-zag line indicates the line of the hills in the distance, and the blue and white background so usual in the Indian color scheme denotes the sky. Her bold touches of green and red and yellow she has learned from Nature's own use of those colors in the green grass and flowers, and the soft tones that were the general tone of ground color in the days of skin garments, are to her as the parched grass and the desert. She makes her strong color contrasts under the glare of the sun, whose brilliancy makes even her bright tones seem softened into tints. This scheme of color has been called barbaric and crude, but then one must remember that in the days when the Indian woman made all her own color, mostly of vegetable dyes, she couldn't produce any of the strong glaring colors they now get in analine dyes.

The white man has tried to teach the young Indian that in order to be a so-called civilized person, he must discard all such barbarisms.

It must be remembered that most of the Indians of the Carlisle school have been under civilizing influences from early youth and have, in many instances, entirely lost the tradition of their people. But even a few months have proved to me that none of their Indian instincts have perished but have only lain dormant. Once awakened it immediately became active and produced within a year some of the designs that you have seen.

I have taken care to leave my pupils' creative faculty absolutely independent and to let each student draw from his own mind, true to his own thought, and, as much as possible, true to his tribal method of symbolic design.

The work now produced at Carlisle, in comparison with that of general schoolwork, would impress one with the great difference between the white and Indian designer. No two Indian drawings are alike and every one is original work. Each artist has his own style. What is more, the best designs were made by my artist pupils away from my supervision. They came to me for material to take to their rooms and some of the designs for rugs that you have seen were made in the students' play hour, away from the influence of others—alone with their inspiration—as an artist should work. It may interest you to know that my pupils never use practice paper. With steady and unhesitating hand and mind, they put down permanently the lines and color combinations that you see in their designs.

We can perpetuate the use of Indian designs by applying them on modem articles of use and ornament that the Indian is taught to make. I ask my pupils to make a design for a frieze for wall decoration, also borders for printing, designs for embroidery of all kinds, for woodcarving and pyrography, and designs for rugs.

I studied the Persian art of weaving from some Persians, because I saw from the start that the style of conventional designing produced by Indian School pupils suggested more for this kind of weaving. We shall use the Navajo method as well, but the oriental method allows more freedom to carry out the more intricate designs. The

East Indian and the American Indian designs are somewhat similar in line and color, especially those of the Kasak make.

I discourage any floral designs such as are seen in Ojibway beadwork. Indian art seldom made any use of the details of plant forms, but typified nature in its broader aspects, using also animal forms and symbols of human life.

With just a little further work along these lines I feel that we shall be ready to adapt our Indian talents to the daily needs and uses of modern life. We want to find a place for our art even as the Japanese have found a place for theirs, throughout the civilized world. The young Indian is now mastering all the industrial trades, and according to the wishes of the Honorable Indian Commissioner, there is no reason why the Indian workman should not leave his own artistic mark on what he produces.[3]

An Autobiography, 1911

I was born in a wigwam, of Indian parents. My father was the fourth son of the hereditary chief of the Winnebagoes. My mother, in her childhood, had had a little training in a convent, but when she married my father she gave up all her foreign training and made a good, industrious Indian wife.

During the summers we lived on the reservation, my mother cultivating her garden and my father playing the chief's son. During the winter we used to follow the chase away off the Reservation, along rivers and forests. My father provided not only for his family then, but his father's also. We were always moving camp. As a child, my life was ideal. In all my childhood I never received a cross word from any one, but nevertheless, my training was incessant. About as early as I can remember, I was lulled to sleep night after night by my father's or grandparent's recital of laws and customs that had regulated the daily life of my grandsires for generations and generations, and in the morning I was awakened by the same counseling. Under the influence of such precepts and customs, I acquired the general bearing of a well-counseled Indian child, rather reserved, respectful, and mild in manner.

A very promising career must have been laid out for me by my grandparents, but a strange white man interrupted it.

I had been entered in the reservation school but a few days when a strange white man appeared there. He asked me through an interpreter if I would like to ride in a steam car. I had never seen one, and six of the other children seemed enthusiastic about it and they were going to try, so I decided to join them, too. The next morning at sunrise we were piled into a wagon and driven to the nearest railroad station, thirty miles away. We did get the promised ride. We rode three days and three nights until we reached Hampton, VA.

My parents found it out, but too late.

Three years later when I returned to my mother, she told me that for months she wept and mourned for me. My father and the old chief and his wife had died, and with them the old Indian life was gone.

I returned to Hampton, and after graduation, some of my teachers prevailed upon me not to return home as I was still too young and immature to do much good among my people.

I went to Northampton, Mass., and through the efforts of some friends there, I entered the Burnham Classical School for Girls, and later when I decided to take up the study of art, I entered the Smith College Art Department, taking the four years' course under Dwight W. Tryon. During my study in Northampton, I worked for my board and lodging and also earned my four years' tuition at Smith College by holding one of the custodianships of the Art Gallery. The instruction I received and the influence I gained from Mr. Tryon has left a lasting impression upon me.

After the four years at Smith College, I went to Drexel Institute, Philadelphia, to study illustration with Howard Pyle, and remained his pupil for over two years.

While at this Institute I used to hear a great deal of discussion among the students, and instructors as well, on the sentiments of

"Commercial" art and "Art for art's sake." I was swayed back and forth by the conflicting views, and finally I left Philadelphia and went to Boston.

I had heard of Joseph DeCamp as a great teacher, so I entered the Cowles Art School, where he was the instructor in life drawing. Within a year, however, he gave up his teaching there but he recommended me to the Museum of Fine Arts in the same city, where Frank Benson and Edmund C. Tarbell are instructors, and for two years I studied with them.

I opened a studio in Boston and did some illustrative work for Small & Maynard Company, and for Ginn & Company. I also did some designing, although while in art schools I had never taken any special interest in that branch of art. Perhaps it was well that I had not over studied the prescribed methods of European decoration, for then my aboriginal qualities could never have asserted themselves.

I left Boston and went to New York City, and while I did some illustrating, portrait and landscape work, I found designing a more lucrative branch of art.

Although at times I yearn to express myself in landscape art, I feel that designing is the best channel in which to convey the native qualities of the Indian's decorative talent.

In 1906, Hon. Francis E. Leupp, Commissioner of Indian Affairs, appointed me to the Carlisle Indian School in Pennsylvania to foster the native talents of the Indian students there. There is no doubt that the young Indian has a talent for the pictorial art, and the Indian's artistic conception is well worth recognition, and the school-trained Indians of Carlisle are developing it into possible use that it may become his contribution to American Art.[4]

Gertrude Bonnin (Yankton Sioux)

Gertrude Bonnin, or Zitkala-Ša (Red Bird, 1876–1938), was born at the Yankton Sioux Agency in South Dakota, where she lived with her mother and attended a bilingual agency school for two years before enrolling in White's Manual Institute, a Quaker-run boarding school in Wabash, Indiana. After graduating from White's Manual Institute she attended Earlham College from 1895 to 1897. While at Earlham she published poems and essays in the school paper, the *Earlhamite*. As a student at Earlham, Bonnin distinguished herself from her predominantly white peers. She excelled academically and delivered a prize-winning speech at a statewide oratorical contest. The *Earlhamite* reprinted an unabridged version of her speech, "Side by Side," as did the Santee Agency school newspaper, the *Word Carrier*. Multiple articles about the event and Bonnin herself also appeared in the *Earlhamite* and in mainstream newspapers like the *Indianapolis Journal* and the *Indianapolis News*, which described her as "a cultivated young woman [whose] pronunciation was without trace of a tongue unfamiliar with English." In all of this press coverage, Bonnin was represented as an exemplary educated Indian—civilized, English speaking, and articulate—an identity that she would later embrace and revise in her periodical writings.

Her success at Earlham College played a part in landing her a teaching position at Carlisle. Although most of the teachers at Carlisle were white missionaries, Bonnin's impressive educational background and teaching experience caught the attention of Carlisle's founder, Pratt. At Carlisle Bonnin taught and recruited Indian students. Her stint at Carlisle was brief; after eighteen months she resigned and went to study at the New England Conservatory of Music in Boston in 1899. One year later she traveled as a violin soloist with the Carlisle Indian School Band on their tour of the northeastern United States at the same time that her three autobiographical essays appeared in the *Atlantic Monthly*: "Impressions of an Indian Childhood," "The School Days of an Indian Girl," and "An Indian Teacher Among Indians." An excerpt of her second autobiographical essay, "School Days of an Indian Girl," is reprinted here.

After her autobiographical essays appeared in the *Atlantic*, she published two books: a collection of oral traditions in *Old Indian Legends* in 1901 and *American Indian Stories* in 1921. She also co-wrote an opera, *The Sun Opera*.

Whereas early in her literary career she engaged the national attention of a mostly white middle-class readership of the *Atlantic* and *Harper's*, she later sought to reach a Native readership by publishing in the *American Indian Magazine*, the official organ of the Society of American Indians. This shift in audience and publishing context shaped Bonnin's artistic and political choices in her periodical pieces. She became a contributing editor to the magazine in the October–December 1915 issue and assumed the editorship of the magazine in 1918 through the Winter 1919 issue. Her involvement with the SAI also ceased with her departure from the magazine. Yet she remained a devoted activist for Indian rights. In 1926 Bonnin and her husband, Raymond Bonnin, co-founded the National Council of American Indians, a pan-tribal organization with local chapters on numerous reservations. Bonnin was also an active member of the General Federation of Women's Clubs.

She also continued to publish in multiple forms. In 1921 she wrote a policy brochure, *Americanize the First American: A Plan of Regeneration*, in which she continued her project of promoting education and citizenship for Indians. She also wrote a series of pieces about the California Indians that were first published in the *San Francisco Bulletin* in 1922 and then reprinted in the *California Indian Herald* as well as in pamphlet form. As both author and activist, Bonnin remained committed to Indian reform until her death in 1938. ("Cheers for the Indian Maiden," *Earlhamite*, March 1896, 187; Cox, "'Yours for the Indian Cause,'" 181–90; Davidson and Norris, Introduction, *American Indian Stories*; Littlefield and Parins, *Biobibliography: Supplement*, 178; Peyer, *American Indian Nonfiction*, 303–5)

School Days of an Indian Girl, 1900

In the January number of the *Atlantic Monthly*, Zitkala-Ša (Miss Gertrude Simmons) dwelt with much simplicity upon the picturesque "Memories of an Indian Childhood." In the magazine for February, she relates the impressions made by her school life.

Miss Simmons' work has literary quality. She has a striking gift of characterization. Her satire is keen. She excels in giving what seems to be the genuine records of the mind of a child, uncolored by later knowledge and experience. We regret that she did not once call to mind the happier side of those long school days, or even hint at the friends who did so much to break down for her the barriers of language and custom, and to lead her from poverty and insignificance into the comparatively full and rich existence that she enjoys today.

We do not for a moment believe that "Zitkala-Ša" desires to injure the cause of her own people, whose titles to the blessings of enlightenment and civilization has so lately found general recognition, but we do feel that the homesick pathos—nay, more, the underlying bitterness of her story will cause readers unfamiliar with Indian schools to form entirely wrong conclusions. Her pictures are not, perhaps, untrue in themselves, but, taken by themselves, they are sadly misleading. The following chapters will serve as examples.

The Cutting of My Long Hair

The first day in the land of apples was a bitter cold one; for the snow still covered the ground, and the trees were bare. A large bell rang for breakfast, its loud metallic voice crashing through the belfry overhead and into our sensitive ears. The annoying clatter of shoes on bare floors gave us no peace. The constant clash of harsh noises, with an unknown tongue, made a bedlam within which I was securely tied. And though my spirit tore itself in struggling for its lost freedom, all was useless.

A paleface woman, with white hair, came up after us. We were placed in a line of girls who were marching into the dining room. These were Indian girls, in stiff shows and closely clinging dresses. The small girls wore sleeved aprons and shingled hair. As I walked noiselessly in my moccasins, I felt like sinking to the floor, for my blanket had been stripped from my shoulders. I looked hard at the Indian girls, who seemed not to care that they were even more immodestly dressed than I, in their tightly fitting clothes. While we marched in, the boys entered at an opposite door. I watched for the three young braves who came in our party. I spied them in the rear ranks, looking as uncomfortable as I felt.

A small bell was tapped, and each of the pupils drew a chair from under the table. Supposing this act meant they were to be seated, I pulled out mine and at once slipped into it from one side. But when I turned my head, I saw that I was the only one seated, and all the rest at our table remained standing. Just as I began to rise, looking shyly around to see how chairs were to be used, a second bell was sounded. All were seated at last, and I had to crawl back into my chair again. I heard a man's voice at one end of the hall, and I looked around to him. But all the others hung their heads over their plates. As I glanced at the long chain of tables, I caught the eyes of a paleface woman over me. Immediately I dropped my eyes, wondering why I was so keenly watched by the strange woman. The man ceased his mutterings, and then a third bell was tapped. Everyone picked up his knife and fork and began eating. I began crying instead, for by this time I was afraid to venture anything more.

But this eating by formula was not the hardest trial in that first day. Late in the morning, my friend Judewin gave me a terrible warning. Judewin knew a few words of English; and she had overheard the paleface woman talk about cutting our long, heavy hair. Our mothers had taught us that only unskilled warriors who were captured had their hair shingled by the enemy. Among our people, short hair was worn by mourners, and shingled hair by cowards.

We discussed our fate some moments, and when Judewin said, "we have to submit because they are strong," I rebelled.

"No, I will not submit! I will struggle first!" I answered.

I watched my chance and when no one noticed I disappeared. I crept up the stairs as quietly as I could in my squeaking shoes—my moccasins had been exchanged for shoes. Along the hall I passed, without knowing whither I was going. Turning aside to an open door I found a large room with three white beds in it. The windows were covered with dark green curtains, which made the room very dim. Thankful that no one was there, I directed my steps toward the corner farthest from the door. On my hands and knees I crawled under the bed and cuddled myself in the dark corner.

From my hiding place I peered out, shuddering with fear whenever I heard footsteps near by. Though in the hall loud voices were calling my name, and I knew that even Judewin was searching for me, I did not open my mouth to answer. Then the steps were quickened and the voices became excited. The sounds came nearer and nearer. Women and girls entered the room. I held my breath and watched them open the closet doors and peep behind large trunks. Some one threw up the curtains and the room was filled with sudden light. What caused them to stoop and look under the bed I do not know. I remember being dragged out, though I resisted by kicking and scratching wildly. In spite of myself, I was carried downstairs and tied fast to a chair.

I cried aloud, shaking my head all the while until I felt the cold blades of the scissors against my neck, and heard them gnaw off one of my thick braids. Then I lost my spirit. Since the day I was taken from my mother, I had suffered extreme indignities. People had stared at me. I had been tossed about in the air like a wooden puppet. And now my long hair was shingled like a coward's! In my anguish I mourned for my mother but no one came to comfort me.

Not a soul reasoned quietly with me, as my mother used to do; for now I was only one of many little animals driven by a herder.

Iron Routine

A loud-clamoring bell awakened us at half past six in the cold winter mornings. From happy dreams of Western rolling lands and unlassoed freedom, we tumbled out upon chilly bare floors back again into a paleface day. We had short time to jump into our shoes and clothes, and wet our eyes with icy water, before a small hand bell was vigorously rung for roll call.

There were too many drowsy children and too numerous orders for the day to waste a moment in any apology to nature for giving her children such a shock in the early morning. We rushed downstairs, bounding over two high steps at a time, to land in the assembly room.

A paleface woman, with a yellow-covered roll book open on her arm and a gnawed pencil in her hand, appeared at the door. Her small tired face was coldly lighted with a pair of large grey eyes.

She stood still in a halo of authority, while over the rim of her spectacles her eyes pried nervously about the room. Having glanced at her long list of names and called out the first one, she tossed up her chin and peered through the crystals of her spectacles to make sure of the answer, "Here."

Relentlessly her pencil black-marked our daily records if we were not present to respond to our names, and no chum of ours had done it successfully for us. No matter if a dull headache or the painful cough of a slow consumption had delayed the absentee, there was only time enough to mark the tardiness. It was next to impossible to leave the iron routine after the civilizing machine had once begun its day's buzzing; and it was inbred in me to suffer in silence rather than to appeal to the ears of one whose open eyes could not see my pain, I have many times trudged in the day's harness heavy-footed, like a dumb, sick brute.

I grew bitter, and censured the woman for cruel neglect of our physical ills. I despised the pencils that moved automatically, and the one teaspoon which dealt out from a large bottle, healing to a row of variously ailing Indian children. I blamed the hard-working, well-meaning, ignorant woman who was inculcating in our hearts her superstitious ideas. Though I was sullen in all my little troubles, as soon as I felt better I was ready again to smile upon the cruel woman. Within a week I was again actively testing the chains which tightly bound my individuality like a mummy for burial.

The melancholy of those black days has left so long a shadow that it darkens the path of years that have since gone by. These sad memories rise above those of smoothly grinding school days. Perhaps my Indian nature is the moaning wind which stirs them now for their present record. But, however tempestuous this is within me, it comes out as the low voice of a curiously colored sea-shell, which is only for those ears that are bent with compassion to hear it.[1]

Letter to the *Red Man*, 1900

Zitkala-Ša writes us the following in explanation of her articles in the *Atlantic Monthly*:

I give outright the varying moods of my own evolution; those growing pains which knew not reason while active. To stir up views and earnest comparison of theories was one of the ways in which I hoped it would work a benefit to my people. No one can dispute my own impressions and bitterness! Perhaps a reason may be assigned to them—that I have left to my friends to do.[2]

A Protest Against the Abolition of the Indian Dance, 1902

There are two sides to every picture.

Zitkala-Ša, whom we know so well at Carlisle, she having been for a time a teacher with us, has made a very readable story in presenting her views on the Indian Dance, and it is a story that wins sympathizing hearts.

She is a Dakota herself, college educated and of considerable travel, and gives a native touch to the narrative that is extremely fascinating, and from her own point of view it may be true to life, but that the savage dance is the greatest possible hindrance to Indian progress is attested by others of her own race, with as much experience and education as Zitkala-Ša can claim; that however is the other side of the picture.

There is a natural way to put an end to such injurious customs.

In the early days of Carlisle it was of nightly occurrence for the crude adult natives to gather in some lonely spot and spend hours in weird song with tom-tom accompaniment.

Those old boys were never told to put away the tom-tom and to stop singing Indian songs but when the band instruments were provided, one of the oldest and most non-progressive of that first party took to the tuba, and it was not long before he could play "In the Sweet by-and-by," and he enjoyed it more than the tom-tom.

As fast as other music and entertainment gained a foothold the tom-tom and weird song were voluntarily dropped.

If amusements or pastimes of a higher order were tactfully introduced to the Indians on the reservation they would not be slow to take them up, and the old order of things would disappear.

The silly Merry-go-round is as demoralizing in character as any Indian dance could well be, and the writer has seen them patronized by Indians of all ages whole families of whom would travel miles across the plains to pay out their money to ride by the hour on the hobbyhorses erected on a prominent bluff where the whistle and steam of the little puffing engine could be seen and heard as far as eye and ear could distinguish.

No dances were carried on when the Merry-go-round was in operation.

Then why would not entertainment of a more elevating character do even a better work toward detracting from the unwholesome dance?

But let Zitkala-Ša in the land of the Dakotas paint her vivid picture in her own choice words, which were published in the Boston *Evening Transcript* last January and [have] since been copied and commented upon by several papers.

Gertrude Bonnin   259

The Story

Almost within a stone's throw from where I sit lies the great frozen Missouri. Like other reptiles, the low murmuring brown river sleeps through the winter season underneath its covering of blue sheening ice.

A man carrying a pail in one hand and an axe in the other, trudges along a narrow footpath leading to the river. Close beside the frozen stream he stands a moment motionless as if deliberating within himself. Then, leaving his pail upon the ground, he walks cautiously out upon the glass surface of the river. Fearless of the huge sleeper underneath, he swings his axe like one accustomed to the use of his weapon. Soon with the handle as a lever he pries up a round cake of ice. Hereupon great moans and yawnings creak up from some unfathomable sleep and reverberate along the quiet river bottom. The sleeping river is disturbed by the mortal's tapping upon its crusty mantle; and—restless—turns, perchance, in its bed, gently sighing in its long winter sleep.

The man stoops over the black hole he has made in that pearly river-sheet and draws up a heavy pail. Apparently satisfied, he turns away into the narrow path by which he came. Unconscious is he of the river's dream, which he may have disturbed; forgetful, too, of the murmuring water-songs he has not released through his tiny tapping! The man's small power is great enough to gain for him his small desire, a pail of winter-buried water!

Here I should have stopped writing had not the man I saw retracing safely his footsteps returned—in fancy—possessed with a strange malady. Under some wild conceit regarding the force of his pigmy hammer stroke, he labors now to awaken the sleeping old river in mid-winter. Vainly he hacks at the edge of acres of ice, while Nature seems to humor the whim by allowing so much as a square inch of the crystal to be broken.

Like our brown river, the soul of the Present Day Indian is sleeping under the icy crust of a transitional period. A whole race of strangers throngs either side of the frozen river, each one tapping the creaking ice with his own particular weapon. While the Dreamer underneath moans in disturbed visions of Hope, these people draw up each his little pail, heavy with self-justification. But where is Spring? The river dreams of springtime, when its rippling songs shall yet flood its rugged banks.

Though I love best to think the river shall in due season rush forth from its icy bondage, I am strongly drawn by an irresistible spirit to wander along the brink. A mist gathers over my sight and the celebrated art galleries of a modern city lure my notice. The geniuses of a cultured nation portray in chiseled stone figures of grace and strength in marvelous imitation of God's own subtle works. Then the inner light, burning and underneath the eyelids, dispels the darkness limiting the art ground, and there within the extended walls are the bronzed figures of Indian dancers. Aye, they are greater than the marble tribe, for they are the original works of the Supreme Artist.

As I passed by a man hacking river ice, I heard him hiss— "Immodest; the Indians' nudity in the dance is shockingly immodest!"

"Why! Does he not wear a dress of paint and loin cloth?" I would have asked; but a silence sealed my lips, and I thought: "False modesty would dress the Indian, not for protection from the winter weather, but to put overalls on the soul's improper earthly garment. I wonder how much it would abash God if, for this man's distorted sense, a dress were put on all the marble figures in art museums. It were more plausible—it seems to a looker-on—to build an annex to the "Infirmary for Ill-Humored People" where folk suffering from false sense of pride and of modesty may be properly nursed.

Again a voice speaks, "This dance of the Indian is a relic of barbarism. It must be stopped!" Then hack! hack! hack!—the little man beats the crystal ice. Before he hangs a mist-tapestry. Woven in wonderful living threads is a picture of a brilliantly lighted hall with mirrored walls. Over its polished floor glide whirling couples in pretty rhythm to orchestral music. The daintiness and exquisite web-cloth of the low-necked, sleeveless evening gowns must be so from the imperative need to distract the mind from the steel frames in which fair bodies are painfully corseted. It may be gauze-covered barbarism, for history does tell of the barbaric Teutons and Anglo-Saxons. It may be a martyrdom to some ancient superstition which centuries of civilization and Christianization have not wholly eradicated from the yellow-haired and blue-eyed races.

I do not know what special step might be considered most barbaric. In truth, I would not like to say any graceful movement of the human figure in rhythm to music was ever barbaric. Unless the little man intends to put an end to dances the world over, I fail to see the necessity of checking the Indian dance. If learned scientists advise and occasional relaxation of work or daily routine with such ardor that even the inmates of insane asylums are allowed to dance their dances then the same logic should hold good elsewhere. The law at least, should not be partial. If it is right for the insane and idiot to dance, the Indian (who is classed with them) should have the same privilege. The old illiterate Indians, with a past irrevocably dead and no future, have but a few sunny hours between them and the grave.

And this last amusement, their dance, surely is not begrudged them. The young Indian who has been taught to read English has his choice of amusements, and need not attend the old-time one. He might spend a profitable winter evening in a library, if such a provision had not been misplaced among the "castles in Spain." Unfortunately for him, there is not even a bookstore where he might buy his reading matter; and because of the inconvenient place from which I get my writing supply, I myself have at times seriously contemplated writing upon the butcher's brown wrapping-paper. But time and opportunity are within the reach of the Indian youth. With these he may yet make some "vigorous self-recovery" against odd circumstances. It is not so with the old Indian. The fathers and mothers of our tribe have not such weapons against their adversity. They are old and (I have heard them say of themselves) worthless; but what American would shuffle off an old parent as he would an old garment from the body?

At this moment I turn abruptly away, from the voices along the river brink wishing the river-hackers might first conspire with nature. Here a pony is ready, and soon a gallop over the level lands shall restore to me the sweet sense that God has allotted a place in his vast universe for each of his creatures, both great and small— just as they are.[3]

Laura Cornelius Kellogg (Oneida)

Laura Cornelius Kellogg (1880–ca. 1949) was born on the Oneida Indian Reservation in Wisconsin. Unlike many of her contemporaries, she did not attend federal boarding schools but rather studied at Grafton Hall, a private school for girls in Fond du Lac, Wisconsin, where she graduated with honors in 1898. Kellogg taught at the Sherman Institute in Riverside, California, between 1902 and 1904 before resigning to study law at Stanford University. Kellogg left Stanford after a few months and, in the fall of 1906, transferred to Barnard College, where she studied law and later social work until May 1907. She also studied at the University of Wisconsin, but she never completed her degree. Kellogg was a founding member of the Society of American Indians. Her views on the reservation differed from those of other members of the SAI. She saw the reservation as a place of opportunity, whereas many of the other members of the SAI believed that the breakup of the reservation offered the best path to citizenship. She eventually distanced herself from the SAI and expanded her concept of transforming reservations into industrial villages in her only published book, *Our Democracy and the American Indian* (1920). While Kellogg is best known for her legacy with the SAI and her book, less known is her lifelong activism for the Six Nations land claims and her other writings, which include short stories, essays, and poetry. (Ackley and Stanciu, *Laura Cornelius Kellogg*, 6, 12; Peyer, *American Indian Nonfiction*, 318–19)

Indian Public Opinion, 1902

The last few issues of Carlisle's publications have so aroused my interest that I cannot refrain from humbly participating in an "Indian Council." Not that the pages of the little paper have been filled, lately, with literature superior than formerly, but the part in it I like better is INDIANS' public opinion.

I feel like living when I hear educated Indians advancing well-balanced ideas. It looks as if we [are] about to redeem our racial mental debility when we have opinions worth expressing, and express them.

For what, after all, is Public Opinion but literature? And literature in time makes and establishes the mental development of a people.

I like much perusing the artistic views of our own Native genius, Zitkala-Ša, on The Indian Dance, and I had to listen to that exponent of Carlisle, Dr. Montezuma, for the practical side bearing upon the subject.[1]

To this extent I agree with the former, that that element of our race which has no future is truly pitiable, that element whose present is a life of constraint and starvation of development, is a heartbreaking thing to look upon, but the latter points out that the present pleasure of the Indian dance is a corruption of sacred rite, and since it is an irreverent imitation, its tendencies cannot be wholesome.

Naturally the beat of the drum wakes up the human desire for recreation long pent up by the dead environment of reserve existence, and thither will go a weak youth, who once in the whirl of such doings forgets the moral and social codes that have replaced those of barbarism, only to wake up on the morrow, a shamefaced idiot, with the manhood gone, that perchance has been Carlisle's hard won years.

So debased pleasure can undo honorable labor, so is ultimate transition retarded.

And can we afford as a race, and individually, to lose thus not only time, which is gold, but honor, the greatest and our all?[2]

John Milton Oskison (Cherokee)

John Milton Oskison (1874–1947) was born in Vinita, Cherokee Nation. He attended Willie Halsell College along with his friend Will Rogers. After graduating in 1894 he studied at Stanford University and graduated with a bachelor's degree in 1898. At Stanford he began publishing articles and short stories. After winning a writing contest sponsored by *Century Magazine* in 1899 while doing graduate work at Harvard, he decided to become a professional writer. He published numerous short stories in popular American magazines such as *Century*, *McClure's*, and *Collier's*. From 1903 to 1906 he was an editorial writer on the New York *Evening Post*, and from 1907 to 1910 he was an associate editor for *Collier's*. He was a founding member of the Society of American Indians, and in 1917 he served as vice-president. His essays on Indian affairs were published in boarding school newspapers and the SAI's magazine, where he was a contributing editor. (Larré, *John Milton Oskison*, 1–4; Littlefield and Parins, *Biobibliography: Supplement*, 261; Peyer, *American Indian Nonfiction*, 382) [1]

The Outlook for the Indian, 1903

> The first and most important step towards the absorption of the Indian is to teach him to earn his living.
> —President Roosevelt, in his last message to Congress

Fortunately for the white race that has extended our frontiers, the "bad" Indian has long ago ceased to exist; fortunately for the Indian who must still face the problem of living, the time has passed when the lawless, cynical white man can appropriate his reservations with impunity and have him "suppressed" when he begins to ask for justice. We are far enough away from the crunching of cavalry hoofs and the rallying yell of warriors to see that there are two sides to the question. Only the most rabid and ignorant enemies of the Indian still maintain that unfortunate, cynical doctrine that "the only good Indian is a dead Indian." And only the most obstinate of our Indians still rail against the domination of the white race.

It is a hopeful fact that the leaders among the various societies formed to protect and befriend the Indian have substituted personal knowledge and close observation for an enthusiastic but ignorant sympathy. They have come to understand that an Indian is a human being with a long and significant history behind him, with a very well-worked-out moral law, and with a tradition of living that is not easy to give up. Likewise, the Indian has come to understand that the white man has a tradition of living to maintain, and that it is not altogether greed and hatred that have sent him forward across frontiers. Tolerance increases.

Now that the races have come to know each other better and have laid aside the old distrust and fear, we hear those who are qualified to speak with authority say that the next inevitable step is the complete absorption of the Indian into the white race, which will result in an ultimate amalgamation of the two. This is an idea that is worth considering. The sooner all the foolish talk about the impossibility of uniting the two people ceases, the better.

Commissioner Jones, in a recent report, calls attention to the fact that the nation has expended over a billion dollars in subduing and attempting to educate the Indians, only to learn of the absolute failure of the "ration system" as a device for making useful or productive citizens of them. That the policy of feeding the Indian at public expense on reservations was the outgrowth of a mistaken philanthropy and was foolish in that it exempted the Indian from the natural and inexorable law that man must earn his living by labor of some kind is now universally recognized. How to rectify the errors growing out of this policy and supplant it by a system that would ultimately induce the Indian to put his hand to the plow is a problem that has engaged the study and activity of Commissioner Jones since his induction into office.

The most radical change inaugurated was the departure from the custom of dealing with the tribe to that of dealing with the individual. The results attending this change, according to Commissioner Jones, have been most gratifying. The manhood of the Indian is appealed to, and he is taught self-reliance and self-respect. As a result of this policy, over 12,000 have been dropped from the ration roll, being wholly self-supporting, and others not yet self-supporting have been put to work. The Indians will become self-supporting, and will adapt themselves to their white neighbors' way of life—there is no doubt of it. But they are not yet ready for the struggle on equal terms; they must be protected from speculators and land-grabbers; they must be led to see what economic independence really means; and their education must be adapted to the needs of their future life. Think of them how we will, we cannot close our eyes to the fact that they are still children, with all of the child's ignorance of modern life, with the child's helplessness in practical affairs. For a little longer the "Great Father" at Washington must direct them.

How constant must be the "Great Father's" vigilance is shown almost every day. It is interesting to compare a part of Mr. Hamlin Garland's last novel, *The Captain of the Gray Horse Troop*, with the story of the Standing Rock cattle leases. In the course of the contest over the Standing Rock land leases, now more than a year ago, it became necessary for the Indians to send a delegation of Sioux chiefs to Washington, where, after waiting two weeks, they met the Senate committee on Indian Affairs. They convinced the senators that the cattlemen's contract, if carried out, would amount to robbery, and would delay the time when the tribe could take up the work of grazing and farming on their own account. The publicity given the matter by the visit of the chiefs led to its being referred directly to President Roosevelt who sent Dr. George Bird Grinnell to Standing Rock. The matter gained wide publicity and it is not improbable that the disclosures made by the Grinnell report will result in the appointment of another agent at Standing Rock. Here is Mr. Garland's tale worked out in actual life almost before the book was off the press. And, as in the novel, there is a distinctly hopeful ending to the story. Everywhere it is true that eternal vigilance is still necessary to ensure the Indians a chance even to earn a living. Moreover they must be taught how to work. It is not yet enough to say, "Here are lands well protected and productive: take them and develop their resources." The Indians do not know how to do it, and they must learn.

The founders of the new Sherman Institute at Riverside, California, have set an excellent example.[2] Here a farm of one hundred acres has been purchased, all under irrigation; ample buildings have been erected to accommodate over three hundred children from the Pacific Coast tribes and those in the Southwest where irrigation must be resorted to in order to raise crops. The idea is to train them in this peculiar method so that the graduates may return to their people equipped for the task of turning deserts into rich fields with the aid of precious water. For the girls there is to be instruction in lace making, dressmaking, fine needlework, basketry, plain sewing, and housework—with all that ranch housekeeping implies. And the peculiar value of an institution like this is that its members can go out of the school to the reservation and take up the work of making a living without readjusting themselves to different methods of work from those prevailing at the training school in a far-away state. If a man is to grow alfalfa to make his land yield a living he is not likely to appreciate half a dozen years of instruction in the planting and cultivation of corn and cotton. For this reason the neighborhood school for industrial training is of the greatest value.

In the Indian Territory, where, for more than twenty years, the tribes have come into competition with the whites as farmers, stock-raisers, teachers, lawyers, and tradesmen, the process of absorption is far advanced and education has also advanced rapidly. The

Cherokees maintain three boarding schools and one colored high school. The enrollment in these four schools is something under five hundred and the expense of maintaining them amounts to about $140.00 a year per capita. For seven months in the twelve one hundred and twenty-four day, or neighborhood, schools, are run, with an average enrollment of 2,200, at a cost of about $14.00 per capita. It is estimated that there are some 8,300 children of school age in the tribe. In the Creek Nation nine boarding schools and fifty-five neighborhood schools are maintained, with an average attendance of over 1,500. The figures for the Choctaw Nation show six boarding, and one hundred and ten day schools, with an enrollment of more than 2,100. Five academies and seventeen primary schools with an approximate enrollment of 850 are supported by the Chickasaw Indians.

Mere figures, of course, have little meaning in themselves, but when it is known that all of these children are coming out of the schools to enter upon a course of life that brings them into contact with the whites—many of the girls to become the wives of white men—they assume importance. They mean that the Indian problem, so far as the tribes of the Territory are concerned, is being solved by extinguishing the Indian as a distinctive individual and merging him with his white neighbors and competitors. They mean that this process is going on more and more rapidly, and that when the Territory is brought into the ranks of the states, Indians and whites alike will be ready to take up the everyday work of a rich and prosperous commonwealth and do it successfully. And that, after all, is the problem in every tribe.[3]

The Problem of Old Harjo, 1907

The Spirit of the Lord had descended upon old Harjo.[4] From the new missionary, just out from New York, he had learned that he was a sinner. The fire in the new missionary's eyes and her gracious appeal had convinced old Harjo that this was the time to repent and be saved. He was very much in earnest, and he assured Miss Evans that he wanted to be baptized and received into the church at once. Miss Evans was enthusiastic and went to Mrs. Rowell with the news. It was Mrs. Rowell who had said that it was no use to try to convert the older Indians, and she, after fifteen years of work in Indian Territory missions, should have known. Miss Evans was pardonably proud of her conquest.

"Old Harjo converted!" exclaimed Mrs. Rowell. "Dear Miss Evans, do you know that old Harjo has two wives?" To the older woman it was as if someone had said to her, "Madame, the Sultan of Turkey wishes to teach one of your mission Sabbath school classes."

"But," protested the younger woman, "he is really sincere, and—."

"Then ask him," Mrs. Rowell interrupted a bit sternly, "if he will put away one of his wives. Ask him, before he comes into the presence of the Lord, if he is willing to conform to the laws of the country in which he lives, the country that guarantees his idle existence. Miss Evans, your work is not even begun." No one who knew Mrs. Rowell would say that she lacked sincerity and patriotism. Her own cousin was an earnest crusader against Mormonism, and had gathered a goodly share of that wagonload of protests that the Senate had been asked to read when it was considering whether a certain statesman of Utah should be allowed to represent his state at Washington.[5]

In her practical, tactful way, Mrs. Rowell had kept clear of such embarrassments. At first, she had written letters of indignant protest to the Indian Office against the toleration of bigamy amongst the tribes. A wise inspector had been sent to the mission, and this man had pointed out that it was better to ignore certain things, "deplorable, to be sure," than to attempt to make over the habits of the old men. Of course, the young Indians would not be permitted to take more than one wife each.

So Mrs. Rowell had discreetly limited her missionary efforts to the young, and had exercised toward the old and bigamous only that strict charity which even a hopeless sinner might claim.

Miss Evans, it was to be regretted, had only the vaguest notions about "expediency"; so weak on matters of doctrine was she that the news that Harjo was living with two wives didn't startle her. She was young and possessed of but one enthusiasm—that for saving souls.

"I suppose," she ventured, "that old Harjo *must* put away one wife before he can join the church?"

"There can be no question about it, Miss Evans."

"Then I shall have to ask him to do it." Miss Evans regretted the necessity for forcing this sacrifice, but had no doubt that the Indian would make it an order to accept the gift of salvation which she was commissioned to bear to him.

Harjo lived in a "double" log cabin three miles from the mission. His ten acres of corn had been gathered into its fence-rail crib; four hogs that were to furnish his winter's bacon had been brought in from the woods and penned conveniently near to the crib; out in a corner of the garden, a fat mound of dirt rose where the crop of turnips and potatoes had been buried against the corrupting frost; and in the hayloft of his log stable were stored many pumpkins, dried corn, onions (suspended in bunches from the rafters) and the varied forage that Mrs. Harjo number one and Mrs. Harjo number two had thriftily provided. Three cows, three young heifers, two colts, and two patient, capable mares bore the Harjo brand, a fantastic "**HH**" that the old man had designed. Materially, Harjo was solvent; and if the Government had ever come to his aid he could not recall the date.

This attempt to rehabilitate old Harjo morally, Miss Evans felt, was not one to be made at the mission; it should be undertaken in the Creek's own home where the evidences of his sin should confront him as she explained.

When Miss Evans rode up to the block in front of Harjo's cabin, the old Indian came out, slowly and with a broadening smile of welcome on his face. A clean gray flannel shirt had taken the place of the white collarless garment, with crackling stiff bosom, that he had worn to the mission meetings. Comfortable, well-patched moccasins had been substituted for creaking boots, and brown cordu-roys, belted in at the waist, for tight black trousers. His abundant gray hair fell down on his shoulders. In his eyes, clear and large and black, glowed the light of true hospitality. Miss Evans thought of the patriarchs as she saw him lead her horse out to the stable; thus Abraham might have looked and lived.

"Harjo," began Miss Evans before following the old man to the covered passageway between the disconnected cabins, "is it true that you have two wives?" Her tone was neither stern nor accusatory. The Creek had heard that question before, from scandalized mis-sionaries and perplexed registry clerks when he went to Muscogee to enroll himself and his family in one of the many "final" records ordered to be made by the Government preparatory to dividing the Creek lands among the individual citizens.

For answer, Harjo called, first into the cabin that was used as a kitchen and then, in a loud, clear voice, toward the small field, where Miss Evans saw a flock of half-grown turkeys running about in the corn stubble. From the kitchen emerged a tall, thin Indian woman of fifty-five, with a red handkerchief bound severely over her head. She spoke to Miss Evans and sat down in the passageway. Presently, a clear, sweet voice was heard in the field; a stout, handsome woman, about the same age as the other, climbed the rail fence and came up to the house. She, also, greeted Miss Evans briefly. Then she carried a tin basin to the well near by, where she filled it to the brim. Setting it down on the horse block, she rolled back her sleeves, tucked in the collar of her gray blouse, and plunged her face in the water. In a minute she came out of the kitchen freshened and smiling. 'Liza Harjo had been pulling dried bean stalks at one end of the field, and it was dirty work. At last old Harjo turned to Miss Evans and said, "These two my wife—this one 'Liza, this one Jennie."

It was done with simple dignity. Miss Evans bowed and stam-mered. Three pairs of eyes were turned upon her in patient, cour-teous inquiry.

John Milton Oskison   273

It was hard to state the case. The old man was so evidently proud of his women, and so flattered by Miss Evans' interest in them, that he would find it hard to understand. Still, it had to be done, and Miss Evans took the plunge.

"Harjo, you want to come into our church?" The old man's face lighted.

"Oh, yes, I would come to Jesus, please, my friend."

"Do you know, Harjo, that the Lord commanded that one man should mate with but one woman? The question was stated again in simpler terms, and the Indian replied, "Me know that now, my friend. Long time ago"—Harjo plainly meant the whole period previous to his conversion—"me did not know. The Lord Jesus did not speak to me in that time and so I was blind. I do what blind man do."

"Harjo, you must have only one wife when you come into our church. Can't you give up one of these women?" Miss Evans glanced at the two, sitting by with smiles of polite interest on their faces, understanding nothing. They had not shared Harjo's enthusiasm either for the white man's God or his language.

"Give up my wife?" A sly smile stole over his face. He leaned closer to Miss Evans. "You tell me, my friend, which one I give up." He glanced from 'Liza to Jennie as if to weigh their attractions, and the two rewarded him with their pleasantest smiles. "You tell me which one," he urged.

"Why, Harjo, how can I tell you!" Miss Evans had little sense of humor; she had taken the old man seriously.

"Then," Harjo sighed, continuing the comedy, for surely the missionary was jesting with him, "'Liza and Jennie must say." He talked to the Indian women for a time, and they laughed heartily. 'Liza, pointing to the other, shook her head. At length Harjo explained, "My friend, they cannot say. Jennie, she would run a race to see which one stay, but Liza, she say no, she is fat and cannot run."

Miss Evans comprehended at last. She flushed angrily, and protested, "Harjo, you are making a mock of a sacred subject; I cannot allow you to talk like this."

"But did you not speak in fun, my friend ?" Harjo queried, sobering. "Surely you have just said what your friend, the white woman at the mission (he meant Mrs. Rowell) would say, and you do not mean what you say."

"Yes, Harjo, I mean it. It is true that Mrs. Rowell raised the point first, but I agree with her. The church cannot be defiled by receiving a bigamist into its membership." Harjo saw that the young woman was serious, distressingly serious. He was silent for a long time, but at last he raised his head and spoke quietly, "It is not good to talk like that if it is not in fun."

He rose and went to the stable. As he led Miss Evans' horse up to the block it was champing a mouthful of corn, the last of a generous portion that Harjo had put before it. The Indian held the bridle and waited for Miss Evans to mount. She was embarrassed, humiliated, angry. It was absurd to be dismissed in this way by—"by an ignorant old bigamist!" Then the humor of it burst upon her, and its human aspect. In her anxiety concerning the spiritual welfare of the sinner Harjo, she had insulted the man Harjo. She began to understand why Mrs. Rowell had said that the old Indians were hopeless.

"Harjo," she begged, coming out of the passageway, "please forgive me. I do not want you to give up one of your wives. Just tell me why you took them."

"I will tell you that, my friend." The old Creek looped the reins over his arm and sat down on the block. "For thirty years Jennie has lived with me as my wife. She is of the Bear people, and she came to me when I was thirty-five and she was twenty-five. She could not come before, for her mother was old, very old, and Jennie, she stay with her and feed her.

"So, when I was thirty years old I took 'Liza for my woman. She is of the Crow people. She help me make this little farm here when there was no farm for many miles around.

John Milton Oskison   275

"Well, five years 'Liza and me, we live here and work hard. But there was no child. Then the old mother of Jennie she died, and Jennie got no family left in this part of the country. So 'Liza say to me, 'Why don't you take Jennie in here?' I say, 'You don't care?' and she say, 'No, maybe we have children here then.' But we have no children—never have children. We do not like that, but God He would not let it be. So, we have lived here thirty years very happy. Only just now you make me sad."

"Harjo," cried Miss Evans, "forget what I said. Forget that you wanted to join the church." For a young mission worker with a single purpose always before her, Miss Evans was saying a strange thing. Yet she couldn't help saying it; all of her zeal seemed to have been dissipated by a simple statement of the old man.

"I cannot forget to love Jesus, and I want to be saved," Old Harjo spoke with solemn earnestness. The situation was distracting. On one side stood a convert eager for the protection of the church, asking only that he be allowed to fulfill the obligations of humanity and on the other stood the church, represented by Mrs. Rowell, that set an impossible condition on receiving old Harjo to itself. Miss Evans wanted to cry; prayer, she felt, would be entirely inadequate as a means of expression.

"Oh! Harjo," she cried out, "I don't know what to do. I must think it over and talk with Mrs. Rowell again."

But Mrs. Rowell could suggest no way out; Miss Evans' talk with her only gave the older woman another opportunity to preach the folly of wasting time on the old and "unreasonable" Indians. Certainly the church could not listen even to a hint of a compromise in this case. If Harjo wanted to be saved there was one way and only one—unless—

"Is either of the two women old? I mean, so old that she is—an—"

"Not at all," answered Miss Evans. "They're both strong and—yes, happy. I think they will outlive Harjo."

"Can't you appeal to one of the women to go away? I dare say we could provide for her." Miss Evans, incongruously, remembered Jennie's jesting proposal to race for the right to stay with Harjo. What could the mission provide as a substitute for the little home that 'Liza had helped to create there in the edge of the woods? What other home would satisfy Jennie?

"Mrs. Rowell, are you sure that we ought to try to take one of Harjo's women from him? I'm not sure that it would in the least advance morality amongst the tribe, but I'm certain that it would make three gentle people unhappy for the rest of their lives."

"You may be right, Miss Evans." Mrs. Rowell was not seeking to create unhappiness, for enough of it inevitably came to be pictured in the little mission building. "You may be right," she repeated, "but it is a grievous misfortune that old Harjo should wish to unite with the church."

No one was more regular in his attendance at the mission meetings than old Harjo. Sitting well forward, he was always in plain view of Miss Evans at the organ. Before the service began, and after it was over, the old man greeted the young woman. There was never a spoken question, but in the Creek's eyes was always a mute inquiry. Once Miss Evans ventured to write to her old pastor in New York, and explain her trouble. This was what he wrote in reply: "I am surprised that you are troubled, for I should have expected you to rejoice, as I do, over this new and wonderful evidence of the Lord's reforming power. Though the church cannot receive the old man so long as he is confessedly a bigamist and violator of his country's just laws, you should be greatly strengthened in your work through bringing him to desire salvation."

"Oh! It's easy to talk when you're free from responsibility!" cried out Miss Evans. "But I woke him up to a desire for this water of salvation that he cannot take. I have seen Harjo's home, and I know how cruel and useless it would be to urge him to give up what he loves—for he does love those two women who have spent half their lives and more with him. What, what can be done?"

Month after month, as old Harjo continued to occupy his seat in the mission meetings, with that mute appeal in his eyes and a persistent light of hope on his face, Miss Evans repeated the question, "What can be done?" If she was sometimes tempted to say to the old man, "Stop worrying about your soul; you'll get to Heaven as surely as any of us," there was always Mrs. Rowell to remind her that she was not a Mormon missionary. She could not run away from her perplexity. If she should secure a transfer to another station, she felt that Harjo would give up coming to the meetings, and in his despair become a positive influence for evil amongst his people. Mrs. Rowell would not waste her energy on an obstinate old man. No, Harjo was her creation, her impossible convert, and throughout the years, until death—the great solvent which is not always a solvent—came to one of them, would continue to haunt her.

And meanwhile, what?[6]

The Indian in the Professions, 1912

My business, or profession, is writing and editing. In my small way, I've tried to make myself an interpreter of the world, of the modern, progressive Indian. The greatest handicap I have is my enthusiasm. I know a lot of Indians who are making good; I know how sturdily they have set their faces toward the top of the hill, and how they've tramped on when the temptation to step aside and rest was strongest. When I try to write about them I lose my critical sense. Then the editors sympathize—"Too bad he's got that Indian bug"—and ask me about the cowboys. Now, I'll write fiction about cowboys, make 'em yip-yap and shoot their forty-fours till everybody's deaf, but I will not repeat the old lies about the Indian for any editor that ever paid on acceptance!

"Most of the Indians that go through Carlisle really *do* go back to the blanket, don't they?" It was an assertion rather than a question, and a modern magazine editor made it to me not a year ago.

"You're wrong," I said. "I can send you accurate statistics compiled by Mr. Friedman, superintendent of the school, which show exactly what has become of the Carlisle graduates. They go back to useful, serviceable lives. They plow and trade, become soldiers and mechanics, enter the professions—teaching, nursing, the law, the diplomatic service, the ministry, medicine, politics, dentistry, veterinary surgery, writing, painting, acting. If you want me to do it, I'll assemble a gallery of individual Indians who are getting to the top of their professions in a friendly, honorable competition with 90 million white Americans that will fill half of your magazine."

Did he want me to do it? Not he! Better for him one Indian who had slumped than a hundred who had pushed ahead. If only Congressman Carter or Senator Curtis would go back to the tepee and the blanket![7] That would be a story worth telling!

Let us develop this profession of reformer; let us develop self-confidence—make ourselves effective, sane, and scientific. Cut out mere complaining, and develop the lawyer's habit of investigation and clear arrangement of facts.

Last Spring, at Carlisle, I heard a Siceni Nori, a graduate of the school of 1894, talk to the graduating class of 1911. Mr. Nori is, I believe, a Pueblo Indian, and is a teacher at Carlisle. I should like to quote all of that good speech to you, changing it here and there to make it fit you. The gist of one paragraph I cannot resist using. It is one in which Mr. Nori ran over a list of Carlisle graduates who are making good in business and the professions:

"If it shall be the pleasure of any one here to take a trip to Cuba and it becomes necessary to have the assistance of a dentist, just look up Dr. James E. Johnson, who is enjoying an annual income of $4,000, and his wife, also a graduate, employed by the government at a salary of $1,200 per annum; or, if you desire to take the water trip, take the Pennsylvania Limited and go to Tiffin, Ohio, where you will find Dr. Caleb Sickles, another graduate and a prominent dentist who is equally successful; then, if you have time, go to Oneida, Wisconsin, where you will find Dr. Powlas, a prominent physician who has the largest practice at his home at DePere, Wis., and is a real leader and missionary among his people. Then proceed to Minnesota and find Carlisle graduates practicing law and other professions in the persons of Thomas Mani, Edward Rogers, and Dr. Oscar Davis. Or, if you took the southern way you would find along the Santa Fe route, Carlisle graduates and ex-students working in the various railroad shops and taking care of sections of that great railroad system, preferred above all other kinds of skilled labor, for they have shown their worth as good workmen. Or, you might meet Chas. A. Dagenett, a graduate, who is National Supervisor of Indian Employment, and who has by experience gained here at this school under the Outing System, been able by untiring effort, to systematize and build up what is really the Carlisle Outing System for the entire Indian Service, and for 300,000 Indians. It is not often possible to find a man who can be equally successful in everything that he attempts, but we have in a Carlisle graduate, Chas. A. Bender, the world-famous pitcher of the Philadelphia Athletics, a crack marksman and a jeweler by trade, and a past-master in all."

Every month I get the *Southern Workman*, the school magazine published at Hampton. Over in the back is a department of "Indian notes," which is inspiring reading. Here are printed bits of news of Indian graduates who are busy in the world. In one paragraph you will read that Elizabeth Bender is taking a nurse's training at the Hahnemann Hospital in Philadelphia; in another that Eli Beardsley has gone to take a job as engineer at the Grand River School in South Dakota; in a third, that Jacob Morgan, a Navajo, is working as a missionary among his people in New Mexico.[8] Month after month the list of those who graduate into the professions lengthens. And not only at Carlisle and Hampton are the professions recruiting Indian members, but Haskell and Sherman Institute, the high schools of Oklahoma and scattered colleges from Dartmouth to the University of Washington are turning them out. With me at Stanford University was an Indian named Jeffe, from Washington. Not only was he a good football player, but one of the best students we had in our law department. Another law student who came to Stanford in my time was a Cherokee named Hughes. He had previously spent two years in Dartmouth. Last fall at Muskogee, I had a good talk with a young Cherokee named Bushyhead, son of a former chief of my tribe.[9] He had just come back from six months in Mexico where he went to learn Spanish. He was fitting himself for an appointment in the Diplomatic Service.

How many here know Little Bison, that thin-faced, keen-eyed Sioux who wants to colonize Nicaragua with American Indians? There's the type of professional man who stirs the imagination! Professionally, Little Bison is a veterinary surgeon—very modestly, he told me once that there isn't a better horse doctor in the country— but he has also been a showman, an artist's model, a companion for an invalid man who wanted to see the ends of the earth before he died. Now he is a colonizer, a practical diplomat having business with the Estradas and the Zelayas of Central America. He comes to my mind, a figure of adventure, out of a tropical upland where the bright-plumed parrots screech. He brings the bright feathers and stories about curing a mule for a native of Nicaragua; about the fine land waiting for development, and about the power 5,000 Indian men would be down there when a revolution broke out.

To my mind Little Bison is a type of promise. He lives by his wits. And that is my definition of a professional man. Not to follow worn trails, but to be ready to break out new ones—let this be the aim of those of us who enter the professions—whatever they be.

The professions are wide open to us. We have the strength and the steadiness of will to make good in them. Prejudice against the

Indian simply does not exist among the people who can make or mar a career. Always the climb for the top will be going on. The Indian who fits himself for the company of those at the top will go up. He will go as swiftly and as surely as his white brother. There is no easy, short road up—either for the Indian or for the white man. Conscientious, thorough training, character, hard work—the formula for success in the professions, is simple. I believe the average Indian would rather work his brain than his hands. That has been accounted our misfortune. *I* think it will be our salvation. There is room for us in the professions, there is a wide market for brains.[10]

Address by J. M. Oskison, 1912

My friends, I am an Indian; I was born and raised among them; but it has taken me a long time to figure out a satisfactory explanation of my interest in them. Naturally, we are not very much interested in people we are familiar with. I find this interest growing all the time. For an explanation my mind has gone back to a process of building up an ideal which went on in my youth.

I never read very much good literature when I was young—mostly the novels that you can buy for five cents and which are published in Augusta, Maine. They were not usually standard works, however full of romance and blood they might be, so it happened that I did not read Aesop's Fables until I went to college. Doubtless, there is a craving in every child's mind which Aesop's Fables satisfies. I did not find them, so I built up a sort of symbolism of my own to take their place.

I remember when I was quite small the family acquired a gray mule about 15½ hands high. He was a solid, square-rigged type of mule. I grew up alongside that mule, and had a lot to do with him personally. At first, I thought he was about the meanest and laziest and orneriest mule I ever heard of. Every time I turned away or dropped the whip, that mule would slow down. It happened that it was I usually who had to make him hustle; one day I would be driving him to the plow, the next day I would be driving him to town for something. Later on, the family acquired some cattle, and I was promoted to the job of cowboy. My first mount, as a matter of course, was that obstinate, lazy gray mule. For a long time I felt that Heaven for me would be to get rid of that mule forever. No such luck. The mule flourished, and grew more vigorous with age.

After awhile, I began to ask myself what there was about this mule that was enduring; what it was that was turning my impatience into genuine liking. It seemed to me that he grew more desirable; a little more of a friend; and it came to a point when I would rather have that gray mule assigned to me than any other animal on the ranch. When I grew older, about 16 or 17, the mule about the same age, I found that he had survived a great many of the horses we had acquired at the same time we bought him. I don't know whether that mule is dead yet. When I left the ranch, and went to college, he was still a pretty good mule, still going strong.

Very slowly, as I have battered away at the world with my pen, an Aesop's Fable of my own has been worked out in my mind. I learned that in the story of the gray mule was a moral, and it was up to me somehow to utilize that moral. Since taking my farewell of him, I have held six positions as writer and editor, each a little better than the one before. I am about to go on to number seven. There was a lesson in that plugging, enduring gray mule that I tried hard to learn. I have tried to apply it, not only to my own life, but, also, by way of explanation, to other Indians who have grown up under my eye and are doing the work of grown-ups. I have thought to myself—and this is a tribute to the Indian—we are a great deal like that gray mule. We are lazy. You have got to spur us on, but we are dependable. You know we are there.

That gray mule could not outrun a pampered yearling, but he always got the yearling! The more I go about among the Indians, the more firmly convinced I am that you can depend on them. They are there. They deliver the goods in the end.

John Milton Oskison   283

From many schools throughout the country, trained Indians have gone out to show their quality. I know a good many of them who have not been at Carlisle or any other Indian school. Indian friends of mine, too, are graduates of Princeton, Harvard, Dartmouth, Columbia, Stanford, and of other colleges, and they have always panned out. School-trained or not, it is a habit of theirs to make good. They have always justified my reading of the gray mule fable.

On behalf of the gray mule, and on behalf of these Indians from other schools and all sorts of trades, I thank you very sincerely for this opportunity to speak to you this evening.[11]

An Indian Animal Story, 1914

Long time ago, when any little boy among the Indians wanted to stay inside the house and watch the men play the wheel and stone game, instead of going out with his bow and arrows to the woods, the old men would call him to the door and whisper:

"Little one, if you stay to watch the gamblers, you will get a striped head like the bullfrog." And then the little boy would ask why the bullfrog has a striped head. And this is the story which the old men would tell:

Way over in the west, beyond the place where the sun goes down, and right next door to Thunder, was the house of Untsaiyi, the greatest gambler that ever lived. People called him "Brass"—he was so hard that he never took any pity on those who came to play with him, but after he had won all the fine things they owned, he would ask them to play for their lives, and when he had won for the last time, he would kill the one who played with him.

In all the time that "Brass" lived beyond the gate of the west, only Thunder ever succeeded in winning any games from him.

Now, the bullfrog had heard about Untsaiyi a great many times, but he did not believe that "Brass" was such a fine gambler as people said he was.

Once, the bullfrog said this to the Wild Boy of the woods.

"Then," said the Wild Boy, "you will know. And before you go, I will call on 'Brass' and fix up a plan. Goodbye!" And the Wild Boy ran off.

After the bullfrog had studied over what the Wild Boy had told him, he thought he would try a game with "Brass." So, he packed up some parched corn and started out to call on Untsaiyi. No one ever came to the house of Untsaiyi who was not given a hearty welcome and asked to eat and drink with him. So, when "Brass" and the bullfrog were eating their supper together, they talked about what they would gamble for when the game began by the light of the fire.

Now, the wild boy had already been to talk with Untsaiyi, and had told him what the last wager was to be. But "Brass" put his hand under his chin as if he was studying hard about what to say, and finally spoke:

"When we get to the last wager, this is what we shall gamble for: the one who wins shall scratch some marks on the head of the one who loses."

"All right" said the bullfrog, "and I am ready to begin."

So, they sat down in the light of the fire and began to play the wheel and stone game. And time after time, as the wheel rolled on the stone, Untsaiyi would cry out:

"You see, I have won!" And then the bullfrog would pay the wager. After a long time the bullfrog had nothing more to bet, and then "Brass" cried out:

"This time, the winner will scratch some deep marks in the head of the loser!" And the bullfrog nodded and sent the wheel rolling.

"You have lost!" cried Untsaiyi, and he came to where the bullfrog sat and ran his fingernails deep across the head of the bullfrog. And to this day you will see the yellow stripes across his head.[12]

Arthur Caswell Parker (Seneca)

Arthur Caswell Parker (1881–1955) was born on the Cattaraugus Seneca Indian Reservation in New York. The family moved to a suburb of New York City in 1891. Parker graduated from a public high school in 1897. He attended Centenary Collegiate Institute and Dickinson Seminary. He also attended Harvard and the University of Rochester. After serving as ethnologist for the New York State Library in 1903–4, he worked as archaeologist for the New York State Museum until 1924. He then served as director of the Municipal Museum in Rochester until his retirement in 1946. Parker joined the Society of American Indians in 1911, serving as secretary-treasurer from 1912 to 1915 and as president from 1916 to 1918. He also served as editor of the SAI's magazine from 1913 until Gertrude Bonnin assumed the position in 1918. Besides his editorials, he wrote several essays, reprinted here, that were published in boarding school newspapers. He also produced collections of Seneca oral stories, a biography of Ely S. Parker, a juvenile novel, and numerous anthropological writings, including the trilogy *Iroquois Uses of Maize and Other Food Plants* (1910), *The Code of Handsome Lake, the Seneca Prophet* (1913), and *The Constitution of the Five Nations* (1916). (Littlefield and Parins, *Biobibliography: Supplement*, 263; Peyer, *American Indian Nonfiction*, 358–60)

Making New Americans from Old, 1911

America is the great mixing bowl of races wherein by some cosmic alchemy the great ruling race of the world is to be produced. Every racial element which is in the country today, or which is coming into the country tomorrow, is a potential element of the American race of the future. One of the first duties of a nation to itself is the insurance of its future quality. This means the Americanizing of the new elements which come to us, and it means likewise the Americanizing of the old elements. The diseases of Americanism do not constitute the healthy ideal. Graft, political corruption and money madness are disorders, not ideals.

The Aboriginal American, the Indian of our country, is destined to become an element in and of the new American race. The Indian cannot always remain an Indian. This is plainly evident. Either he must continue to suffer and to witness the degeneration of his tribe and its individuals, or he must become so imbued with the spirit of the new America that he absorb its teachings and save himself. The old America with its traditions is forever beyond his grasp. The new America with its wealth of opportunity is before him, and he must grasp it with a grip that knows no breaking.

Thus must the old American strive and attain. I say *he must* but left to himself he will not. Do you wonder why he will not? All races are not the same in many respects, and the aboriginal American race is not an *imitative race* as some are, but it is a race that loves and clings to that which itself has created. There is virtue in this. If the Indian will not grasp civilization unaided it must be brought to him. The race which supplanted the Indian in his own ancient home has its duty. This brings me back to the proposition that one of the first duties of a nation is to insure its future quality. The white American cannot afford to neglect the Indian American, for to do so would mean the injury of the future race. Realizing these facts, the government and the churches have expended time and money for the education and Christianizing of the Indian. Mighty work has been done, and one has only to review the history of the Indian schools and missions, to realize that greater Christian zeal, however, are urgent necessities.

The Indians whom I know best are the Iroquois of New York and Canada. In New York there are some 5,000 Iroquois living as a distinct people within the environments of civilization. They have outlived the conditions and necessities of barbarism, their cultural stage at the time of the discovery. They are surrounded by white people and have absorbed a large percentage of white blood. The average so-called New York Indian is in reality at least one-quarter white, and the percentage of white blood is yearly increasing, so that many nominal Indians are in reality white people. Notwithstanding, these mixed bloods are forced by the system under which they live to retain, develop, conserve, and propagate all the factors and elements that go to make up the peculiar problem that we call the Indian problem.

Strange to say, the Iroquois of New York, with all their boasted independence, are today a dependent people. This is not entirely their fault, for it is the result of a combination of circumstances not entirely of their own making. Treaties and concessions on the part of the State and various churches, have led them to believe that their bridges, roads, their schools and teachers must be built and maintained by the State, and that all churches, missions and ministers must be maintained by mission boards. Because of this they feel that there must be no effort on their own part. The memory of Sullivan's campaign still lingers, and the fraudulent treaties of the Genesee Valley and of Buffalo Creek have left their sting, and with it a feeling that no work that the white man can do will ever undo the wrongs which they suffered. Whatever may be the merits of the case, the effect has been to create a feeling of dependence. Contrast, however, the Canadian Six Nations of Iroquois who maintain their own schools, pay their teachers, build their own roads and bridges, pay a medical superintendent and support a national hospital and dispensary. Then note what efficient men and women independent action has produced. The same is true of the Canadian Six Nations' churches. Most of them, the English Church excepted, are supported almost entirely by the Indians themselves, with a result of greater interest and better attendance. With our New York Indians, the gospel of self-help must be inculcated.

To create and foster this spirit manual training schools are needed. These schools should be equipped for both the young and for adults. Men must know how to work, and for what purpose, before they can produce efficiently. A large portion of the New York Indians are fully competent, but those who are not should be placed on proper footing. Then when a man, a boy, or a girl is trained for a position he should be helped to secure one if he is unable to find one for himself. It is sheer folly to educate our Indians as tinners, printers and wagon builders, and then send them back to the reservation where there is no call for these trades.

With the means of reform just indicated, the churches would find it far easier to spread the higher Christian ideal of self, of home, and of ethical living. The influences, which now tend most to destroy, are the drink curse, and the lure of the Indian show. With higher ideals developed these things would lose their charm.[1]

Progress for the Indian, 1912

In almost any conference of importance in which race progress is being discussed the most ordinary observer will discover that the Indian has two radically distinct classes of earnest champions. Each of these classes, though they differ widely as to what the Indian should be, is laboring to secure what it believes to be his best interests.

The first division consists of those who find so much to admire in the Indian as he was that they desire him to always remain substantially as he was. The romance of his life and history, his essentially religious nature, his interesting social organization, his mode of life in the open, his distinctive arts, and his intense love of freedom present such an appeal that they argue since the Indian is happy in his own culture there should be no effort to destroy that culture by the innovations of civilization. They ask why all men should be made to conform to the ideals of Anglo-American civilization, why the Indian should be made to unlearn the lore of his fathers, why he should be taught to desire the luxuries and enervating pleasures of modern life, why he should be plunged into the complexities of an economic system which produces so many miseries that primitive life could not produce. They ask why, when civilized man loathes and deplores these things and looks longingly to the freedom and simplicity of the aborigine, this same aborigine should be made to abandon his pristine Eden for an acquaintance with these same deplorable things. They ask if this is not unjust. They ask why the Indian should be tainted with the leprosy of civilization when the health of barbarism leaves his blood virile and his wants but few.

Among the aborigines of America there was no such thing as tuberculosis, few or no specific blood diseases, no need of jails for the criminal or asylums for the orphaned, drug crazed, or insane, no drunkenness, no frenzied scramble for gold, and no concentration of power over food and other necessities of life. Men in those days were strong and the women likewise were strong. The weak were not bred. Every man then knew where he might find food and shelter, every man and women had an occupation. Every man knew that his children would have a home after this death and he knew that his house would never be robbed by any member of his tribe. He knew that his nation's power rested upon his ability to fight. He was conscious that he was in reality a factor in his social group. The national councils of his people were simple, his code of ethics inflexible, his every right defined, and his status unquestioned. Who then could justly wish to wreck such simplicity and plunge him who enjoyed it into a sea of complexity filled with strange, ravenous fish? Who would wish to tear the Eskimo from his polar home and divest him of his wonderful ingenuity? Who would wish to make the Cree forget to use the simple things he found about him? Who would seek to rob the Sioux of his picturesque bonnet and shirt and take away his tepee? Who would wish to destroy the strange and wonderful social system of the northwest coast or blot out the unique art of that region? Why should the Pueblo be torn from his adobe town house and transplanted to a half-built shack of mill lumber? Why should the wonderfully evolved governmental system of the Iroquois be supplanted by any other political system? Why, indeed, should any Indian abandon his splendid traditions, his reverent religion, and his picturesque ceremonies for a mess of civilized pottage that is even now turning sour with age and infection? In a word, why should not broad America have room for her native people and leave them as they are? Why not allow the Indian to be himself? Why educate him, why civilize him, why Christianize him? Why teach him new arts foreign to his nature when his own native arts breathe of his very spirit? Why give him books of foreign literature and surfeit him with an education ill suited to his native environment? Why deculturate him and at the same time rave over his beautiful native products? Why not leave the Indian as he is and allow him to live and do as his own intellect or fancy directs?

The second division of the Indian's friends endeavor to answer the "why." They advocate for the Indian as for every man every good thing that enlightenment can bestow upon human kind, and assert that no man should be denied the right to enjoy the best and greatest things that all men and wide nature have produced. The conception of what is best and greatest differs of course as education, environment, and taste differ in the various classes of critics. The advocate of progress holds that every race that lives and grows must advance. He argues that progress is an inflexible law of growth, that when either animals or plants cease to develop they ripen and die. They use the analogy that when water ceases to run it becomes stagnant—and so with a nation or social group. To have reached its present stage, they explain, or any other former stage, has meant growth and development. Cessation of growth has meant stagnation and often degeneration. Innovations have been accepted, new conditions have brought new methods of meeting them. The struggle with unfavorable conditions has taught how to meet and overcome them. The persistent endeavor to advance, the struggle to attain, and the desire to obtain that which is better gives to a race its strength.

Arthur Caswell Parker   291

Today, in the age of rapid development, when developed man has extended his power over the earth, gradually encroaching upon native races, those native races can only survive as they respond to the conditions and requirements that the advanced culture thrusts upon them. With a million civilized people (so-called, rightly or not matters not), surrounding a small tract of land known as a "reservation," containing from 500 to 80,000 native people, what salvation have these native people as such? Indians they may be, but can they, under the circumstances, live now as Indians lived before the whites came and bought or stole their land? Surrounded on all sides and with their native environment gone, do not their needs become the same as those of the whites about them? Do you not find them eating the same food, when they can get it, wearing the same clothing and wishing to, using the same tools and utensils, even in preference to their native ones? Do you not find them depending every largely upon every device of the dominant culture for necessities, conveniences, and luxuries? How then, or why then, can one reasonably expect them to live in tepees and wear buckskins and war bonnets? How can they, when hunting ranges are diminished or obliterated and game extinct? Must not the Indian by force of circumstances turn to new things, accept new things, use new things, and employ the same methods of procuring these new things as are employed by the race that produced them and caused the change of conditions?

Between the conservationist and the extreme progressionist there should be a sane middle ground on which the best elements of both may be found.

The man who would have an Indian continue now as he was four centuries ago fails to tell us how he could exist, though possessed of every unadulterated traditional virtue. He does not tell us how the Indian is to be given back what was once his. He does not tell us how the Indian is to deal with the "white problem." History has shown that even when laws are enacted prohibiting white men from living in the Indian country, it is still utterly impossible to keep the worst individuals of the white and other races from ignoring them and finding an asylum among the Indians, to the detriment of the Indians. They do not tell us how white men are going to be kept from trading with Indians and from using every influence to obtain used and unused Indian land. They do not tell us how, when good white men are free to mingle with the Indians, the Indians are going to be prevented from wanting the food and wares of white men and the education and refinements of white men.

Suppose twenty Indians should be permitted by law to camp in Battery Park, New York City. Dressed in all their primeval glory and having no knowledge of the English language or business methods, how could they live except by charity, by selling their wares to white men, or by making an exhibition of themselves? Would not poverty, disease, and death be their speedy lot if they were compelled to subsist upon what they could produce there for themselves without trading with non-Indians?

On the other hand the extreme progressionists take the opposite view. They assert that every element that makes an Indian an Indian should be expunged and supplanted by the elements of culture that make a white man a white man. They insist upon the Indian giving up his language, his religion, his folk-lore, his tribal relations, and his "Indianness," and becoming a white man in thought and appearance, forgetting that this is a basic error resulting from confusing civic and ethnic elements.

Many an unfortunate Indian youth who has been schooled by this class has forgotten his mother tongue and has learned to despise his tribal history and look upon his ancestors as savage beasts deserving of no respect. He may have discoursed learnedly of Plato and Socrates, of Sanskrit verbs or Semitic substantives, of trigonometry and the nth power of *pi,* of the heroes of Thermopylae, of the astronomy of the Arabs, of the migrations of the Indo-Aryans, and the social system of the neo-Goths, but he may never have known of his own flexible language, of the philosophy of his own people's sages, of Tecumtha or Hiawatha, of the heroes of the Pequoit massacre or those of Wounded Knee, of Chilcat art or Zuni pottery. To him a *katchina* or a *kiva*, a totemic system or linguistic stock, folklore and tradition, the Wallum Olum or the codices of the Aztecs, the Pawnee Hako or the Objiwa Mide Wiwin, mean nothing but pagan mummery.

Many an educated Indian who wears a white collar and a frock coat has been pointed to with pride by his tutors because he knew nothing of the "heathen ways" of his ancestors. Yet this very Indian when he commences to mingle with cultured men and women in the civilized world finds himself at a distinct disadvantage. He is flooded with questions he cannot answer, and his audience soon turns away in weariness, if not disgust, to welcome with open arms his unlettered brother clad in show buckskins and eagle feathers, whose English is abominable but sufficiently vivid to explain the picturesque things of his native life. The "de-Indianized" in his white collar then commences to think. He commences to study his people, learn their ways, and understand their system of thought. Then the whole scheme comes to him as a revelation. He feels that he has been outraged and robbed. Straightway he commences to "re-Indianize" himself. If his tutors have taught him to despise his heathen father and mother too deeply he is very likely to take the directly opposite view and pride himself on the idyllic side of their life. Thus do the wrongly educated Indians "go back to the blanket," figuratively, and become strenuous champions of the "old regime." It was an unjust and one-sided education that caused the revulsion of feeling. Despite what one may say I think the ordinary man who thinks broadly will respect the Indian for his pride in his people. He who holds his head high is apt to find more room on the sidewalk of life than he who hangs his head in shame.

Now then, where shall the sane middle ground be found? May it not be found in admitting that under the circumstances the Indian must give up certain things and take others in their places?

May it not be found in asserting that the Indian need not entirely "deculturate" himself, but go on developing the best that is inherent to him? Will it not be well to admit that absolute uniformity of thought, method, and outward appearance are not absolutely necessary and that some virtue may be found in things and ways other than our own?

The writer of this article believes that as long as the Indian finds efficiency in his native ideas there is no absolute need of causing him to abandon those ideas. Every race as a result of its racial history develops certain characteristics, practices, or habits. The Frenchman would not copy the Englishman or use an English method of expressing himself, neither would the German imitate, except for profit, Japanese art or music. How incongruous any one of us would find the singing of the Russian national hymn by a Chinese coolie, who yet claimed to possess self-respect! How we would despise the Italian for donning the garb of a Turk and strolling down Broadway singing, "Erin go bragh." We consider the abandonment of racial characteristics of virtue as indicative of shame or lack of pride and appreciation of one's own culture, and we either laugh in derision or secretly despise the man who has so little dignity that he can find nothing in his blood worthy of standing for. Each man and every race should develop and be entitled to develop its own virile qualities and its own inherent virtues. For the Indian to cast aside all that goes to make him such and abandon all that his fathers have produced would be conducive of great harm. Without pride a race becomes dispirited, inefficient, incompetent, and the prey of every stronger force. The Indian of America may wear his own style of swimming suit and use his own special swimming stroke. He will progress faster and keep afloat better by so doing. He may swim in his own way and win if he will, but take the stones out of his pocket and the leaden weights from his feet. If this is done the Indian will not have to be upheld by a life preserver or be towed by a man of a lighter color.

If the Indian, now, will cast aside certain outgrown habits that bind him to past ages and will adjust himself to modern conditions, if he will rise to the demands of modern social and material culture, and *develop his own best qualities, arts, and virtues,* he may add materially, not only to art and literature but to philosophy and politics. Those Indians who have not become degenerated by the vices and diseases of civilization will transmit to the future race many healthy qualities and add to its brilliancy and virility. A review of the lives and achievements of men and women possessing Indian blood who have adjusted themselves to civilization substantiates this contention. It is not the dream of an enthusiast but the verdict of a statistician.

Under conditions as we find them now the Indian must buy, trade, or sell, he must own real and personal property. He must, therefore, know how to buy advantageously, how and when to sell, how to acquire, hold, and protect his property. He must learn how to resist the diseases and overcome the temptations and vices that civilization brings. It is therefore manifest that he must acquaint himself with these ways and customs in order that he may exist in health, live in more or less comfort, and protect his property. Otherwise the Indian will always be at disadvantage, he will fail to utilize the forces and the property within his grasp. He will be preyed upon, be robbed and shifted about if he still persists in clinging to his own methods to the exclusion of all others. This will not be because he is an Indian but because civilization in its present phase is competitive and predatory. We thrive on the weaknesses, the necessities, and the ignorance of others. We use as capital our greater strength, our stored-up supplies, and our superior knowledge. At the same time, seeing the misery this creates, we seek to alleviate it, and yet somehow generally in such a way that the advantage is still ours. This we call "hard-headed" business. We weaken our patients by prohibiting or making impossible the exercise through which we ourselves became strong; we administer anesthetics instead of mental and moral stimuli.

Howsoever unfortunate these things may be, yet, with all its crudities, this state of society is the one the Indian must successfully compete with or be destroyed. Whether the current phase of civilization is right or wrong it is nevertheless the state of society in which we live. Below its surface we drown, above it we are tempest driven upon but vapory supports, on its surface we may swim but we must still swim to survive. If we cease to struggle on we are drawn back by the current and down by sheer gravity. It is motion, progress, achievement that gives the right to live. Adjustment to present environment alone can save the man or beast that has lost its earlier environment. If there can be no adjustment there can be no hope for survival.

Any race which becomes satisfied with its present condition, believing that it has reached the ultimate goal, and refusing to consider a state beyond and another world to conquer, has reached its western shore and may only look out into the deep to see a setting sun. Even those who believe that their condition, their social or economic system, is the criterion, needing only proper remedies to correct the faults, are wrong. Like the diseased and dying limb of a pine tree overshadowed by a new and higher one, the old must perish even before it is truly perfect. Nothing can save it. The law of growth, the necessities of the tree, demand that the newer and higher limb receive the sap and grow in full vigor until another, ever higher, in turn shuts out the sun and the lower one drops wilted and dying from very lack of light and nourishment. So stage by stage races have developed. It will not avail to cling to the lower limb. Modern man is in the top branches of this ethnic tree; his slower brothers cling below on branches brittle and decayed. Many have dropped into the abyss below and we call their bones, for lack of better names, the Man of Spy, of Neanderthal, of Calaveras, or the *pithecanthropus erectus*.

The Indian is not inferior as a race or as an individual except as he is made so or so chooses to be. He has ability, even if much of it is

Arthur Caswell Parker   297

dormant, and he has capacity. With a white man's fighting chance he has always demonstrated this. The great need of teaching the Indian to appreciate and measure his own culture in the full knowledge of others is apparent. To this end the writer strongly believes in the necessity of an Indian college or university. Others, both Indian and non-Indian, share in this belief. In such an institution graduates of the higher schools might be trained in the art, literature, history, ethnology, and philosophy of their people. Along with such subjects might be taught political and social science and such other academic branches as might be found necessary.

The writer is not alone in the belief that the American Indian has something permanent to contribute to civilization. By a conservative policy alone he cannot contribute, however. To bring his contribution to humanity he must move upward and movement means progress. It is this belief of the race in itself that leads the Society of American Indians to state as one of its objects, "To promote and co-operate with all efforts looking to the advancement of the Indian in enlightenment that leaves him free as a man to develop according to the natural laws of social evolution," and then at the same time to state as another object, "To present in a just light the true history of the race, to preserve its records, and emulate its distinguishing virtues."[2]

Needed Changes in Indian Affairs, 1912

With every thoughtful student of human development, I believe that the Indian possesses every ability and capacity for development and that he is capable of any attainment possible for men, providing his environment is made normal. This postulates that the Indian is equal in inherent capacity and therefore not an inferior.

Many mistakes and much misery have been produced by dogmatically asserting the contrary. Hampered by a false environment and artificial social conditions thought necessary to restrain him, the Indian has found it difficult to develop along normal lines. The education, civilization, and incentive came from without and not from within. It was a gift and not a growth. When the contrary was occasionally true, the Indian's social and legal position prevented his highest success.

That some Indians attained great distinction as leaders in the white world proves the vitality of the race and demonstrates its capacity. The Indian is a capable, useful American when he is permitted to be. There can be little doubt that the majority of Americans desire justice and progress for the Indian. Americans as a rule believe in fair play. As the law stands this is now difficult to give. An uncertain and indetermined status makes it possible for dishonest interests to prey upon the Indian so affected.

There often has been the lack of fair play and often no redress. The law blocks the way. The Indian has never been the subject of searching sociological study. Basic causes for conditions have never been studied. Hence the "problem." There must be a new beginning. Scientific system must supplant disorder. To prepare for such a change it is first necessary to understand the laws that now affect the Indian. Obsolete and injurious laws must be repealed; needful laws must be enacted. The exact status of every tribe, band, or class of Indians must be determined as far as existing law affects his status. In this way a true legal basis will be found on which to build anew. The legal position of the Indian is now so involved that with the further changes that come through allotments, the payment of claims, new contracts, through intermarriage and changes of administration and policy, matters only grow more complex. Laws made for the "blanket Indian," of two generations ago are still in force to make life miserable for the educated Indian of today seeking to compete in modern life. Competent men are declared incompetent, an Indian congressman is arrested for selling his own land, an Indian attorney is prevented from buying a cow with his own money, and an educated Indian leaves his children to discover that with all his education and civilization he is declared incompetent to make a will disposing of his property. These "incompetent" men, on the other hand, had been fully trusted with the legal and financial interests of their white neighbors. They were only incompetent because of obsolete Indian law.

The answer to many discouraging remarks about Indian capacity and progress is to point to the legal position into which the Indian is thrust. A reservation Indian is enslaved by his reservation Indian environment. To remedy such a state of affairs was the object of the Carter Indian Code Bill (H. R. 18334, 62nd Congress, Second session). This bill was drafted by the Society of American Indians and introduced by Congressman Charles D. Carter. It provides for a new epoch in Indian affairs, and when passed will simplify the work of the government in dealing with the Indian and give the Indian a foundation upon which he may stand securely. It will make possible a rapid transition from a lower stage to a higher one and render justice more a common matter. It will reduce the cost of administrating Indian affairs and save large amounts of money both for the government and for the Indian. It will pave the way for freedom and self-government and mark the passing of "ward" and "subject" and ultimately give the Indian American now possessing "diminutive rights" every right that the nation vouchsafes to its sovereign people.[3]

Henry Roe Cloud (Winnebago)

Henry Roe Cloud (1884–1950) was born as Wo-Na-Xi-Lay-Hunka (War Chief) on the Winnebago Reservation in Nebraska. He attended the Genoa Industrial School, the Santee Normal Training School, and the Mount Hermon School before attending Yale University. After graduating from Yale in 1910, he spent a year at Oberlin Seminary College and then transferred to the Auburn Theological Seminary, where he earned his bachelor of divinity degree. He also received a master's degree in anthropology from Yale in 1914, making him the first full-blood Native American to earn a bachelor's and master's degree from Yale. One year later he founded the American Indian Institute in Kansas, a Christian preparatory school for Indians. He acted as the institute's president, principal, chief fundraiser, and editor of its journal, the *Indian Outlook*. Roe Cloud later became superintendent of Haskell Institute. He was a founding member of the Society of American Indians and an advocate for Indian education. (Littlefield and Parins, *Biobibliography: Supplement* 191; Peyer, *American Indian Nonfiction*, 388–89; Pfister; *Southern Workman*, March 1921, 125)

Education of the American Indian, 1915

Education is for life—life in the workaday world with all its toil, successes, discouragements, and heartaches. Education unrelated to life is of no use. Education is the leading-out process of the young until they themselves know what they are best fitted for in life. Education is for complete living; that is, the educational process must involve the heart, head, and hand. The unity of man is coming to the forefront in the thought of the day. We cannot pay exclusive attention to the education of one part and afford to let the other part or parts suffer. Education is for service; that is, the youth is led to see the responsibilities as well as the privileges of his education so that he will lend a helping hand to those who are in need.

Indian education offers no exception to these general definitions. The educational needs of the Indian can be best seen in the light of his problems. He has before him two problems—the white man's and his own peculiar racial problem. The one confronting the white child is the Indian's also, for, if the goal for the Indian is citizenship, it means sharing the responsibilities, as well as the opportunities, of this great Republic.

The task of educating the American young is a stupendous one. The future welfare of the American nation depends upon it. Children everywhere must be brought to an appreciation of the great fundamental principles of the Republic as well as to a full realization of its dangers. It required long, toilsome marches of peoples beyond the seas to give us our present-day civilization. Trial by jury came through William the Conqueror. America's freedom was at the cost of centuries of struggle. America's democracy is both the direct and the indirect contribution of every other civilized nation. Our wide-open door of opportunity was paid for by untold sacrifice of life and labor. It involves the story of the sturdy and brave frontiersman, the gradual extension of transportation facilities westward, the rise of cities on the plains. So great and rapid has been this progress, that already the cry of the conservation of our natural resources is ringing in our ears.

Along with these great blessings, there are the national dangers stalking through the land. I need but mention them. The stupendous economic development of the United States has meant the amassing of great and unwieldy wealth in few hands. It has meant the creation of a wide gap between the rich and poor. Industries have been revolutionized by the introduction of machinery. There has now grown up the problem of the relation of labor and capital. Our railroad strikes and mine wars are but symptoms of this gigantic problem.

Immigration and the consequent congestion in our cities have put the controlling political power into the hands of the "boss." There is the tenement problem of physical degeneracy and disease. It requires no prophet to foresee the increase of these problems and dangers, owing to the war now raging across the sea. The desolation of those countries, the inevitable tax burdens, will mean an even greater influx of immigration into this country. There is the problem of "fire water," that has burned out the souls of hundreds of thousands of men, to say nothing of the greater suffering of their wives, mothers, and children. There is the big national problem of race prejudice. Is America truly to be the "melting pot" of the nations?

These are the problems confronting white youth, and, I repeat, they are the Indian's also.

Besides these, the Indian has his own peculiar race problems to meet. There is the problem of home education. Education in the Indian home is almost universally lacking. The vast amount of education which white children receive in their homes—a great many of them cultured and Christian homes, where, between the ages of ten and fourteen, children read book after book on travel, biography, and current events—goes to make up for deficiencies in the public schools. The Indian youth go back from school into homes that have dominant interests altogether different from those he has been taught at school. I have seen many a young man and woman bravely struggle to change home conditions in order to bring them into keeping with their training, and they have at last gone down! The father and the mother have never been accustomed, in the modern sense, to a competitive form of existence. The father has no trade or vocation. The value of a dollar, of time, of labor, is unknown in that home. The parents have not enough insight into educational values to appreciate the boy's achievements and to inspire him further. What is to be done under such circumstances? In many cases the youth finds himself face to face with a shattered home. Bad marriage conditions, the very core of his social problem, stare him in the face. Many a young man and woman, realizing these home conditions, have gone away to establish homes of their own. As soon as the thrifty Indian accumulates a little property his relatives and tribesmen, in keeping with the old custom of communal ownership of property, come and live at his expense. There was virtual communal ownership of property in the old days under the unwritten laws of hospitality; but the omission, in these days, of that corresponding equal distribution of labor plays havoc with the homes of young Indians.

The Indian has his own labor problem. He has here a race inertia to overcome. The sort of labor he is called upon to do in these days is devoid of exploit. It is a change from sporadic effort to steady, routine labor calling for the qualities of self-control, patience, steady application, and a long look ahead. Shall he seek labor outside the reservation? Shall he work his own allotment? What bearing have his annuity money and his lease money on his labor problem? Do they stifle effort on his part? Do they make him content to eke out a living from year to year without labor? If he works, how is he to meet the ubiquitous grafter with his insistence upon chattel mortgages? How is he to avoid the maelstrom of credit into which so many have fallen?

The health problem of the Indian race may well engage the entire attention and life-work of many young Indian men and women. What about the seventy to eighty thousand Indians now suffering from trachoma? What about the thirty thousand tubercular Indians? Is this due to housing conditions?

There is also the legal problem. Is the Indian a ward of the Government, or a citizen? What are his rights and duties? His legal problem involves his land problem. Ought he to pay taxes? Will he ever secure his rights and be respected in the local courts unless he pays taxes? Is not this question most fundamental?

Shall the Indian youth ignore the problem of religion? Of the many religions on the reservation, which one shall energize his life?

Shall it be the sun dance, the medicine lodge, the mescal, or the Christian religion? Shall he take in all religions, as so many do? What do these different religions stand for?

There is, finally, the whole problem of self-support. If he is to pursue agriculture he must study the physical environment and topography of his particular reservation, for these control, in a large measure, the fortunes of his people. If the reservation is mountainous, covered with timber, he must relate his studies to it. If it is a fertile plain, it means certain other studies. It involves the study of soils, of dry farming, irrigation, stock-farming, and sheep raising. The Indian must conquer nature if he is to achieve race adaptation.

My friends, here are problems of unusual difficulty. In the face of these larger problems—city, state, and national, as well as the Indian's own peculiar race problems, and the two are inextricably interwoven—what shall be the Indian's preparation to successfully meet them? What sort of an education must he have? Miss Kate Barnard has told us something of the problem as it exists in Oklahoma. Into this maelstrom of political chicanery, of the intrigue and corrupting influences of great vested interests, shall we send Indian youth with only an eighth-grade education? In vast sections of that Oklahoma country ninety per cent of the farms of white men were under mortgage last year. It means that even they, with their education and inheritance, are failing. Well might one rise up like Jeremiah of old and cry out, "My people perish for lack of knowledge"—knowledge of the truth as it exists in every department of life. This only can make us truly free.

The first effort, it seems to me, should be to give as many Indians as are able, all the education that the problems they face clearly indicate they should have. This means all the education the grammar schools, the secondary schools, and the colleges of the land can give them. This is not any too much for the final equipment of the leaders of the race. If we are to have leaders who will supply disciplined mental power in our race development, they cannot be merely grammar-school men. They must be trained to grapple with these economic, educational, political, religious, and social problems. They must be men who will take up the righteous cause among their people, interpret civilization to their people, and restore race confidence, race virility. Only by such leaders can race segregation be overcome. Real segregation of the Indian consists in segregation of thought and inequality of education.

We would not be so foolish as to demand a college education for every Indian child in the land, irrespective of mental powers and dominant vocational interests; but, on the other hand, we do not want to make the mistake of advocating a system of education adapted only to the average Indian child. If every person in the United States had only an eighth-grade education with which to wrestle with the problems of life and of the nation, this country would be in a bad way. We would accelerate the pace in the Government grammar schools of such Indian youth as show a capacity for more rapid progress. For the Indian of exceptional ability, who wishes to lay his hand upon the more serious problems of our race, the industrial work, however valuable in itself, necessarily retards him in the grammar school until he is man-grown. He cannot afford to wait until he is twenty-five to enter the high school. This system is resulting in an absolute block upon the entrance of our ablest young people into the schools and colleges of the land which stand open to them. There are hundreds of the youth of Oriental and other native races in our colleges. As an Indian it is impossible for me to believe that the fact that there are almost no Indians under such training today is due to a failure of my race in mental ability. The difficulty lies in the system rather than in the race. According to the census of the last decade, there were 300,000 college men and women to 90,000,000 of people in the United States, or 1 to every 300. In the same proportion there should be 1000 college Indian men and women in the United States, taking as our total population 300,000, or 1 in 300. Allowing for racial handicaps let us say there should be at least 500 instead of 1000 Indian college men and women. Actually there is not 1 in 30,000, and most of these escaped in early life the retarding process in the Government schools.

This is not in any way disparaging to the so-called industrial education in the Government Indian grammar schools, such as Carlisle, Haskell, Chilocco. Education that seeks to lead the Indians into outdoor vocational pursuits is most necessary. Our Government Indian Bureau feels the need for vocational training among the Indians, and I am very glad that it does. Productive skill we must have if we are to live on in this competitive age.

Others before me, such as Dr. Walter C. Roe, have dreamed of founding a Christian, educational institution for developing strong, native, Christian leadership for the Indians of the United States.[1] I, too, have dreamed. For, after all, it is Christian education that is going to solve these great problems confronting the Indian. Such an institution must recognize the principle that man cannot live by bread alone, and yet at the same time show the dignity and divineness of toil by the sweat of one's brow. The school must teach self-support. The Indian himself must rise up and do for himself, with the help of Almighty God. It must be Christian education because every problem that confronts us is, in the last analysis, a moral problem. In the words of Sumner, "Capital is another word for self-denial." The gift of millions for Indian education is the people's self-denial. Into whatever activity we may enter for life work, we must pay the price of self-control if we are to achieve any degree of success. The moral qualities, therefore, are necessary for our successful advance. Where shall we look for our final authority in these moral questions? We must look to nothing this side of the "Great Spirit" for our final authority. Having, then, brought into the forefront of the Indian race men of sound morality, intellectual grasp, and productive skill, we shall have leaders who are like the great oak tree on the hill. Storm after storm may break upon them, but they will stand, because they are deeply rooted and the texture of their souls is strong.[2]

Elizabeth Bender (White Earth Chippewa)

See the Essays section for a profile of Elizabeth Bender (1888–1965).

Training Indian Girls for Efficient Home Makers, 1916

I do not intend to tire the reader with long drawn out stories of broken treaties, the misappropriation of Indian money, nor do I intend to dwell on the subject of how we have been starved and pampered on various reservations. Lamenting over past abuses, hanging around Indian trading stores, demanding certain rights, does not solve the Indian Problem. We hear a great deal about developing leaders for leadership and are apt to forget that our girls are to be the sources of such leadership, too, for they represent our homemakers and homekeepers.

In traveling over this great country of ours, I have noticed that the best schools, the most productive farms, the most sanitary conditions exist only where educated fathers and mothers have given their sons and daughters the proper home life. But as I have traveled through the Indian country, I have not seen many homes on this order. The conditions are just the reverse. The unkempt homes, which are breeding places for filth and disease, outnumber the homes of cleanliness and Christian training, and thousands and thousands of acres of Indian lands, rich in undeveloped resources, are lying idle.

The time was when the Government school system met the necessary requirements, but it lacks in the fact that it does not teach our girls and boys the real value of labor and the cost of materials. They are not impressed with money values and how much it means to make a living for themselves.

Can we expect to develop great, strong Christian leaders in spite of such home conditions? Yes, we can. We can take our youth away

308

from home, send them off to such schools as Haskell, Carlisle, or Hampton for a period of years, give them an even better education than these now offer, and have them associate with high minded instructors who shall teach them that the home is the very core of any civilization, that the ideal home shall permeate its environment and bring it into keeping with that of their school. When we shall have done this no girl will be ashamed of her people or disgusted with her lot.

Often in the Indian country we find father speaking intelligent English, using the latest implements in farming, thrifty and industrious. But you wonder why his home does not show the result of his labor. You will have to look farther. Does the mother speak English? Does she know anything about food values? Has she had the training of Home Economics and Domestic Science? Does she know anything about organizing Mothers' Clubs and Girls' Clubs for the advancement and betterment of her community? You will find that that side of her education has been neglected. As no people advance any faster than their women and the home is considered to be the core of the Indian problem, my plea is that these Indian girls should receive a fair chance.

Nearly all the large Indian schools have trade schools in which our young men are taught the various trades, but the Indian girls must day after day do the menial drudgery of the school, working in the laundry, washing dishes, with little time for recreation and play.

More and more we are beginning to appreciate the fact that the Indian girl along with this sort of work must be given a thorough course in Home Economics and Domestic Science. The Indian girl was naturally a homemaker even in the days of savagery. She it was who pitched tent, tilled the little garden, and at that early stage made something of a home for her roaming people.

Carlisle, for the first time in its history, has installed such a course. We have this year built a model home cottage, in which the girls get a real taste of home-life for a month. Here our girls are being trained how to cook over a common stove, to take care of kerosene lamps, and to prepare three meals a day in the most wholesome and economical way. In this model cottage she is to learn the art of cooking cereals, vegetables, and the preparation and serving of family meals. Invalid cookery, caning of fruits and vegetables, jelly making and pickling will be a part of the course. She will also learn how to do the plain, everyday sewing, so needful in a home of this kind.

I believe that this sort of training will give her a broader outlook on life and make her realize the tremendous responsibility that confronts her as a homemaker. She will look upon her lot as a sacred calling and appreciate the dignity and nobility of labor.

Along with Home Economics and Domestic Science, have her realize that she, too, has a social problem. Have her study sociology in its broadest sense so that she shall know the relation of character building to health, recreation, business, and racial welfare.

One writer tells us that "Education is not simply the art of developing powers and capacities of the individual; it is rather the fitting of individuals for efficient membership. It should fit one for social service. It should create the good citizen."

My plea is for a broader and more comprehensive education for the girl than has ever been given before.

Lastly, we must teach our girls to go out as strong, Christian leaders, for not only must they be good homemakers but also soul savers. I have been in some schools where this side of Christian education was sadly lacking. Do we not boast of belonging to a Christian Nation and are we not all seeking after the same God? Then teach my people more about the Great Spirit, so that they too shall be morally strong. Our girls as well as our boys must have great and compelling ideals. These are practical lines along which our girls should be educated. I think that something on this plan will produce the homes we wish to see in the Indian country, the Great West, the land of wonderful opportunities.

We are a people that have always lived in the country, fished in the rivers, lived on its hills, raced upon its plains and that is where our homemakers belong. The West is where we wish to solve the Indian Problem, building up better schools, better churches, and better homes.[1]

A Hampton Graduate's Experience, 1916

After being graduated from Hampton in 1907, I accepted a Government appointment in Montana, and in the fall of 1909 started on my new and untried work—that of a teacher among my own people.

I was sent to work among the Blackfeet Indians who are located in the northwestern part of Montana. They are on a large reservation comprising many thousands of acres of excellent grazing land, which, however, is not well adapted to farming owing to the short season. According to tradition, the name "Blackfeet" was given to these Indians by another tribe with whom they had been fighting, and by whom they had been chased across a broad expanse of burned prairie, thus making their moccasins black.

It was with a feeling of uncertainty that I got off at the little station in Montana on that cold, raw October night, and made my way into a dark and dingy waiting room. In one corner of the room was a sputtering lamp that tried to give a little light through a black chimney. As I glanced about, I saw a long-haired Indian sprawled upon the floor, wrapped in his blanket, snoring contentedly, and not at all concerned with the casual stranger who had happened in. On the bench was an Indian mother, cuddling in her arms a sickly-looking baby and trying to soothe its fretfulness. I learned afterward that they were all of the same family, and were there to take a midnight train in order to see if they could get medical aid which the government doctor could not adequately give the sick infant.

After an hour's wait, the stage arrived and conveyed me to the small town of Browning which was two miles from the station. The stage stopped at the Kipp Hotel, and there I was to put up for the night. As I entered, many men were sitting around the heater; some were smoking and one or two cowboys were rolling cigarettes. Gradually the conversation ceased, and the stranger was the center of interest.

The next morning I called at the agent's office and made it known that I was the new teacher. He welcomed me cordially and told me that the school team would be up at noon to get the beef supply and I could go back with it. The school was situated seven miles from the railroad station, beautifully located in the Cut Bank Valley. Looking westward one could see the Rocky Mountains in all their ruggedness and grandeur. Old Chief Mountain stood out grim and silent, separating the Blackfeet Reservation from the Dominion of Canada. Eastward one could see the rolling plains dotted with herds of cattle and horses belonging to these Indians.

My first day in school was a very trying one. I had, in the primary room, boys and girls ranging from five to fifteen, some of whom could speak English, but others had no command of the language. I asked the children what had been the lesson of the previous day and no one volunteered to tell. After a long silence one little girl had courage enough to tell me that they had not had any school, although they had entered the first of September.

On Saturdays and Sundays the parents came to see their children. Their coming was heralded by the barking of the many dogs that always follow the train of an Indian team.

On Saturdays the children were dressed in clean dresses and their hair tidily combed for the occasion. What a contrast they were to the parents, who came wearing their gaily colored blankets and shawls, moccasins on their feet, and the fathers often with their hair in long braids. The fathers and mothers often painted their faces in vivid red and yellow. Yet these same parents were willing to send their children to school, and were anxious to have them get the things they themselves had not had the opportunity of getting. They all congregated in the girls' sitting room and enjoyed themselves visiting their children. On the floor one would perhaps see an old grandmother squatting and smoking her pipe filled with Indian tobacco, "kinnikinic."

Our school children celebrated the Holidays in much the same way people would in any community. However, many of the parents looked on, not knowing what was being said, but paternal pride showed itself when their children took part in the school program.

The children enter school the first of September and remain until about the middle of June, with an occasional visit home on Saturday. They have lessons only two hours and a half daily, devoting the rest of the time to industrial work. When the mild Chinook winds begin to blow, and Mother Nature begins to waken the sleeping buds and flowers, the Indian child gets the wanderlust. He longs for that home, humble though it may be, and for that pony of his which has been idle all winter, and which has fattened on the bunch grass, severe as the winter may have been on the range. The Blackfeet have many horses and we are not surprised to learn that the boys learn to ride almost as soon as they are able to walk. These spring days are days of worry to the teacher. Sometimes, when she goes to her schoolroom, only girls are to be seen, as the boys have decided to round up their ponies, or those who have not the courage to go home are off drowning ground squirrels. Indian police are sent out to various homes to round up the truants. Sometimes they manage to get them back in two or three days, but more often it takes ten.

The teacher who enters the Indian Service is called upon to do many things besides actual academic work. One fall when school opened I had to assume the duties of matron for a month. This was a most trying time, as in the case of the Blackfeet children many came back to school fresh from a summer of camp life, and not always as clean as one would like to have them. Then there were homesick children to cheer; the arranging of details in laundry, sewing room, kitchen, dining room and buildings; the getting of sleepyheads out of bed every morning; keeping a watchful eye on those who tried to evade work; taking care of sick and children, doctoring trachomatous eyes; and many other duties.

Another time I was the children's cook for three weeks. One would hardly expect that accomplishment in a teacher, but Hampton does expect it of her graduates, and I knew what my training had been. One thing I remember very vividly in those three weeks of experience, and that was what the children said, "Miss Bender sure can cook good beans."

I got the parents interested in the field-day sports which were held in the spring. Then, with the aid of a supervisor and the principal, we got the parents to donate $84 to purchase basketballs, footballs, a baseball outfit, and indoor games to be used when the weather was severe and the children had to be confined in small playrooms. Up to this time they had had nothing in the way of games, and consequently the boys had spent much of their time sneaking off to the school dairy herd and breaking calves to ride.

I became well acquainted with some of the parents and visited them in their homes. Some had comfortable homes that were orderly and neat, but the majority of them had only one room, no floor but the dirt, and two windows, those usually with an eastern exposure. Many of the homes are excellent breeding places for trachoma and tuberculosis.

This brings me to the horrors of trachoma and my observation of it among the Plains Indians. It is a disease that without medical attention gradually impairs the sight until blindness results. Upon the examination of one hundred and fifty children in our school, forty-three were found to be afflicted with trachoma. The Government sent out specialists about three years ago, and they found that, out of the Indian population of 300,000, 50,000 had trachoma.

When the treatment of trachoma began I was called on to treat all cases with bluestone. There was a marked improvement in all the cases that we had treated for over six months. I do not know how soon they would have been pronounced cured, as I left in March, having received a transfer to the Fort Belknap Reservation. Here the conditions were even worse. Someone told me that this was "the one-eyed reservation," and it seemed almost true. Here we had fifty children enrolled, and all but six had trachoma. I cite these instances because I feel so strongly these problems that are confronting our people, and they are problems that we can all help to remedy, whether our vocation in life is that of a teacher, carpenter, nurse, or a blacksmith. If you cannot get a doctor to treat this disease, be interested enough to treat the cases in your own community.

Think of it! Nearly 30% of all Indian children are in danger of becoming blind. Nearly 17,000 Indian boys and girls are in danger of complete blindness.

We may talk about demanding our rights, but unless we are willing to assume responsibilities we cannot presume to make such a demand. The missionary field for service and for consecrated workers is broad. What a wonderful opportunity for some of our young men to become doctors, fitted to cope with trachoma and tuberculosis. Without medical attention thousands of men and women will not be self-supporting, and they will be deprived of their usefulness.

We need strong Christian workers in the "Indian Country." A number of the Indians are Christians, but the teacher who works among them sees the horrors of the grass dance, sun dance, the medicine lodge, and the use of mescal.

My white friends say, "Let them continue these old dances, they are so picturesque." Is there any picturesqueness when a performer in the sun dance drops dead from exhaustion? Such a scene I witnessed up at Glacier National Park, where the Indians were dancing day and night for the benefit of guests at this summer resort. The day when the sun dance and medicine dance played an important part of their religious rites has passed. This form of religious ceremony has deteriorated with the advance of civilization, and we need to give the Indian Christianity and not paganism.[2]

Acknowledgments

I am grateful to a number of people who have helped to make this collection possible.

This recovery project builds on my dissertation. I thank my dissertation advisor, Miles Orvell, for encouraging me to pursue this book project. I also thank the other members of my dissertation committee, James Salazar and Sue-Im Lee, for their guidance.

To my editor at the University of Nebraska Press, Matt Bokovoy, who offered unwavering support for this project, I am truly grateful. Many thanks to Heather Stauffer, Joeth Zucco, Sally Antrobus, and everyone else at the press for their help. I also thank Hilary Wyss, Cari Carpenter, and the anonymous readers for their thoughtful feedback at various stages of this project.

Many thanks to my colleagues at SUNY College at Old Westbury. I am especially grateful to the Campus Professional Development Committee for awarding me generous funding to complete this project.

Various librarians and archivists assisted me with my research queries. I thank Barbara Landis and the staff at the Cumberland County Historical Society, Maggie Dittemore and the staff at the John Wesley Powell Library of Anthropology, Jenny C. Freed at Earlham College's Lilly Library, Mallory Covington at the Oklahoma Historical Society, and Lin Fredericksen at the Kansas Historical Society.

I thank Bridget Chapman and Tatum Petrich for their comments on drafts and for cheering me on throughout the writing process.

And, finally, I thank my family for their encouragement and support.

Notes

Introduction

1. The Seneca Indian School has had several names, including the Wyandotte Mission; the Seneca, Shawnee, and Wyandotte Industrial Boarding School; and the Seneca Boarding School. The school was founded in 1871 in Wyandotte, Oklahoma, under the auspices of the Society of Friends. Children between the ages of four and eighteen attended the school, which initially offered a curriculum through the fourth grade, later expanding to the eighth and ninth grades in the 1920s. Classes began in spring 1872, with fewer than fifty students. The low enrollment reflected the resistance among Seneca, Shawnee, and Wyandot parents to sending their children away to boarding school. In 1876 the government began to assume a more active role in Indian education, and it oversaw all the missionary schools in Indian Territory, including the Seneca Indian School (Bieloh, "Bad Water," 58). Due to recruitment efforts and increased pressure by the federal government, the enrollment increased to more than 135 by 1885 (Gibson, "Wyandotte Mission," 140). Over time the school earned a reputation for its "steady stream of dedicated and competent administrators and teachers" and for its success in transforming so-called "savages" into students. Unlike other church-sponsored schools that failed, the Seneca Indian School thrived, resulting in its nickname as the "Marvel of the Wilderness" (Gibson, "Wyandotte Mission," 140).

2. Here I borrow a term from an editorial in which the editors of the *Hallaquah* announced the death of their beloved fellow "Indian school-girl editor" Lucy Grey. I use the terms "Indian," "Native American," and "Native" throughout the introduction and annotations as well as in the author profiles, as these are the terms most often used by the writers themselves. I use the term "indigenous" to refer to a broader pan-tribal identity. I also identify writers by their tribal affiliation whenever possible.

3. Arizona Jackson (Wyandot) and Lula Walker (Wyandot) founded the *Hallaquah* with Ida Johnson (Wyandot?) and were associate editors

for the first three issues; Jackson, Walker, and Johnson assumed the editorship in the March–April 1880 issue. Lula Walker was an older sister of Bertrand N. O. Walker, who later published poetry under his Wyandot name Hen-toh and animal stories in *Tales of the Bark Lodges* (1919).

4. See Batker, *Reforming Fictions*; Kilcup, *Native American Women's Writing*; Washburn, "New Indians"; Littlefield and Parins, *American Indian*; and Peyer, *American Indian Nonfiction*. See also Hoxie's edited collection *Talking Back to Civilization*, which contains several essays that appeared in the *Quarterly Journal of the Society of American Indians* (later renamed the *American Indian Magazine*).

5. See Stanciu, "'That Is Why I Sent You,'" and Zink, "Carlisle's Writing Circle."

6. Gaul echoes Wyss's view in her work on Catharine Brown's letters. She writes, "Those critics who tend to see Brown as a passive tool of the missionaries neglect to recognize the ways that her simple act of writing was an assertion of agency, a way to create certain effects or acts" (Gaul, *Cherokee Sister,* 35). Those effects or acts, as Gaul further explains, were "geared toward making arguments that will change minds on politicized issues surrounding Cherokees' status in the United States and lead to increased donations to missions, both of which would benefit the Cherokees in strategic ways" (35).

7. Bonnin's final editorial appeared in the Winter 1919 issue of the *American Indian Magazine*. After she left the magazine it underwent a number of changes under the editorship of Thomas L. Sloan (Omaha). As Hazel W. Hertzberg explains, the new *American Indian Magazine* was a marked departure from its predecessor under the editorship of Parker and Bonnin: "None of the signed articles were written by Indians. It was not to be, like its predecessor, a magazine of Indian opinion written largely by Indians, but rather a magazine about Indians written mostly by whites, and yet at the same time the official publication of the Society" (Hertzberg, *The Search*, 190). Publication of the magazine ceased with the August 1920 issue.

8. As the scholarship of Brooks, Cohen, and Round shows, alphabetic literacy, writing, and print culture played constitutive roles in early indigenous communities. Networks of print were established in enough indigenous communities by the 1880s "to support a new generation of Native writers and alphabetically literate activists" (Round, *Removable Type*, 224). This new generation, which includes the boarding school

students and prominent Native American public intellectuals featured in this collection, transformed the tools of the boarding school by engaging in literacy and print practices that were already being produced and consumed in indigenous communities. The work of Brooks, Cohen, and Round encourages us to see federal boarding schools as one key site within extensive networks of print culture that gave rise to a new generation of Native American writers, editors, and printers at the turn of the twentieth century.

9. For more on the pan-tribal networks that early twentieth-century Native American public intellectuals cultivated and maintained through their work in the Indian Service and the Society of American Indians, see Hertzberg, *Search for an American Indian Identity*, and Vigil, *Indigenous Intellectuals*.

10. See Francis Paul Prucha's discussion of "the friends of the Indian" in *Americanizing the American Indians*. As Prucha explains, "the friends of the Indian" was a group of white reformers who dominated late nineteenth-century Indian policy and "with an ethnocentrism of frightening intensity, they resolved to do away with Indianness" (Prucha, *Americanizing*, 1).

11. For more on Pratt's educational program for adult Indian prisoners at Fort Marion, see Fear-Segal, *White Man's Club*.

12. For exemplary scholarship on the founding of Hampton Institute, see Anderson, *The Education of Blacks in the South*, and Engs, *Educating the Disfranchised and Disinherited*.

13. It is worth noting that the founding of Carlisle marked a shift away from the heavy emphasis on Christian teachings at missionary schools to the federal government's approach to Native American education. After the Civil War, missionary schools were phased out as the federal government gained more control over the education of Native Americans. Christianity was still important to Pratt's model but was not its primary focus. Rather, his educational program focused on teaching Native American students English as well as the character-building habits of discipline, work, and cleanliness.

14. According to Littlefield and Parins (*American Indian*, 320): "The apprentice printers received a full course in composition and as much experience as possible in the job, stone, and press work. They were taught layout, operation and management of the equipment, as well as management of the steam engine and boiler that drove the machinery." This

training prepared many apprentice printers to enter the printing trade and the publishing industry.

15. Letters served multiple and often competing purposes in federal boarding schools as well as early missionary-run boarding schools, as demonstrated in the scholarship of Wyss, *English Letters*; Gaul, *Cherokee Sister*; and Child, *Boarding School Seasons*. For boarding school students and their families, letters were important communication and community-building tools. Parents of federal boarding school students who were not able to write in English would often write letters to their children with the aid of the agent or missionary (Adams, *Education for Extinction*, 251).

16. In *Individuality Incorporated*, Joel Pfister explains the shift that occurred after Pratt was forced to resign from Carlisle. Assuming the position of Indian commissioner in 1905, Francis Leupp defined himself against Pratt's intent to eradicate Indian cultures: "I like the Indian for what is Indian in him. . . . Let us not make the mistake, in the process of absorbing them, of washing out whatever is distinctly Indian" (qtd. in Pfister, *Individuality Incorporated*, 23). From the moment Pratt left Carlisle until it closed in 1918, the school reflected the government's shift toward pluralism and exhibited an increased acceptance of Indianness, especially through its encouragement of the study of Native artistic traditions.

17. As Littlefield and Parins explain, the *Red Man* "was first published as *Eadle Keahtah Toh*, meaning 'big morning star,' which appeared in March 1880 as a four-page, three column monthly" printed at Carlisle. In 1888 the name of the school newspaper was changed to the *Red Man*. It was merged with the *Indian Helper* in 1900 to form the *Red Man and Helper* (Littlefield and Parins, *American Indian*, 318–19).

18. Due to the poor condition of the June 1907 issue of *Talks and Thoughts*, I could not transcribe and reprint Bender's essay in full.

19. For more on the myth of the vanishing Indian, see Dippie, *The Vanishing American*.

20. In her well-known preface to *Old Indian Legends* (1901), Zitkala-Ša asserts that the oral tradition "strongly suggests our near kinship with the rest of humanity and points a steady finger toward the great brotherhood of mankind" (Zitkala-Ša, *American Indian Stories*, 5–6).

21. Advertised as "a magazine not only *about* Indians, but mainly *by* Indians," the *Indian Craftsman* (later known as the *Red Man*) was estab-

lished in February 1909 to serve as an outlet for a developing art-craft printing department at Carlisle. As Littlefield and Parins explain, Angel De Cora, a Winnebago, and William Deitz (Lone Star), a Sioux, both of whom taught in the school's native arts department, directed the magazine's art work, while Edgar K. Miller, formerly an instructor of printing at the Chilocco Indian School, directed the new printing shop. The *Indian Craftsman* was modeled after Gustav Stickley's illustrated magazine, the *Craftsman*, and contained articles about Indian affairs and news related to the school as well as student writings. Many of the stories and legends written by students and published in the *Indian Craftsman* (and later the *Red Man*) were reprinted by newspapers and magazines in the East. It also contained photographs and illustrations by De Cora, Deitz, and their students. Their artwork contributed considerably to making the magazine "a showpiece of Indian printing" (Littlefield and Parins, *American Indian,* 315). In fact, as Littlefield and Parins note, the magazine became so popular that the publishers of Stickley's magazine demanded that Carlisle change the name of its newspaper, which it did in February 1910, to the *Red Man*. Much of the magazine remained the same, although over time more emphasis was placed in the content on the possibilities of Indian citizenship, farming and agricultural "progress" of the Indian, and vocational training. In 1917 the *Red Man* ceased publication and then merged with the *Carlisle Arrow* to form the *Carlisle Arrow and Red Man* (Littlefield and Parins, *American Indian,* 314–15).

Letters

1. *Hallaquah*, January 1880, n. pag.
2. *Hallaquah*, January 1881, n. pag. Jackson was a student at Earlham College in Indiana at this time. According to Earlham College Libraries Friends Collections and College Archives, Jackson was the first Native American to attend the college. It is worth noting that Gertrude Bonnin (Yankton Sioux), also known as Zitkala-Ša, attended Earlham College from 1895 to 1897.
3. Susan Longstreth was a Quaker from Philadelphia and devoted benefactor of federal boarding schools, including the Seneca Indian School. Although letters to benefactors were commonplace in boarding school newspapers, this letter is particularly noteworthy because Longstreth had supplied funding and materials so that Jackson and her two female class-

mates, Ida Johnson and Lula Walker, could found the *Hallaquah* in December 1879. There is no way of determining just how the letter came to be published in Carlisle's *Eadle Keahtah Toh*, which was edited by Pratt and Marianna Burgess, who oversaw all the publications in the Carlisle Printing Office. It is possible that Jackson herself submitted the letter for publication or Longstreth did (Carlisle's literary society was named after Longstreth, which suggests her close affiliation with the school).

4. Jackson opens her letter by explaining that she had completed her examinations at Earlham College, earning grades in the mid-80s and 90s. By representing herself as a successful college student, Jackson's letter supported school authorities' practice of publishing letters by "model students" for other students to emulate and to demonstrate the success of their educational programs. Indeed, in her letter Jackson authorizes herself as what school authorities deemed an exemplary educated Indian girl—civilized and adept at writing in English.

5. A review of John B. Gough's lecture on temperance appeared in the January 1881 edition of the *Hallaquah*.

6. Huldah Bonwill was also a benefactor of federal boarding schools.

7. *Eadle Keahtah Toh*, April 1881, n. pag.

8. *School News*, June 1880, n. pag.

9. Editorial comment.

10. *School News*, February 1881, n. pag.

11. Luther Standing Bear (*Land of the Spotted Eagle*, 234) recounts a conversation he had with his father, Chief Standing Bear, when his father visited him for the first time at Carlisle. Standing Bear credits his father, "the man who had been the greatest influence" in his life, with inspiring him "to learn all I could of the white man's ways."

12. Years later, when reflecting back on his experiences at Carlisle, Standing Bear underscored the ultimate destructiveness of the school's efforts to transform Native American children: "But the change in clothing, housing, food, and confinement combined with lonesomeness was too much, and in three years nearly one half of the children from the Plains were dead and through with all earthly schools. In the graveyard at Carlisle most of the graves are those of little ones" (Standing Bear, *Land of the Spotted Eagle*, 234). Illness and death were common at federal boarding schools; see Trafzer et al., *Boarding School Blues*, 20–21.

13. An English-only policy was strictly imposed on students at federal boarding schools from the 1880s until the 1930s. Students were often

severely punished for speaking Indian languages. At Carlisle, Pratt and other school authorities sought to enforce the English-only policy by praising students who conformed to it and representing those students as role models in the pages of the school's newspapers. Carlisle's *School News* contains numerous letters like Standing Bear's and short compositions that stress the importance of speaking only English at school. For more on the English-only policy, see Adams, *Education for Extinction*; Spack, *America's Second Tongue*; and Trafzer et al., *Boarding School Blues*.

14. *School News*, April 1882, n. pag.

Editorials

1. Walker was the first and only male editor of the *Hallaquah*. The Oklahoma Historical Society maintains the most comprehensive run of the *Hallaquah*, December 1879–May 1880 and January 1881–November 1881.

2. Due to insufficient federal funding, the Seneca Indian School failed "to provide the children with healthy living conditions" and was prone to outbreaks of highly contagious diseases like scarlet fever, measles, typhoid fever, and malaria (Bieloh, "Bad Water," 58, 60).

3. According to the tribute written by the matron, Lucy Grey was seventeen years old when she died. She moved to Indian Territory from Kansas two years before her death. When she was twelve years old she converted to Christianity (*Hallaquah*, August–November, 1881).

4. The Cumberland County Historical Society in Carlisle, Pennsylvania, houses an extensive collection of Carlisle Indian Industrial School publications, including the *School News*.

5. The former motto was "Tahenan upi qa ounkiya biye,—Come over and help us." As Phillip H. Round explains, "Come over and help us" was the motto of the Massachusetts Bay Colony seal, which depicted a Native American calling to Europe for help (Round, *Removable Type*, 66).

6. The first issue of *Talks and Thoughts* appeared in March 1886. Its twenty-one-year run ceased with the July 1907 issue. Students wrote all the content. Unlike the editors of the *Hallaquah* and the *School News*, the editors of *Talks and Thoughts* did not write recurring editorials that appeared on an editorial page, but they did contribute their own content to the paper and were responsible for editing and printing it.

The February 1891 issue of *Talks and Thoughts* is the earliest issue that I have been able to locate, and it is available online through the UC

San Diego Library, Special Collections and Archives Online Journals, http://roger.ucsd.edu/record=b2425214~s9. To my knowledge, no complete run of *Talks and Thoughts* exists. Only five libraries maintain issues of *Talks and Thoughts*. The New York Public Library houses the most comprehensive but incomplete collection of the paper; it is available in print form, from June 1891 through 1907.

7. *Talks and Thoughts*, January 1892, 1.

Essays

1. *School News*, June 1880, n. pag.
2. *School News*, September 1880, n. pag.
3. *School News*, October 1880, n. pag.
4. Pratt's "Florida Boys" were a group of fifteen men in their twenties who accompanied Pratt from Fort Marion to Hampton and then to Carlisle. Their names, according to Fear-Segal, were the first listed in Carlisle's student record files, and Pratt relied heavily on these students for vital support during the school's first year (Pratt, *Battlefield and Classroom*, 25). Roman Nose traveled to reservations to recruit students, as he recounts in his autobiographical essay "Roman Nose Goes to Indian Territory," which appeared in the October 1880 issue of the *School News*.
5. For more on the experiences of and ledger book drawings by the Fort Marion prisoners, see Glancy, *Fort Marion Prisoners*.
6. *School News*, December 1880, n. pag.
7. *School News*, January 1881, n. pag.
8. *School News*, February 1881, n. pag.
9. Roman Nose's disparaging remarks about the Native American children's traditional dress suggest he has been influenced by school authorities like Pratt into denigrating Native cultures. His remarks parallel how he was represented by school authorities in other Carlisle newspapers. For example, commentary about him in the June 1890 issue of the *Red Man* (3) reads: "Henry C. Roman Nose, one of the Florida prisoners, from Cheyenne Agency, who came to Carlisle when the school first opened in 1879, and remained two years, says he lives in a square tent covered with duck. It is his own. He has never worn Indian dress since he went back, and is now serving the Government as tinner, the trade he learned at Carlisle. He receives $20 a month." As this commentary suggests, Roman Nose continued to practice the lessons of Carlisle even after he returned to

the reservation. This was an especially important message to send other students and parents, as school authorities were highly concerned about the number of students who would "return to the blanket" and resort to their Indian way of life after leaving school. Roman Nose continued to wear the clothes of civilization and practiced civilization's two major teachings: self-sufficiency and hard work. He also lived in a tent—not a tepee—and owned it during the Dawes era, when the government aimed to break up reservations and tribal communities by making Indians into farmers, Christians, and individuals.

10. *School News*, March 1881, n. pag.
11. *School News,* August 1880, n. pag.
12. *Talks and Thoughts,* June 1891, 1, 4.
13. *Talks and Thoughts,* April 1892, 4.
14. *Talks and Thoughts,* November 1893, 1.
15. *Talks and Thoughts,* January 1895, 6.
16. *Talks and Thoughts,* May 1896, 3.
17. Lee entered Hampton in 1894, not 1893. See his essay "Transition Scenes," this volume, where he notes that he came to Hampton in 1894.
18. *Talks and Thoughts,* April 1896, 7.
19. *Talks and Thoughts,* November 1896, 4.
20. *Talks and Thoughts,* February 1897, 2–3.
21. *Talks and Thoughts,* March 1899, 3.
22. *Talks and Thoughts,* May 1904, 4.
23. *Talks and Thoughts,* December 1904, 4.
24. *Talks and Thoughts,* February 1905, 3.
25. *Carlisle Arrow,* May 7, 1909, n. pag.
26. *Red Man*, February 1911, 252–54.
27. Use of "cooler" may have been an error.
28. *Red Man*, September 1911, 15–16.

Short Stories and Retold Tales

1. *Talks and Thoughts*, September 1892, 1.
2. *Talks and Thoughts*, March 1892, 4.
3. *Talks and Thoughts*, April 1892, 1, 4.
4. *Talks and Thoughts*, March 1893, 1. This story is unsigned but is attributed to Hand in Fear-Segal, *White Man's Club*, 131.
5. *Talks and Thoughts*, April 1893, 1, 7.
6. *Talks and Thoughts*, February 1893, 1.

7. *Talks and Thoughts*, March 1893, 2.
8. *Talks and Thoughts*, July 1895, 3, 7. What incidents at Sleepy Hollow are meant is not known.
9. *Talks and Thoughts*, September 1895, 1.
10. *Talks and Thoughts*, April 1903, 4. This story is unsigned but is attributed to Bear in Littlefield and Parins, *Biobibliography: Supplement*, 7.
11. *Talks and Thoughts*, May 1903, 4. This retold tale is unsigned but is attributed to Bear in Littlefield and Parins, *Biobibliography: Supplement*, 7.
12. *Talks and Thoughts*, February 1905, 1. This story is unsigned but is attributed to Bear in Littlefield and Parins, *Biobibliography: Supplement*, 8.
13. *Indian Craftsman*, January 1910, 24–25.
14. *Red Man*, April 1910, 47–48.
15. *Talks and Thoughts*, January 1904, 4. This story is unsigned but is attributed to Bender in several sources, including Littlefield and Parins, *Biobibliography: Supplement*, 10.
16. *Talks and Thoughts*, April 1904, 1, 4. This legend was told by Bertha Mountain Sheep and written by Anna Bender. Mountain Sheep (Crow) attended Hampton from 1903 to 1908 (Brudvig, *Hampton*).
17. *Talks and Thoughts*, November 1904, 1, 4. This legend was told by Bertha Mountain Sheep and written by Anna Bender.
18. *Red Man*, November 1910, 131–32.
19. *Carlisle Arrow*, June 7, 1912.
20. *Red Man*, October 1910, 78–79.
21. *Red Man*, January 1911, 204.
22. *Red Man*, January 1911, 206–7.
23. *Red Man*, January 1913, 208.
24. *Red Man*, June 1913, 467–68.

Francis La Flesche

1. *Morning Star*, May 1886, 3.
2. Originally in the *Southern Workman*, October 1900, 554–56. Reprinted in La Flesche, *Ke-ma-ha: The Omaha Stories*, 3–8. This story was included in a collection of stories La Flesche wrote for young adult readers. The collection *Ke-ma-ha* was not published until 1995 (Peyer, *American Indian Nonfiction*, 293).
3. *Southern Workman*, November 1905, 587–94.
4. *Southern Workman*, August 1913, 427–28.

Carlos Montezuma

1. Although linguistically distinct, the Apaches and Yavapais were close neighbors and were often regarded as a combined tribal entity.
2. *Indian Helper*, October 14, 1887.
3. *Red Man*, February 1898, 1–2.
4. *Red Man and Helper*, May 16, 1902.
5. *Red Man and Helper*, September 19, 1902.
6. *Red Man and Helper*, November 14, 1902.
7. *Red Man and Helper*, October 16, 1903.

Charles Alexander Eastman

1. *Southern Workman*, December 1888, 128.
2. *Red Man*, February–March 1899, 9.
3. *Red Man*, December 1899, 2.
4. *Red Man*, May 1900, 4.
5. *Red Man*, June 1900, 2.
6. *Red Man*, June 1900, 8
7. *Southern Workman*, April 1903, 225–27.
8. *Reader: An Illustrated Monthly Magazine*, May 1903, 539–42. A similar version of this essay, "The Indian in Literature," appeared in *Oglala Light*, May 1903. That version was unavailable to reprint here.
9. *Southern Workman*, May 1911, 273–78.
10. *Red Man*, December 1914, 133–40.

Angel De Cora

1. *Southern Workman*, June 1897, 115–16.
2. Editorial note reads: "Paper read by Miss Angel De Cora, instructor in native Indian art, Carlisle School, Pennsylvania, before the Department of Indian Education at the annual convention of the National Educational Association, held at Los Angeles, Cal., July 8–12, 1907."
3. *Southern Workman*, October 1907, 527–28. In contrast to Pratt, Commissioner of Indian Affairs Francis E. Leupp and other reformers encouraged the study of Native arts and crafts because they saw it as "an effective means of 'industrializing' their charges and thereby speeding up the process of adaptation" (Peyer, *American Indian Nonfiction*, 325).
4. *Red Man*, March 1911, 279–85.

Gertrude Bonnin

1. Originally in the *Red Man*, February 1900, 8. Full text of "The School Days of an Indian Girl" is reproduced in Zitkala-Ša, *American Indian Stories*, 87–103. Although the editorial comment is unsigned, it was likely written by Richard Henry Pratt, as he maintained strict editorial control over the white-run publications printed at Carlisle and the representations of Native Americans contained within them. Pratt attempts to take credit for Zitkala-Ša's literary success by reminding her of "the friends" who helped her become who she is. Pratt also sought to cast doubt over the veracity of Zitkala-Ša's account of her boarding school experience by stating, "Her pictures are not, perhaps, untrue in themselves, but, taken by themselves, they are sadly misleading." It is worth noting that Pratt censored the version of the essay he reprinted in the *Red Man* without providing any indication that the original text had been altered in any way. As literary scholar Amelia V. Katanski observes, there are no ellipses, for instance, to signal that content has been excised (*Learning to Write "Indian,"* 121). Two chapters from the original essay have been omitted—"The Snow Episode," during which a schoolteacher spanks one of Zitkala-Ša's classmates several times with a slipper, and "The Devil," in which Zitkala-Ša takes revenge upon the image of the devil in the Bible by "scratching out his wicked eyes" with a pencil (*American Indian Stories*, 95). Both moments are commonly interpreted by scholars as "incidents of rebellion," so it is unsurprising that they have been expunged (Lukens, "American Indian Story," 148). Pratt further eliminates the paragraph in which Zitkala-Ša recounts the death of her "dear classmate" (*American Indian Stories*, 96). That paragraph, according to literary scholar Margaret Lukens, offers "the most damning charge against the white missionaries" for their "inattention to the Indian children's physical ailments" (Lukens, "American Indian Story," 149). It is telling that Pratt chose to omit mention of the incident in the pages of the *Red Man*.

2. *Red Man*, April 1900, 8.

3. Originally in the *Red Man and Helper*, 22 August 1902. Reproduced in Zitkala-Ša, *American Indian Stories*, 235–38. Editorial comment characterizes the Indian dance as "savage," "unwholesome," and a "hindrance to Indian progress." At the same time it seeks to discredit Bonnin's defense of the dance.

Laura Cornelius Kellogg

1. Zitkala-Ša's "A Protest Against the Abolition of the Indian Dance" and Carlos Montezuma's "The Indian Dance" are reprinted in this volume.
2. *Red Man and Helper*, 10 October 1902. This essay appears with Kellogg's book, short stories, essays, public speeches and congressional testimonies, and poem in *Laura Cornelius Kellogg*, edited by Kristina Ackley and Cristina Stanciu. I thank Cristina Stanciu for sharing her copy of the 10 October 1902 issue of the *Red Man and Helper* with me.

John Milton Oskison

1. All the writings reprinted here, with the exception of "An Indian Animal Story," are reprinted in Larré, ed., *John Milton Oskison: Talks of the Old Indian Territory and Essays on the Indian Condition* (2012).
2. The Sherman Institute was an off-reservation boarding school that opened in 1902.
3. *Southern Workman*, June 1903, 270–72.
4. Reprinted in Peyer, *Singing Spirit*, 128–35; in Allen, *Voice of the Turtle*, 136–44; in Littlefield and Parins, *Native American Writing*, 80–86; and Larré, *John Milton Oskison*, 248–54.
5. According to Larré, the "certain statesman" Oskison refers to is Reed Smoot, and the "wagonload of protests that the Senate had been asked to read" refers to the Reed Smoot case. Smoot, an apostle of the Mormon Church and accused polygamist, was elected senator of Utah in 1903, and many petitions were subsequently filed for his expulsion from the Senate (Larré, *John Milton Oskison*, 559–61).
6. *Southern Workman*, April 1907, 235–41.
7. Charles D. Carter (Chickasaw) was a congressman from Oklahoma and a member of the Society of American Indians. Charles Curtis, of Kaw ancestry, was a senator from Kansas. He was elected vice-president of the United States in the Hoover administration in 1929.
8. Elizabeth Bender (White Earth Chippewa) was a Hampton graduate and member of the SAI. Select essays by Bender are reprinted in this book. Eli Beardsley (Pueblo) attended Hampton on and off from 1906 to 1910. Jacob Morgan graduated from Hampton in 1900 and then completed post-graduate work there in 1903. He later became president of the Navajo Progressive Association, Navajo tribal

chairman (1938–42), and vice-chairman of the American Indian Federation (Brudvig, *Hampton*).

9. Dennis Wolfe Bushyhead was a principal chief of the Cherokees from 1879 to 1887.

10. *Red Man*, January 1912, 201–4.

11. *Red Man*, May 1912, 396–98.

12. *Indian School Journal*, January 1914, 213.

Arthur Caswell Parker

1. *Word Carrier of Santee Normal Training School*, September–October 1911, 20.

2. *Southern Workman*, November 1912, 628–35.

3. *Word Carrier of Santee Normal Training School*, November–December 1912, 22.

Henry Roe Cloud

1. As an undergraduate at Yale, Roe Cloud befriended Walter and Mary Roe and assisted the couple in their missionary efforts among the Southern Cheyennes and Arapahos in Oklahoma. He took "Roe" as his middle name as a sign of respect for them. For more on Roe Cloud's relationship with Walter and Mary Roe, see Pfister, *Yale Indian*.

2. *Southern Workman*, January 1915, 12–16. Roe Cloud published essays on his missionary experiences and on Indian education in the *Word Carrier* and *Word Carrier of Santee Normal Training School*, which are available online through the Minnesota Digital Library's Minnesota Newspapers Collection at mndigital.org.

Elizabeth Bender

1. *Red Man*, January 1916, 154–56.

2. *Southern Workman*, February 1916, 109–12.

Bibliography

Ackley, Kristina, and Cristina Stanciu, eds. *Laura Cornelius Kellogg: Our Democracy and the American Indian and Other Works*. Syracuse: Syracuse University Press, 2015.

Adams, David Wallace. *Education for Extinction: American Indians and the Boarding School Experience, 1875–1928*. Lawrence: University Press of Kansas, 1995.

Alexie, Sherman. *The Absolutely True Diary of a Part-Time Indian*. New York: Little, Brown and Company, 2007.

Allen, Paula Gunn, ed. *Voice of the Turtle: American Indian Literature, 1900–1979*. New York: Ballantine–One World, 1996.

Allred, Christine Edwards. "'Real Indian Art': Charles Eastman's Search for an Authenticating Culture Concept." In *True West: Authenticity and the American West*, ed. William R. Handley and Nathaniel Lewis, 117–39. Lincoln: University of Nebraska Press, 2004.

Anderson, James D. *The Education of Blacks in the South, 1860–1935*. Chapel Hill: University of North Carolina Press, 1988.

Annual Report of the Commissioner of Indian Affairs to the Secretary of the Interior. Washington DC: GPO, 1891.

Barrett, Carole A., Harvey J. Markowitz, and R. Kent Rasmussen, eds. *American Indian Biographies*. Pasadena CA: Salem Press, 2005.

Batker, Carol J. *Reforming Fictions: Native, African, and Jewish American Women's Literature and Journalism in the Progressive Era*. New York: Columbia University Press, 2000.

Bender, Elizabeth. "The Land of Hiawatha." *Talks and Thoughts*, June 1907, I, 4.

Berkhofer, Robert F. *White Man's Indian: Images of the American Indian from Columbus to the Present*. New York: Knopf, 1978.

Bieloh, Christina. "Bad Water and Epidemics: The Wages of Neglect at the Seneca Indian School." *Chronicles of Oklahoma* 87 (2009): 56–75.

Blaeser, Kimberly. "Learning 'The Language the Presidents Speak': Images and Issues of Literacy in American Indian Literature." *World Literature Today* 66, no. 2 (1992): 230–35.

Bonnin, Gertrude. Editorial Comment, *American Indian Magazine*, Summer 1919, 61–63.

Brooks, Joanna, ed. *The Collected Writings of Samson Occom, Mohegan: Leadership and Literature in Eighteenth-Century Native America*. New York: Oxford University Press, 2006.

Brooks, Lisa. *The Common Pot: The Recovery of Native Space in the Northeast*. Minneapolis: University of Minnesota Press, 2008.

Brudvig, Jon L. *Hampton Normal and Agricultural Institute's American Indian Students, 1878–1923*. 1996. http://www.twofrog.com/hampton.html.

Brumble, H. David, III. *American Indian Autobiography*. Berkeley: University of California Press, 1988.

Carlisle Indian School Digital Resource Center. 2015. http://carlisleindian.dickinson.edu.

"Cheers for the Indian Maiden." *Earlhamite*, March 1896, 187.

Child, Brenda. *Boarding School Seasons: American Indian Families, 1900–1940*. 1998. Reprint, Lincoln: University of Nebraska Press, 2012.

Cohen, Matt. *The Networked Wilderness: Communicating in Early New England*. Minneapolis: University of Minnesota Press, 2010.

Coleman, Robert C. *American Indian Children at School, 1850–1930*. Jackson: University Press of Mississippi, 1993.

Coskan-Johnson, Gale P. "What Writer Would Not Be an Indian for a While?: Charles Alexander Eastman, Critical Memory, and Audience." *Studies in American Indian Literatures* 18, no. 2 (Summer 2006): 105–31.

Cox, James H. "'Yours for the Indian Cause': Gertrude Bonnin's Activist Editing at *The American Indian Magazine*, 1915–1919." In *Blue Pencils and Hidden Hands: Women Editing Periodicals, 1830–1910*, ed. Sharon M. Harris, 173–97. Boston: Northeastern University Press, 2004.

Deloria, Philip J. *Playing Indian*. New Haven: Yale University Press, 1998.

Dippie, Brian W. *The Vanishing American: White Attitudes and U.S. Indian Policy*. Middletown CT: Wesleyan University Press, 1982.

Earlham College Bulletin. Richmond, Indiana: Earlham College, 1916. Earlham College Libraries, Friends Collection and College Archives, September 10, 2015. http://library.earlham.edu/c.php?g=82612&p=533775.

Eastman, Charles Alexander. *Indian Boyhood*. 1902. Reprint, New York: Dover, 1971.

———. *From the Deep Woods to Civilization*. 1913. Reprint, New York: Dover, 2003.

———. "The Indian's View of the Indian in Literature." *Reader: An Illustrated Monthly Magazine*, May 1903, 539–42.

———. *The Soul of the Indian*. 1911. Reprint, New York: Houghton Mifflin, 1971.

"Educated Indians." *New York Times*, February 5, 1887, 5.

Engs, Robert Francis. *Educating the Disfranchised and Disinherited: Samuel Chapman Armstrong and Hampton Institute, 1839–1893*. Knoxville: University of Tennessee Press, 1999.

Enoch, Jessica. "Resisting the Script of Indian Education: Zitkala-Ša and the Carlisle Indian School." *College English* 65, no. 2 (2002): 117–41.

Fagg, John, Matthew Pethers, and Robin Vandome. "Introduction: Networks and the Nineteenth-Century Periodical." *American Periodicals* 23, no. 2 (2013): 93–104.

Fear-Segal, Jacqueline. "The Man on the Bandstand at the Carlisle Indian Industrial School." In *Boarding School Blues: Revisiting American Indian Educational Experiences*, ed. Clifford E. Trafzer, Jean A. Keller, and Lorene Sisquoc, 99–122. Lincoln: University of Nebraska Press, 2006.

———. *White Man's Club: Schools, Race, and the Struggle of Indian Acculturation*. Lincoln: University of Nebraska Press, 2007.

Fisher, Dexter. "Zitkala-Ša: The Evolution of a Writer." *American Indian Quarterly* 5, no. 3 (1979): 229–38.

Fitzgerald, Michael Oren, ed. *The Essential Charles Eastman (Ohiyesa): Light on the Indian World*. Bloomington IN: World Wisdom, 2007.

Gaul, Theresa Strouth. *Cherokee Sister: The Collected Writings of Catharine Brown, 1818–1823*. Lincoln: University of Nebraska Press, 2014.

Gere, Anne Ruggles. "An Art of Survivance: Angel De Cora at Carlisle." *American Indian Quarterly* 28, nos. 3 and 4 (2004): 649–84.

Gibson, A. M. "Wyandotte Mission: The Early Years, 1871–1900." *Chronicles of Oklahoma* 36, no. 2 (1958): 137–54.

Glancy, Diane. *Fort Marion Prisoners and the Trauma of Native Education*. Lincoln: University of Nebraska Press, 2014.

Hafen, Jane P. *Dreams and Thunder: Stories, Poems, and the Sun Dance Opera*. Lincoln: University of Nebraska Press, 2001.

Hale, Frederick. "Acceptance and Rejection of Assimilation in the Works of Luther Standing Bear." *SAIL* 5, no. 4 (1993): 25–41.

Hertzberg, Hazel W. *The Search for an American Indian Identity: Modern Pan-Indian Movements*. 1971. Reprint, Syracuse NY: Syracuse University Press, 1981.

Hoxie, Frederick E., ed. *Talking Back to Civilization: Indian Voices from the Progressive Era*. Boston: Bedford–St. Martin's, 2001.

"Indian School Commencement." *Sentinel,* June 1891, 2.

Jaskoski, Helen, ed. *Early Native American Writing: New Critical Essays*. New York: Cambridge University Press, 1996.

Katanski, Amelia V. *Learning to Write "Indian": The Boarding-School Experience and American Indian Literature*. Norman: University of Oklahoma Press, 2005.

Kilcup, Karen, ed. *Native American Women's Writing, 1800–1924: An Anthology*. Malden MA: Blackwell Publishers, 2000.

La Flesche, Francis. *Ke-ma-ha: The Omaha Stories of Francis La Flesche*. Ed. James W. Parins and Daniel F. Littlefield Jr. Lincoln: University of Nebraska Press, 1995.

Larré, Lionel, ed. *John Milton Oskison: Talks of the Old Indian Territory and Essays on the Indian Condition*. Lincoln: University of Nebraska Press, 2012.

———. "John Milton Oskison and Assimilation." *American Indian Quarterly* 37, nos. 1–2 (2013): 3–33.

Littlefield, Daniel F., and James W. Parins. *American Indian and Alaska Native Newspapers and Periodicals, 1826–1924*. Vol 1. Westport CT: Greenwood, 1984.

———. *A Biobibliography of Native American Writers, 1772–1924: A Supplement*. Metuchen NJ: Scarecrow Press, 1985.

———. "Introduction." In *Tales of the Bark Lodges*, by Bertrand N. O. Walker, vii–xvi. Jackson: University Press of Mississippi, 1995.

Littlefield, Daniel F. Jr. and James W. Parins, eds. *Native American Writing in the Southeast: An Anthology, 1875–1935*. Oxford: University Press of Mississippi, 1995.

Lomawaima, K. Tsianina. *They Called It Prairie Light: The Story of the Chilocco Indian School*. Lincoln: University of Nebraska Press, 1994.

Lukens, Margaret A. "The American Indian Story of Zitkala-Ša." In *In Her Own Voice: Nineteenth-Century American Women Essayists*, ed. Sherry Lee Linkon, 141–55. New York: Garland, 1997.

Lyons, Scott Richard. *X-Marks: Native Signatures of Assent*. Minneapolis: University of Minnesota Press, 2010.

Maddox, Lucy. *Citizen Indians: Native American Intellectuals, Race, and Reform*. Ithaca: Cornell University Press, 2005.

Martínez, David. *Dakota Philosopher: Charles Eastman and American Indian Thought*. St. Paul: Minnesota Historical Society Press, 2009.

Molin, Paulette Fairbanks. "'Training the Hand, the Head, and the Heart': Indian Education at Hampton Institute." *Minnesota History* 51 (Fall 1988): 82–98.

Parker, Arthur C. "Editorial Comment: The Permanent Value of Indian School Papers." *Quarterly Journal of the Society of American Indians*, January–March 1915, 5–6.

Parker, Robert Dale. *Changing Is Not Vanishing: A Collection of American Indian Poetry to 1930*. Philadelphia: University of Pennsylvania Press, 2011.

Peyer, Bernd C., ed. *American Indian Nonfiction: An Anthology of Writings, 1760s–1930s*. Norman: University of Oklahoma Press, 2007.

———, ed. *The Singing Spirit: Early Short Stories by North American Indians*. Tucson: University of Arizona Press, 1989.

Pfister, Joel. *Individuality Incorporated: Indians and the Multicultural Modern*. Durham: Duke University Press, 2004.

———. *The Yale Indian: The Education of Henry Roe Cloud*. Durham: Duke University Press, 2009.

Pratt, Richard Henry. *Battlefield and Classroom: An Autobiography by Richard Henry Pratt*.1964. Ed. Robert M. Utley. Norman: University of Oklahoma Press, 2003.

Prucha, Francis Paul. *Americanizing the American Indians*. Lincoln: University of Nebraska Press, 1978.

Round, Phillip H. *Removable Type: Histories of the Book in Indian Country, 1663–1880*. Chapel Hill: University of North Carolina Press, 2010.

Ruoff, A. Lavonne Brown. Foreword. In *Early Native American Writing: New Critical Essays*, ed. Helen Jaskoski, vii–x. New York: Cambridge University Press, 1996.

Smith, Dwight L. *Indians of the United States and Canada: A Bibliography*. Santa Barbara: ABC–Clio, 1974.

Spack, Ruth. *America's Second Tongue: American Indian Education and the Ownership of English, 1860–1900*. Lincoln: University of Nebraska Press, 2002.

Stanciu, Cristina. "'That Is Why I Sent You to Carlisle': Carlisle Poetry and the Demands of Americanization Poetics and Politics." *American Indian Quarterly* 37, nos. 1–2 (2013): 34–76.

Standing Bear, Luther. *Land of the Spotted Eagle.* 1933. Lincoln: University of Nebraska Press, 2006.

———. *My People the Sioux.* 1928. Reprint, Lincoln: University of Nebraska Press, 1975.

Szasz, Margaret. *Education and the American Indian: The Road to Self-Determination, 1928–1973.* Albuquerque: University of New Mexico Press, 1974.

Tetzloff, Lisa. "Elizabeth Bender Cloud: 'Working for and with Our Indian People.'" *Frontiers* 30, no. 3 (2009): 77–115.

Trafzer, Clifford E., Jean A. Keller, and Lorene Sisquoc, eds. *Boarding School Blues: Revisiting American Indian Educational Experiences.* Lincoln: University of Nebraska Press, 2006.

Trennert, Robert A. "Educating Indian Girls at Nonreservation Boarding Schools, 1878–1920." *Western Historical Quarterly* 13, no. 3 (1982): 271–90.

Vigil, Kiara M. *Indigenous Intellectuals: Sovereignty, Citizenship, and the American Imagination, 1880–1930.* New York: Cambridge University Press, 2015.

Walker, Bertrand N. O. "A Personal Sketch of Bertrand Nicholas Oliver Walker." *Chronicles of Oklahoma* 6, no. 1 (March 1928): 89–93.

Washburn, Kathleen. "New Indians and Indigenous Archives." *PMLA* 127, no. 2 (2012): 380–83.

Warrior, Robert. *The People and the Word: Reading Native Nonfiction.* Minneapolis: University of Minnesota Press, 2005.

———. *Tribal Secrets: Recovering American Indian Intellectual Traditions.* Minneapolis: University of Minnesota Press, 1995.

Weaver, Jace. *That the People Might Live: Native American Literatures and Native American Community.* New York: Oxford University Press, 1997.

What Hampton Graduates Are Doing in Land-Buying, in Home-Making, in Business, in Teaching, in Agriculture, in Establishing Schools, in the Trades, in Church and Missionary Work, in the Professions, 1868–1904. Hampton VA: Hampton Institute Press, 1904.

Wilson, Raymond. *Ohiyesa: Charles Eastman, Santee Sioux.* Urbana: University of Illinois Press, 1983.

Wong, Hertha Dawn. *Sending My Heart Back Across the Years: Tradition and Innovation in Native American Autobiography*. New York: Oxford University Press, 1992.

Wyss, Hilary E. *English Letters and Indian Literacies: Reading, Writing, and New England Missionary Schools, 1750–1830*. Philadelphia: University of Pennsylvania Press, 2012.

Zitkala-Ša. *American Indian Stories, Legends, and Other Writings*. Ed. Cathy N. Davidson and Ada Norris. New York: Penguin, 2003.

Zink, Amanda J. "Carlisle's Writing Circle: Boarding School Texts and the Decolonization of Domesticity." *Studies in American Indian Literatures* 27, no. 4 (2015): 37–65.

Zuck, Rochelle Raineri. "'Yours in the Cause': Readers, Correspondents, and the Editorial Politics of Carlos Montezuma's *Wassaja*." *American Periodicals: A Journal of History and Criticism* 22, no. 1 (2012): 72–93.

Index

Southern Workman; *Talks and Thoughts*

panthers, 143–46
Parker, Arthur C., 11, 12, 25–26, 178, 286–300
Pawnee, 66, 132–33, 294
Peace Pipe, 30
Philadelphia, 96
Pima, 214
pipes, 114–15, 169, 234
Pipestone Indian School, 30
pneumonia, 54
Ponca, 220
Pontiac, 228
porcupine quills, 137
pottery, 236–37
Powlas, Dr., 280
Pratt, Capt. Richard Henry: and Gertrude Bonnin (Zitkala-Ša), 252, 330n1; and Henry Caruthers, 65, 66, 68, 69, 70, 71, 73; and civilizing mission of Carlisle, 22; editing work, 324n3; and Florida Boys, 326n4; mentioned in commencement address, 204, 205; monitors *School News,* 20; as Native education reformer, 14–15, 16; resigns from Carlisle, 24, 322n16; in Standing Bear's letter, 44; uses Native writing as propaganda, 8
printing as vocation, 41, 42
prison, 69–70
professions, 278–82, 304
progress, 289–307
Pyle, Howard, 238, 250

Quarterly Journal of the Society of American Indians, 10, 11, 12, 286.

See also *American Indian Magazine*

rabbits, 138–39
racism, 56–57
Ramona (Jackson), 227
rattlesnakes, 114
readerly Indians, 8
Red Cloud, 217–18
Red Man, 239, 322n17, 323n21
religion: and art, 236; of Henry Caruthers Roman Nose, 67; choice of, 304–5; and civilizing mission, 196, 202, 203; Native, 84–85, 90–92; at Seneca Indian School, 38. See also Christianity
religious ceremony, 174, 231. See also ceremonial dances
reservations: Charles Eastman's view of, 225; Laura Cornelius Kellogg's view of, 264; Carlos Montezuma's view of, 185–86, 191, 195–96, 199; John M. Oskison's view of, 267
Roe, Mary, 332n1
Roe, Walter C., 307, 332n1
Rogers, Edward, 280
Roman Nose, Henry Caruthers, 20, 65–73, 326n4, 326n9
Romayn, Capt., 72
Roosevelt, Theodore, 268
rug weaving, 248–49

Savannah, 70
scalping, 76, 102–3, 113, 114, 128, 165, 202
Schanandoah, Chapman, 118–19
school. See education